The
Legal Pathway of God

The Way, the Truth & the Life

O.T. Blalock, Jr.

xulon PRESS

Preface

The initial response of many people upon learning of this book will likely be, *Not another book about the Bible... I have read the Bible so many times and so many books about the Bible that I have become mentally saturated.* Those who have studied the gospel in seminaries or in Bible schools or in churches around the world will wonder what else they could possibly learn. Perhaps others have accumulated commentaries on the Bible for years, so what will this book reveal that other biblical teachers, preachers, ministers and evangelists have failed to glean from the Bible over the years? Others may say, "What is different about this book that makes it worth reading?"

I know of no other book that centers upon God's plan and purpose for man that biblically tracks the legal pathway that God was required to follow to redeem and restore man after the first Adam, as God's appointed ruler over the earth, disobeyed Him and conveyed his God-given power and authority to Satan. As you follow the biblical history of the battle raging between God and Satan in the spirit realm, you will be able to make a knowledgeable decision as to whom you choose to obey.

After following the legal pathway through the Bible from Genesis through Revelation, you will be able to readily discern that fellowship with God becomes possible only after a person enters into a blood-covenant relationship with Him. Not only will you be able to understand that God has a plan and purpose for your life, but you will fully understand how one is spiritually redeemed and restored to a righteous relationship with the only true God of the universe with the ability to experience intimate fellowship with Him as well.

The onset of writing this book began when the Holy Spirit, the third person of the Trinity, revealed to me that God did not have the legal right to send His Son into the world until He could find a man who would do for Him that which He had promised to do for all mankind. He then began to reveal through biblical scriptures why the Son of God had to enter the world as the Son of Man and why He had to perform all things as man and not as deity. He enabled me to see beyond the cross, the spiritual side of the sufferings of Jesus as the Son of Man to fulfill the demands of the law to justify sinful man before God. The Holy Spirit confirmed that neither the Jews nor the Roman soldiers slew Jesus and where He spent the three days and nights that His body was in the tomb. Many other truths are revealed, all of which will enable you to know with absolute certainty who is the Truth, and the Life, and the only Way to God.

As the Holy Spirit started opening up the scriptures to me, He said, "Write a book," which I have endeavored to accomplish by following in His footsteps. May the Lord bless you and may this book serve as a gateway into His holy presence.

Chapter One

The Beginning of a Spiritual Journey

A multitude of religions and religious sects exist in the world today; all profess to know and serve the same God. If each religion or religious denomination or sect claims exclusivity regardless of different beliefs, do all religions lead to a spiritual relationship with the same God? The obvious question arises, "How can I know and recognize the real God who created all things and who rules over the universe? Can I, through the practice of a religion, develop a relationship with Him based on good works and human efforts?"

Perhaps to some individuals God resembles an ATM machine dispensing favor and wealth based upon individual desires and demands, as is often represented today in the world of prosperity. Many voices are saying various things as religions and religious sects flood the world, proclaiming that they all lead to a relationship with the same God. Each religious denomination has its own doctrine or dogma, which establishes the borders or parameters of its religious belief. Thus the adherent or believer remains confined within that religious box. If each independent belief enables an individual to experience a spiritual relationship with the true God of the universe, then why are there so many religions being practiced?

So what does the Bible reveal concerning God and His plan and purpose for creating man, as well as His relationship with man and the future events that will take place in the world in which we live? The Bible informs us that God is sovereign as well as altogether holy and righteous. He cannot violate His character or His nature of absolute holiness. He is all powerful, all knowing, and omnipresent. God is the ever existent One, the Creator, the giver and sustainer of life. He is the unchanging supreme Ruler of the universe. God is Spirit (John 4:24) and He rules and reigns in the supernatural realm and remains beyond the sense-realm of man unless He chooses to manifest Himself to him.

In today's world is the Bible considered to be relevant in the personal lives of individuals or in our societies or in the functioning of our governments? Or has it become simply another book to add to our library? Have the laws and commands of God as relating to man become passé? Does the Bible merely contain some random writings inspired by man over thousands of years that are subject to the various interpretations of men? Or does it contain truth that cannot be disputed which eternally affects the life and future of everyone? Some might argue that the Bible contains contradictions within its scriptures or accounts of miraculous events that never could have happened. Undoubtedly many individuals consider the Bible to be just an antiquated book that has little, if any, relevance to their lives.

Yet the Bible is more than just a history of the feats and failures of man. It provides us with the reason for man being created; the relationship God desires for man to have with Him; the conditions under which relationship with Him becomes a reality; the past, present and future of man, and the hope of spending eternity with Him in a new world cleansed of all sin, corruption and rebellion.

The Bible reveals that the testaments or covenants entered into between God and man became legal documents governing the conduct and responsibilities of both parties. Both God and man made promises to engage in or to refrain from specific activity. The covenants became solemn sacred written agreements between them, with penalties being imposed for failure to perform the promises that were made. Greater understanding of the Bible becomes a reality when we realize that both the natural realm in which man lives and the supernatural spirit realm from which God rules and reigns are involved. In the natural or material realm, man is dependent upon his five senses to apprehend and understand spiritual realities that prevail in the world. Natural man cannot see or hear or detect with his five senses the things that exist or occur in the unseen supernatural realm, which encompasses the entire universe (1 Cor 2:9-16).

The Bible gives an account of how spiritual warfare originated in the supernatural realm between God and one of His fallen archangels (who became Satan) and how it has prevailed down through the ages. As humanity approaches the end of the age, evidence proves, for the most part, that natural man is unable to spiritually discern between the god of this world and the true God who created all things and who rules and reigns in the supernatural realm. The majority of people go about their daily lives and activities unaware of the ongoing spiritual conflict or how it arose or how it affects them. Individuals, for the most part, tend to remain undiscerning about who spiritually influences them and the events that occur daily in this world in the unseen realm of the spirit.

God had a specific purpose and plan for creating man and placing him upon planet Earth as opposed to any other planet in the universe. Each one of us was created a free moral agent with the freedom to choose whom we will serve. We will see how the rebellious choice of Adam had a severe adverse effect upon all of his offspring, including each one of us. We will follow the scriptural account of man's plight after he became alienated from God, to learn whether we are able to justify ourselves by our own works and good deeds before a holy God. We will discover the legal pathway that God was required to follow in order to provide us with the opportunity of being restored to an eternal righteous relationship with our Creator, to enjoy intimate spiritual fellowship with Him.

The focus of this book centers upon God's holy nature and His relationship with man, which dictated the legal course that God followed in fulfilling His covenant promises to mankind. Often it has been said that God can do anything. If that is fact, can God violate His righteous nature, His covenants with man, or the laws He has made, to fulfill His promises to man and to restore him to his original position as ruler over the Earth?

We will follow the battle raging between Satan and God to see the *modus operandi* being employed by the devil to prevent us from knowing and developing a relationship with the only true and living God. Also we will discover Satan's efforts to establish his eternal kingdom of darkness upon planet Earth. As we examine scripture to determine the plan and purpose of God for creating man, we will see that the Bible does not say that the God of the universe was just lonely or in need of fellowship. We will understand that God had already created a host of spirit beings, called angels, for the purpose of serving and worshiping Him. We will also find that God, who is holy and altogether righteous, created man for a specific purpose that required obedience rather than just the performance of religious duties or rites. We will learn that the Son of God came into the world as man to accomplish a great deal more than just surrendering His life on the cross for mankind.

The Bible states that Jesus, the only begotten Son of God, came to destroy the works of the devil (I John 3:8). The works of the devil are sin and death. After His resurrection, Jesus declared that He held the keys of hell and death (Rev 1:18). So how could the works of the devil be destroyed and the keys of death and Hell be in the possession of Jesus, the Son of Man, when Satan continues to roam about in this world as a roaring lion seeking whom he can devour (I Peter 5:8)? How is Satan able to transform himself into an angel of light, which enables his ministers to also transform themselves into ministers of righteousness (2 Cor 11:14, 15)?

If Jesus literally destroyed the works of the devil and robbed him of his power, how could the devil continue to tempt man and influence him to sin and commit lawlessness? How is the devil able to harass, oppress, vex, or even possess man in today's world if he is a defeated foe? We need only to look about in our own communities, cities, nations, or political arenas to see that man is becoming more and more evil and wicked, even to the point of killing fellow human beings in the name of his god as the devil continues to visit his deception upon mankind.

Does a contradiction exist in the scriptures of the Bible? Does the Bible not say, *Jesus disarmed satanic principalities and powers and made a public spectacle of them, triumphing over them in it...* (2 Cor 2:15)? Did Jesus engage in mortal combat with Satan to seize the keys of hell and death from him? How and when did Jesus conquer him if the devil remains alive and free to exercise his control over man through the power of sin? How could the Bible tell us that Satan will eventually rule the world through the anti-christ (I John

2:18) before Christ the Son of Man returns to this earth, if in fact Jesus is the victorious warrior?

The emphasis of Christian teaching and preaching down through the centuries has centered upon Christ Jesus coming into the world and performing all things as the Son of God or as deity. Yet Jesus personally proclaimed that He came to accomplish all things as man and not as deity. Although He acknowledged that He was the only begotten Son of God in the flesh, He never said that He came to accomplish anything on behalf of humanity as the Son of God, but only as the Son of Man. When Christ Jesus was born into the world, why was it necessary for Him to be conformed to man in all things? Why was He unable to accomplish all things from His position in heaven as the second Person of the Trinity or on earth as the divine Son of God in His glorified body?

If He only died on the cross, in the same manner as many other men suffered death, then what did Jesus accomplish that others were unable to do? If death by crucifixion was all that was required to redeem man from Satan's kingdom of darkness, then why could any earthly man not accomplish that which was required of Jesus? Since the death of Christ Jesus on the cross, Jewish people have been persecuted and even slain for allegedly executing the only begotten Son of God. Did they actually slay Him or were they performing their required duty under the Old Testament Covenant?

After His death on the cross, did Jesus actually face the judgment of God once for all mankind and suffer the wrath of God in hell? If so, did He actually do battle with Satan and defeat him and destroy his works and take the keys of hell and death from him? If Christ suffered in hell for three days and three nights, which some Christian ministers and teachers dispute, what happened during the time He was there? How could He have been resurrected from the dead, laden with the sins of all mankind? Does the Bible actually give us the words that the Son of man uttered to the Father during His different stages of sufferings?

The Bible answers these and many other questions that man has raised since His appearance upon planet Earth. Once we understand the legal course of action that God was required to follow to regain and restore that which was forfeited to Satan, we will be able to recognize and know the Truth and the Life and the Way that eliminates all other religions of the world as a means of enabling us to be united with the only all-powerful and all-loving God of the universe.

Chapter Two

Spiritual Warfare Originated In Heaven

Let us begin by examining (John 3:16, 17), one of the most quoted scriptures of the Bible. *For God so loved the world that He gave His only begotten Son, that whoever believes in Him should not perish but have everlasting life.* God's reason for sending His Son was His love for the world, which included more than just mankind who was created to occupy and rule over it. The following verse states: *For God did not send His Son into the world to condemn the world, but that the world through Him might be saved.* From what or whom or why was it to be saved? Does the Bible not say, *The earth is the Lord's and everything in it, the world and all who live in it* (Ps 24:1, NIV)? If man was made by God in His image and placed on planet Earth, then what prevented the Son of God, as the second Person of the Trinity, from accomplishing all things from His heavenly position rather than having to appear on planet Earth?

The heavens and holy angelic beings were created before God made man. Three archangels are identified as Michael, Gabriel, and Lucifer (Dan 10:13, 8:16; Luke 1:19). The archangels, together with the angels assigned under each of their commands, were created as free moral agents to worship, obey, and serve God in the supernatural realm throughout the universe. The Bible reveals that Lucifer was one of the wisest and most powerful angels, who served in the heavenly Garden of Eden (Isa 14:12), the dwelling place of God. The name Lucifer (Hebrew *Heylel*) means brightness or morning star, which describes his extraordinary angelic appearance. Lucifer, as well as all angelic beings, was created with the righteous spiritual nature of God and was given the freedom to choose to obey or disobey Him.

According to Holy Scripture, spiritual warfare broke out in the heavenly or supernatural realm when Lucifer attempted to exalt himself above the throne and authority of God. Due to his rebellious sinful actions, he suffered spiritual death inasmuch as Lucifer's spiritual nature changed from being holy to evil, which eternally severed his holy relationship with God. He remained an evil, but powerful angelic spirit being after he was removed by God from his exalted position in the heavenly Garden of Eden.

The prophets Isaiah and Ezekiel described Lucifer's original heavenly existence, the reason for his rebellion, as well as his fall from grace. These passages of scripture were addressed to the kings of Babylon and Tyre, but they obviously have a double reference. The passages also relate to Satan, who exerted his evil power and influence in the supernatural realm over the two kings who ruled at that time (John 14:30). The prophet Isaiah describes Satan's fall from heaven by using the fall of the king of Babylon as his example. Biblically Babylon came to be known as a symbol of Satan's kingdom of darkness on the Earth after the tower of Babel was built by man to exalt himself before God (Gen 11:3, 4). Even after God destroyed the tower, Babylon has remained the symbol of man's violent rebellion against the authority of God. Throughout biblical history Satan has continued to be the spiritual king of

Babylon and is the author of all false religions that keep mankind bound in his kingdom of darkness.

Ezekiel described Lucifer in his original sinless condition as being the seal of perfection, full of wisdom and perfect in beauty. He was in Eden, the Garden of God; every precious stone was his covering. He was the anointed cherub who covered the throne of God; God established him; he was on the holy mountain of God; He was perfect in his ways from the day he was created until iniquity was found in him. By the abundance of his trading or speaking evil of God, he became filled with violence within and he sinned; therefore, he was cast as a profane thing out of the mountain of God. God removed him as the cherub who covered His throne. Lucifer's heart was lifted up because of his beauty. He corrupted his wisdom for the sake of his splendor and was cast to the ground. He defiled his sanctuaries by the multitude of his iniquities, by the iniquity of his trading or slandering God (Ezek 28:12-18).

Lucifer was determined to sit upon the throne of God and to exalt himself above the authority of God to become the ruler over God's Kingdom of Righteousness. But God removed him from his position of great dignity and honor as one of His three archangels and cast him out of the heavenly Garden of Eden to planet Earth, thereby severing the righteous relationship that existed between the two of them. Apparently one third of the angelic spirit beings were assigned under each of the three archangels' command since Scripture states: *war broke out in heaven: Michael and his angels fought with the dragon; and the dragon and his angels fought, but they did not prevail, nor was a place found for them in heaven any longer. So the great dragon was cast out, that serpent of old, called the Devil and Satan, who deceives the whole world, was cast to the earth, and his angels were cast out with him*

(Rev 12:7-9). The angels assigned under Lucifer's command were apparently deceived by him and were also complicit in his rebellion against God.

Biblical evidence confirms that Satan was cast out of the heavenly Garden of Eden. His absence becomes apparent when one examines the explicit instructions that God gave to Moses on Mount Sinai. God told Moses to build a tabernacle for Him to dwell in among His people during the Israelites' journey of 40 years in the wilderness. Only two archangels were represented in the Holy of Holies, in which the Mercy Seat of the Ark of the Covenant was located. Their wings touched over the mercy seat of the Ark of the Covenant. Scripture states that *two cherubim of beaten gold were made of one piece. One cherub was located at each end of the Mercy Seat. They faced one another; the faces of the cherubim were toward the mercy seat. The cherubim covered the mercy seat with their uplifted wings* (Ex 37:7-9).

The mercy seat of the Ark of the Covenant in the Holy of Holies in the earthly Tabernacle of Moses represented the throne of God on earth, which constituted a shadow or pattern of His dwelling place in the heavenly Garden of Eden. The two cherubim undoubtedly represent the remaining archangels, Michael and Gabriel, who cover the throne of God in heaven with their uplifted wings, which confirms that the third archangel, Lucifer, who originally covered the heavenly throne of God, was no longer present in the heavenly Holy of Holies.

As a result of Lucifer's attempt to usurp God's authority and rule, he was not only evicted from heaven, but he also became Satan, the prince (Eph 2:2) of demons or evil spirits. Satan means adversary (I Pet 5:8), which is actually the personal name of the devil (Rev 12:9). Devil means slanderer or false accuser. Literally, the word "devil" describes what Lucifer became upon rebelling against God's rule in heaven. His nature changed from being holy and obedient to wicked and rebellious. He became the original source of sin, evil, and death in the universe, as well as *the arch enemy of God (Luke 10:19)*.

God pronounced through the prophet Isaiah what the final eternal destiny of Lucifer will be. *How art thou fallen from heaven, O Lucifer, son of the morning! For thou hast said in thine heart, I will ascend into heaven, I will exalt my throne above the stars of God: I will sit also upon the mount of the congregation, in the sides of the north* (the dwelling place of God, Ps 48:1, 2): *I will ascend above the heights of the clouds; I will be like the most High. Yet thou shalt be brought down to hell, to the sides of the pit* (Isa 14:9-15, KJV).

When Lucifer served in the presence of the Lord as the covering archangel, he undoubtedly became intimately familiar with God and His ways. Accordingly, after he was removed from his exalted position, he was knowledgeable of the various aspects of God's power, authority, and laws governing His holiness. He understood how God ruled and reigned. Upon suffering spiritual death, the devil became eternally separated from the Lord and became unable to perform any righteous creative acts. He is limited to mimicking God's actions and patterns of conduct in his dealings with man for the purpose of deceiving and inducing man to obey and serve him as the god of this world.

When Satan was cast out of heaven, the Bible does not say that God granted him permission or authority to rule and reign over planet Earth. The earth continued to belong to the Lord who created it. The Lord had the legal right to establish His Kingdom of Light upon it. Nevertheless, Satan continued his rebellion by setting up his kingdom of darkness over the Earth as another defiant act against the authority of God. He further demonstrated his determination to oppose God by setting up his kingdom of darkness for the purpose of ruling over the Earth as a god. Satan's evil nature, resulting from his disobedience in the heavenly Garden of Eden, was destined to become more wicked as an enemy of God.

Following Satan's rebellion against God, two opposing principal spiritual forces began to rule in the universe. First, the all-powerful and holy Triune being of God—God the Father, God the Son and God the Holy Spirit (Gen 1:26)—together with His holy angels, exercised supreme authority over all things. God remained the only source of holiness, eternal life, light and good. Second, the lesser spiritual force became Satan and his fallen angels, or evil spirits, who represent darkness, evil, death, and destruction (John 10:10, Prov 4:19). In Scripture light represents the spiritual life and holiness of God as well as the kingdom of God (I John 1:5, Matt 4:16), whereas darkness often represents sin and spiritual death as well as the evil nature of Satan.

Scripture records the condition of the earth after Satan was thrust out of heaven with great force, like a bolt of lightning (Luke 10:18). *The earth was without form, and void; and darkness was on the face of the deep. And the Spirit of God was hovering over the face of the waters* (Gen 1:2). The earth was in chaotic condition, blanketed in darkness representative of Satan's spiritual kingdom.

Chapter Three

God's Plan and Purpose for Man

The first three chapters of the book of Genesis provide us with the biblical history of creation. God created the planets and heavenly bodies, including the Earth. He established order upon planet Earth after Satan was cast down from heaven. God created all creatures and every living thing that moves on the water or upon the earth. God blessed them and commanded that they be fruitful and multiply. He commanded the earth to bring forth the living creature according to its kind: cattle and creeping things, and beasts of the earth each according to its kind. And God saw that it was good.

His final act involved the centerpiece of His creation when He made man in his own image. He called him Adam. The Lord God created man of the dust of the ground and breathed into his nostrils the breath of life; and man became a living being. He created woman and Adam named her Eve. God said that a man shall leave his father and mother and be joined to his wife and they shall become one flesh. He gave them dominion over every living thing that moves on the earth. He created them male and female and blessed them and commanded them to be fruitful and multiply and fill the earth and subdue it. He saw that everything that He had made was indeed very good.

God established His spiritual kingdom of righteousness in the natural or material realm upon planet Earth as a mirror image of His heavenly kingdom, which exists in the unseen supernatural or spirit realm. God said, *Let Us make man in our image, in our likeness* (Gen 1:26). The personal pronoun *us* is translated in Hebrew as *Elohiym* and refers to the triune being of the Godhead: God the Father, God the Son, and God the Holy Spirit. God created Adam a little lower than Himself as a sinless spirit being in the image of His Son, the Second Person of the Trinity, who is the express image of the invisible God (Col 1:15, Heb 1:1-3). According to Scripture, all things were created through Him and for Him. He is before all things and in Him all things consist or are held together (Col 1:15-17).

God made man a triune being consisting of a spirit with a soul, clothed in a body of flesh (I Thes 5:23), which enabled him to exist in the natural environment of planet Earth. When God, who is Spirit (John 4:24), breathed His holy spiritual nature into Adam, he as man became a righteous natural living being. God created Adam in His image and imparted unto him His holy eternal spiritual nature that enabled him to experience an intimate spiritual relationship with Him in His Kingdom of Light upon the Earth. Adam's relationship with God required obedience and imposed responsibility upon him rather than just the performance of religious duties or engaging in religious activities.

Man was ordained by God to rule over His kingdom on earth.

Not only was man created a free moral agent in the image of God, but he was empowered to rule and reign under God's authority upon the earth in the mirror image of the Son of God (Rom 5:14), who is enthroned in the heavens.

Not only was Adam commanded by God to rule over planet Earth, but to also subdue it. Subdue is defined by Webster: *to bring into subjection, conquer or control.* If everything God made was *very good,* then who or what remained to be brought under the dominion and rule of His Kingdom of righteousness, which Adam was mandated to establish upon the earth? Only the kingdom of darkness (Luke 11:18), which was established upon planet Earth and ruled by Satan after he was cast out of heaven, remained to be conquered. In essence, God commanded Adam to rule in His Son's image over His Kingdom upon the earth and to subdue Satan in order to bring Satan and his kingdom of darkness under submission to God's Kingdom of Light.

The Lord God planted a garden eastward in Eden, which represented His Kingdom of Light upon the earth. *And out of the ground the Lord God made every tree grow that is pleasant to the sight and good for food.* The Tree of Life was also in the midst of the garden together with the Tree of the Knowledge of Good and Evil (Gen 2:7-10). Then the Lord God put man in the Garden of Eden to tend and keep it. And He commanded him saying, *Of every tree of the garden you may freely eat; but of the tree of knowledge of good and evil you shall not eat, for in the day that you eat of it you shall surely die* (Gen 2:15-17).

God placed before man the Tree of Life and the Tree of Death.

The earthly Garden of Eden was created as a type of the heavenly Garden of Eden for the purpose of providing man a holy environment in which to live on planet Earth. Unlike the heavenly Garden of Eden, both good and evil were present in the earthly Garden of Eden, as represented by the Tree of Life and the Tree of The Knowledge of Good and Evil.

Undoubtedly God set before Adam, who was created a free moral agent, both trees to determine if he would remain faithful to Him. It was absolutely necessary for Adam to obey God's commands in order for him to remain in a righteous relationship with his Creator, who empowered him to serve as ruler over His Kingdom of Light upon the earth. Many years later a similar command was given by God to His people, the nation of Israel, in the wilderness. He said to them, *you shall therefore be holy, for I am the Lord your God. And you shall keep My statutes, and perform them; I am the Lord who makes you holy* (Lev 20:7, 8). Since the Lord God is holy, then we also must be holy to experience a living spiritual relationship with Him and to enjoy fellowship with the One in whose image we are created and through whom we derive authority and power to rule over the evil one.

The same command God gave to Adam applies to us today inasmuch as we are given a choice of obeying either God or Satan. The greatest deception that Satan can visit upon us is to influence each one of us, from a very early age, to focus upon our self-image and self- gratification rather than upon our relationship with the living God. As a result, we become self-centered in our thinking rather than God-centered. This allows the devil to appeal to us through the lustful appetites of our fleshly nature, to influence us to obey him rather than the Lord.

Within the earthly Garden of Eden the Tree of Life represented the Son of God, who is the only source of eternal holy life and empowerment. For the Lord said, *To him who overcomes I will give to eat from the tree of life, which is in the midst of the Paradise of God (Rev 2:7). Blessed are those who do His commandments, that they may have the right to the tree of life, and may enter through the gates into the city, the New Jerusalem, which will come down out of heaven at the end of the age* (Rev 22:14).

The Tree of the Knowledge of Good and Evil represented Satan, the author of sin and death (Heb 2:14). At that point in time, Satan was the only one in the universe to have experienced both righteousness in serving God and evil in his rebellion against Him. Adam was clearly warned by God that he would surely die, spiritually as well as physically, if he obeyed the devil by partaking of the Tree of the Knowledge of Good and Evil. God only required man to remain obedient to His commands as opposed to the performance of any religious duties or rites in order for him to remain in a holy relationship with his Creator. So long as Adam remained in a righteous relationship with his Creator, he was able to recognize God's presence and to personally commune with Him without fear or shame even though both he and Eve were naked (Gen 2:25). In His original, righteous, spiritual condition, Adam was immortal and did not come under Satan's rule, since Satan only derives his authority over man through the power of sin (John 8:34; Rom 5:12).

The Tree of Life offered Adam the opportunity to receive the anointing and the abundant eternal life of God (John 10:10). Whereas partaking of the Tree of the Knowledge of Good and Evil would condemn him to eternal separation from God resulting in his spiritual and physical deaths, in that order. In addition, any disobedient act would make Adam and his offspring subject to eternal punishment in hell with Satan if he became their spiritual master (Ps 9:17; Matt 5:29, 30).

Although we do not live in or have access to an earthly Garden of Eden, we nevertheless are born into the world facing the same spiritual decision as Adam and Eve. Yet we fail to recognize the importance of becoming familiar with the two spiritual forces who rule over the world in which we live. Accordingly, from early childhood we become vulnerable to not only the influence and deception of the devil, but we also are unable to recognize that God, our Creator, works through the spirit or heart of man whereas Satan works primarily through our minds by appealing to the desires of our physical nature.

Satan, as represented by the serpent (Rev 20:2), immediately instituted his plan of action to usurp Adam's God-given dominion and authority over him and to destroy God's Kingdom of Light on the earth. Even though Satan failed in his attempt to exalt himself above the rule of God in the heavenly Garden of Eden, he was determined to overcome Adam and seize his God-given power and authority to prevent him from eternally ruling over him as God's earthly representative. Since the devil cannot overpower the Lord God, he immediately displayed his determination to defeat and destroy man, who is created in God's image. Satan obviously knew the reason why God created man and placed him in the Garden of Eden on Earth. He recognized that it was imperative for him to act with haste before man could partake of the Tree of Life and become empowered to subdue him and again subject him to the humiliation of defeat.

Satan's initial ploy involved deceiving and enticing Eve to obey him. He knew from personal experience that her disobedience would violate God's command and would invoke the penalty of death upon her. He approached Eve with the apparent intent of also using her to influence Adam to disobey God. Satan undoubtedly understood God's purpose and plan for creating man and for placing him on planet Earth rather than on any other planet in the universe. He realized that God had instituted His plan to establish His kingdom of righteous upon the very planet to which he had been cast out of the heavenly Garden of Eden.

Now the serpent was more cunning than any beast of the field, which the Lord God had made. And he said to the woman, Has God indeed said You shall not eat of every tree of the garden? And the woman said to the serpent, We may eat the fruit of the trees of the garden; but of the fruit of the tree which is in the midst of the garden, God has said, You shall not eat it, nor shall you touch it, lest you die. Then the serpent said to the woman, You will not surely die. For God knows that in the day you eat of it your eyes will be opened and you will be like God, knowing good and evil. So when the woman saw that the tree was good for food, that it was pleasant to the eyes, and a tree desirable to make one wise, she took of its fruit and ate. (Genesis 3:1-6)

Satan prevailed upon Eve to rebel against God's command.

In tempting Eve, the serpent first challenged God's authority and His command that man remain obedient to Him. Then he influenced Eve to question God's penalty of death for disobeying Him. He also reminded her that she would become wise like God. The devil utilized the same subtle approach of appealing to the desires of her soul and the desires of the flesh, which he continues to employ in the world today to lead us to rebel against the commands and laws of God.

Satan was well aware of the penalty for disobedience. He knew that Eve would encounter the same fate—spiritual death—that he had suffered after committing his rebellious acts against God in the heavenly Garden of Eden. Satan defeated Eve by appealing to the lust of the flesh, the lust of the eyes, and the pride of life (I John 2:15, 16). He succeeded in corrupting the world through lust (II Pet 1:4), which he continues to do daily in his efforts to permanently establish his spiritual kingdom of darkness over planet Earth and to rule over man as a god.

Eve further ignored God's command and *gave to her husband, who was with her and he ate* (Gen 3:6). Immediately, their righteous spiritual nature was changed from that of God to that of Satan. They immediately became aware of their fallen nature and attempted to clothe themselves in a righteousness of their own making by using fig leaves. When they heard the sound of the Lord God walking in the garden in the cool of the day, Adam and his wife hid themselves from the presence of the Lord God among the trees of the garden.

> Then He said to Adam, Where are you? Adam replied, I heard Your voice in the garden, and I was afraid because I was naked; and I hid myself. God asked him, Who told you that you were naked? Have you eaten from the tree of which I commanded you that you should not eat? Adam responded, The woman whom You gave to be with me, she gave me of the tree, and I ate. The Lord God asked the woman, What is this you have done? She replied, The serpent deceived me, and I ate. (Gen 3:7-13)

Upon partaking of the forbidden fruit, both Adam and Eve suffered spiritual death, causing their spiritual nature to be changed from holy to unrighteous, which severed their intimate spiritual relationship with their

Creator. Their eyes were opened to evil as well as to good. They immediately became conscious of themselves or self-conscious upon losing their righteous relationship with God. They became spiritually separated from Him because of the change in their spiritual nature. Their righteous spiritual lifeline to the Lord was severed and their natural five senses gained ascendency over their spirits. God's word tells us: *Do you not know that to whom you present yourselves slaves to obey, you are that one's slaves whom you obey, whether of sin leading to death, or of obedience leading to righteousness? (Rom 6:16).* Man came under the power of Satan and began to be dominated by his five senses rather than by his spirit, which caused him to focus upon himself and his personal desires, surroundings, and welfare instead of his relationship with God. The tactics of the devil remain the same today in his efforts to spiritually blind us as we endeavor to navigate our way in this life.

Scripture does not indicate that Adam engaged in conversation with Satan or that he deceived, enticed, or forced Adam to obey him. Therefore, Adam obviously exercised his own free will in forfeiting his God-given power and authority over to Satan. His rebellious act imposed legal restrictions upon God as to how He could regain and restore to man that which Adam lost through his act of disobedience. Since man willfully forfeited to Satan his God-given power and authority, then only by man could it be regained and restored. God as deity could not arbitrarily invade Satan's kingdom of darkness and subdue Satan to recover the power and authority that He had bestowed upon man. If Adam had originally chosen to submit to God by partaking of the fruit of the Tree of Life rather than disobeying God, then he would have been anointed with the power to not only resist the devil, but to also subdue him (James 4:7).

Satan, by successfully enticing Eve and Adam to disobey God, corrupted the holy nature of the human race, thereby severing man's righteous spiritual relationship with his Creator. Adam's offense of disobedience caused judgment to fall upon all men, resulting in all of Adam's offspring being condemned to spiritual and physical deaths and after physical death to the judgment of God (Heb 9:27). Consequently Satan became the mass murderer of all time.

The word death in scripture, as relating spiritually to the man who sins, means a separation or a cutting off from God, whereas physical death means the separation of the inner man from the outer man; the soul and spirit from the body (Jam 2:26). Man remains physically alive even though he is born into the world spiritually dead or spiritually separated as an offspring of the first man Adam (Matt 8:22, Col 2:14, I Tim 5:6). The inner man remains conscious in soul and spirit regardless of his spiritual or physical state.

How did Adam partake of spiritual fruit in the Garden of Eden?

When God sent His Son into the world as the Son of man, He explained the spiritual truth and reality of eating spiritual food. Partaking of spiritual food relates to man exercising his free will to either obey God, who is holy and who rules the universe, or to obey Satan, who is condemned to eternal punishment in hell. We are created with the freedom to choose whom we will serve. We are at liberty to choose eternal life with God by obeying Him or eternal separation from God, followed by His punishment if we obey Satan and remain in his kingdom of darkness. As we will see later in scripture Jesus, the Son of Man, said:

I am the bread of life. Your fathers ate the manna in the wilderness, and are dead. This is the bread which comes down from heaven that one may eat of it and not die. I am the living bread which came down from heaven. If anyone eats of this bread, he will live forever; and the bread that I shall give is My flesh, which I shall give for the life of the world. (John 6:48-51)

Jesus referred to the reality that He would offer Himself in the flesh as the sin-bearing sacrifice on the cross at Calvary (I Peter 2:24) to provide sinful man the opportunity to be set free from the rule of Satan and to receive the eternal life of God by being restored to a living spiritual relationship with Him. The Son of Man used an earthly example to explain a spiritual truth. He explained that He would offer Himself in the flesh so that man could partake of Him spiritually and not physically. He said, *It is the Spirit who gives life; the flesh profits nothing. The words that I speak to you are spirit, and they are life* (John 6:63). In essence Jesus stated that He is the *Tree of Life* and those who obey His teachings and commands will partake of Him spiritually and will be redeemed from Satan's kingdom of darkness.

Chapter Four

The Effect of Adam's Transgression Upon Mankind

As a result of Adam's act of disobedience, all of mankind inherited his rebellious spiritual "DNA" making us a prisoner of sin (Isa 61:1; Luke 4:18). Adam as head of the human race chose death rather than life, not only for himself but for the entire human race. As a consequence all of his off-spring, including each one of us, have been born into the world with the sinful spiritual nature of Satan, who lawfully gained Adam's authority to become the spiritual head of the human race. As the result of one rebellious trespass by Adam, sin entered the world and all mankind was condemned to death (Rom 5:16-21). By their willful disobedient acts, Adam and Eve exchanged the Kingdom of Light and the holiness of God for the kingdom of darkness and the evil nature of Satan not only for themselves, but for all of humanity.

Satan succeeded in deceiving Adam and Eve and destroying the image of God in them, and causing all of mankind to suffer spiritual death through their transgression. Even though man suffers spiritual death, which is eternal separation from God, he does not cease to remain an eternal spirit being. The severance of their intimate spiritual relationship with God resulted in Adam and Eve being cast out of God's presence in the earthly Garden of Eden before they could partake of the Tree of Life.

Before evicting Adam and Eve from the Garden of Eden, the Lord God said: *Behold, the man has become like one of Us, to know good and evil. And now, lest he put out his hand and take also of the tree of life, and eat, and live forever—therefore the Lord God sent him out of the garden of Eden to till the ground from which he was taken* (Gen 3:22, 23). The casting out of Adam and Eve makes it clear that Adam did not partake of the Tree of Life before he disobeyed God's command. If Adam had partaken of the Tree of Life before violating God's command of holiness, he would have been empowered to rule and reign over the Earth and to resist and to subdue Satan according to God's original command.

If Adam had been permitted to partake of the Tree of Life, which represented eternal life, after disobeying God's command, he would have lived eternally in a fallen or evil spiritual condition as an enemy of God without hope of being redeemed or delivered from slavery to sin under Satan's rule. For when Adam, who was a type of Him who was to come (Rom 5:14), obeyed Satan instead of God, he entered into spiritual union with the enemy of God.

God drove out Adam and placed cherubim at the east entry of the Garden of Eden and a flaming sword which turned every way, to guard access to the tree of life (Gen 3:22-24). The cherubim, who were angelic spirit beings, were assigned by God as guardians to prevent spiritual access to the Tree of Life by fallen sinful man. The sin of Adam interposed a spiritual barrier between God and fallen mankind. Man became doomed to the dominion of darkness (Col 1:3) after being thrust out of the Kingdom of Light (Col 1:12) because his spiritual nature became the same as that of Satan. God, who is altogether holy, cannot and will not allow sin to dwell in His presence or to go unpunished (Prov 11:21, John 3:36).

Before the Lord God evicted Adam and Eve from His presence in the Garden of Eden, He promised to put enmity between the devil and the woman, and between the devil's seed and her Seed or Offspring. God said that the Seed of woman would bruise the devil's head or break his lordship over man and the devil would bruise His heel (Gen 3:15). God did not say seeds as of many, but as of one, speaking of the Son of God who would be sent into the world as the Son of man (Gal 3:16) to become a life-giving Spirit (1 Cor 15:45). God served notice that the incarnation of His Son as man would be as the "seed of woman" and not in the traditional way as the seed of man. Earthly man could not be the father of her seed, since physical and spiritual death are imparted through all of the offspring of Adam. The seed of woman had to be fathered by the Holy Spirit to enter the world as the immortal sinless Son of Man (Luke 1:35). God promised Adam that He would send His Son clothed in human flesh to redeem and to restore by His obedience that which the first Adam lost through His disobedience.

Contrary to the deception that Satan has visited upon humanity, no earthly man is able to redeem himself, much less anyone else, because he is born into the world a captive of Satan through the power of sin. A natural or earthly man *can by no means redeem his brother or give himself to God as a ransom for him* (Ps 49:7), despite the deceptive teachings Satan has fostered through a multitude of false religions to spiritually enslave mankind. How can a man who is conceived in sin and born a sinner become a sinless substitutionary sacrifice for another when he must face the judgment of God himself for his own transgressions? God, who rules the universe, is the only power greater than

Satan. Only God, who created man through His Son by His Spirit in His image, is able to redeem, recreate, and restore us spiritually to a righteous relationship unto Himself. False religions inspired and crafted by Satan can in no wise free us from the bondage of sin. They only serve to keep us as his spiritual prisoner and to prevent us from becoming spiritually united with our Creator.

God requires a blood sacrifice for the atonement of man's sins.

Before casting Adam and Eve out of the Garden of Eden, the Lord God revealed that an innocent blood sacrifice was required to atone for the sins of man before he could enter into a spiritual relationship with Him. He demonstrated His mercy and His grace toward man by making tunics of skin for Adam and Eve and clothing them (Gen 3:21). In order to clothe them in animal skins, God first had to provide the animals and then slay them by shedding their innocent blood. As revealed later in Scripture, God demonstrated that not only would He provide the atoning sacrifice for all of mankind, but He would also be the One to slay the substitutionary sin-bearing sacrifice by shedding His innocent blood on behalf of sinful humanity to provide man with the opportunity to be restored to a righteous relationship with Himself.

The blood, of the sacrificial animal, made temporal atonement by reason of the innocent life that was offered. The innocent blood that was shed testified that God's judgment had been carried out against the sin-bearing sacrificial animal in sinful man's stead. The atonement enabled man to have an external relationship with God and forestalled the judgment of God falling upon spiritually unregenerate man. *The blood of sacrificial animals sanctified man for the purifying of the flesh*—or the outward man only (Heb 9:13). It was unable to change the spiritual nature of man. Animal sacrifices had to be offered continually by sinful man to appease God, whose wrath is aroused by man's disobedience. In His forbearance, God passed over the sins that were committed when acceptable animal sacrifices were offered to Him. Thus, He demonstrated His righteousness, that He might be just and the justifier of all who express their faith in the Seed of woman, who would become the supreme substitutionary sacrificial sin offering once for all mankind (Rom 3:25, 26). The sacrificial sin offering represented far more than just a religious ritual or practice.

All of the efforts of man cannot put away the guilt of sin for *without shedding of innocent blood there is no remission* (Heb 9:22). Repentance and good works on the part of man do not constitute "blood-shedding." The shedding of natural man's blood, corrupted by sin, cannot make man holy. So how can any earthly offspring of Adam deliver man from condemnation to eternal death and punishment as earthly false religions declare?

The sin of man invoked the curse of God upon Satan, the Earth, and man.

Biblically, sin is viewed as an offense against God or as a breach of His Law and imposes the sentence of physical death upon man as well as divine punishment. *Vengeance is Mine; I will repay,* says the Lord. And again, *The Lord will judge His people.* As a sinful human being, *It is a fearful thing to fall into the hands of the living God* (Heb 10:30, 31).

Adam's rebellious act also invoked the curse of God upon the devil and upon the earth, which remains today. *So the Lord God said to the serpent: Because you have done this, you are cursed more than all cattle, and more than every beast of the field; on your belly you shall go, and you shall eat dust all the days of your life* (Gen 3:14). The Lord's curse upon Satan was so severe that He characterized the devil and his existence as the lowest form of life on planet Earth. God was compelled to withdraw His blessings from fallen man and to place a curse upon Satan and every living thing, including mankind, as well as upon the Earth. Satan, who is the archenemy of God, became the pseudo-ruler over God's creation, the world system, and over fallen man. God's curse will remain in effect until Satan is eternally confined to hell at the end of the age, but not before he becomes ruler through the Antichrist over the entire world system for a period of seven years (Dan 9:24-27, Rev 6:19).

Even though the Earth legally belongs to the Lord (Exodus 19:5, Deut 10:14) Satan gained Adam's God-given authority to spiritually rule over it (Eph 6:12).

To the woman God said: I will greatly multiply your sorrow and your conception; in pain you shall bring forth children; your desire shall be for your husband, and he shall rule over you. Then to Adam He said, Because you have heeded the voice of your wife, and have eaten from the tree of which I commanded you, saying You shall not eat of it: Cursed is the ground for your sake; in toil you shall eat of it all the days of your life. Both thorns and thistles it shall bring forth for you, and you shall eat the herb of the field. In the sweat of your face you shall eat bread till you return to the ground, for out of it you were taken; for dust you are, and to dust you shall return. (Genesis 3:16-19)

Since the fall of Adam, man has been born into this world spiritually blind as to the reality of God and Satan. Inasmuch as we, the offspring of the first

Adam, enter the world spiritually separated from God, we never have the opportunity to experience intimate spiritual fellowship with our Creator as Adam originally enjoyed. At birth we are unable to spiritually discern the presence of the devil and for the most part, we remain unaware of his evil presence and his deceptive practices in the world today, as well as his ultimate goal of exalting himself as ruler over the entire world as a god.

Upon defeating Adam, Satan became the spiritual ruler over the Earth.

As the head of the human race, Adam's transgression resulted in humanity becoming Satan's spiritual captive. Scriptures tell us that *He who sins is of the devil, for the devil has sinned from the beginning* (I John 3:8); *Most assuredly, I say to you, whoever commits sin is a slave of sin (Rom. 8:34); for by whom a person is overcome, by him also he is brought into bondage* (2 Pet 2:19). Adam's rebellious act resulted in Satan becoming the new spiritual master of the human race through the power of sin (Rev 3:13) as well as the ruler of this world (John 12:31, 14:30). Satan succeeded in corrupting and defeating the very species that God had created to subdue him. Thus he became the pseudo-ruler of the earth as *the prince of the power of the air* (Eph 2:2) and continues to rule over the worldly system as *the god of this age* (2 Cor 4:4).

Satan succeeded in destroying the holy image of God in man and substituted his image of rebellion and evil. Man became incapable of delivering himself or his offspring from the power of sin since *In Adam all die* (I Cor 15:22). For all sin and fall short of the glory of God (Rom 3:23) and the wages of sin is death (Rom 6:23). Adam's rebellious sin has prevailed in spiritual and physical deaths over offspring fathered by fallen man throughout the ages.

Adam's transgression made us subject to the influence, control and manipulation of the devil, who is the great deceiver (Rev 12:9) and the father of lies (John 8:44). Most individuals remain unable to discern the devil's presence, his activities, his influence, and his control over the world's system as well as his involvement in their lives as they continue to blindly serve him.

Chapter Five

Satan's Evil Influence and Rule Over Man

Adam's transgression imposed an evil effect upon humanity. *Man became carnal*, a natural man, *sold under sin* (Rom 7:14). Webster defines carnal as having to do with or being preoccupied with bodily or sexual pleasures. Scripture informs us: *Now the works of the flesh are evident, which are: adultery, fornication, uncleanness, lewdness, idolatry, sorcery, hatred, contentions, jealousies, outbursts of wrath, selfish ambitions, dissensions, heresies, envy, murders, drunkenness, revelries, and the like* (Gal 5:19-21).

Man began to follow in the footsteps of his spiritual slave master Satan and to express the corrupt desires of his sinful nature. He began to despise the authority of God as ruler over him. This attitude prevails in today's world, when even the Ten Commandments cannot be displayed in a public place in the United States of America, which was founded on biblical principles. Even the name of Jesus cannot be invoked in public prayer on government property without the individual becoming subject to punitive repercussions. Scripture tells us,

Those who live according to the flesh set their minds on the things of the flesh. For to be carnally minded is death, because the carnal mind is enmity against God; for it is not subject to the law of God, nor indeed can be. So then, those who are controlled by the desires of the flesh cannot please God. (Romans 8:5-8)

Man became a slave of sin and presented his members as slaves of uncleanness, and of lawlessness leading to more lawlessness (Rom 6:17, 19). Living proof is constantly manifested in the lives of men that *The whole world lies under the sway of the wicked one* (I John 5:19).

Man began to manifest the murderous nature of his master Satan.

Man immediately began to manifest the attributes of his slave-master by becoming more and more sinful under Satan's influence and dominion. The nature of Satan was immediately manifested in the life of Cain, the first off-spring of Adam and Eve. Adam must have instructed his sons, Cain and Abel, about offering an acceptable blood sacrifice for the atonement of their sin as God performed for him in the Garden of Eden. Cain rebelled against God's instructions and ignored the fact that God will not allow sinful man to enter into his presence without a blood atonement being made. Cain defied God by bringing an unacceptable offering to the Lord of the fruit produced from the earth, which is under the curse of God.

Since *Abel was a keeper of sheep, but Cain was a tiller of the ground* (Gen 4:2), perhaps Cain felt it was beneath his dignity to humble himself and nego-tiate with Abel for an animal that was suitable to offer to God as an atoning sacrifice for his sins. Abel, in obedience to God, brought of the firstborn of his flock as a sacrificial offering and the Lord respected Abel and accepted his offering, but He did not respect or accept Cain and his offering. Cain became very angry and the Lord asked him why he was angry. The Lord told him if he obeyed His instructions, his sacrifice would be accepted. If he disobeyed, the guilt of sin would overcome him, but he should rule over it (Gen 4:6-7). Not only did Cain rebel against God in refusing to offer a blood sacrifice as atonement for his sins, but he became enraged because God accepted his younger brother's blood sacrifice as atonement. So he rose up and killed his brother Abel.

"By faith, Abel offered to God a more excellent sacrifice than Cain, through which he obtained witness that he was righteous" (Heb 11:4). The blood of Abel testified to God as to the murderous act of Cain long before Cain responded to God's questions. The cry of Abel's blood rose directly to the judgment-seat of God and witnessed against his brother who had killed him, *For the life of the flesh is in the blood* (Lev 17:11). The voice of Abel's blood cried out for judgment against his guilty brother and brought vengeance from God upon Cain as well as his offspring. Does anyone today wonder how many millions of voices throughout the world are crying out to God for judgment against those who aborted them in their mothers' wombs by shedding their innocent blood?

Satan exercises his control over mankind through the power of sin.

Adam's offspring, down through the present age, began to *walk according to the course of this world, according to the prince of the power of the air, the spirit who works in the sons of disobedience* (Eph 2:2). Man began to conduct himself *in the lust of his flesh, fulfilling the desires of the flesh and of the mind and became by nature a child of wrath* (Eph 2:3). As a consequence, the wrath of God was aroused by the rebellious nature of man (Deut 9:7; 2 Kings 22:13; 2 Chron 34:21).

The mind of man became no longer able to focus upon God because his mind was set on what his fallen or sinful nature desired (Rom 8:5), a mindset that continues to prevail in today's world. The sinful nature of man desires that which is contrary to the holiness of God and keeps him in conflict with God, making him an enemy of God (James 4:4). After Satan became man's adversary and slave-master through the power of sin, man began to develop the attributes of his evil ruler and to love the earthly world and the things in the world more than his Creator. All that is in the world; the lust of the flesh, the lust of the eyes, and the pride of life began to control the lives of men and the lives of their offspring (I John 2:15, 16). The worldly desires of the natural man overpowered and squelched the spirit of man, leading him to primarily pursue worldly pleasures and success that stimulate and satisfy the desires of the flesh, rather than first seeking to obey God and to honor Him. For the most part, the carnal nature of man remains unchanged as he endeavors to rule over his personal life and worldly affairs, while suppressing the commandments and the law of God and even the public mention of His name.

Man ceased to be spiritually alive unto God upon losing his righteous spiritual nature. He became unable to spiritually apprehend God or to commune with Him, except through the realm of his five senses. Man could not spiritually receive the things of the Spirit of God, for they became foolishness to him; nor could he know them, because they can be only spiritually discerned (1 Cor

2:14). The Spirit of God does not dwell in spiritually unregenerate man. As an enemy of God he is unable to commune with the living God or to experience a spiritual relationship with Him, regardless of what false religious beliefs or practices proclaim.

Satan as the head of the kingdom of darkness, together with one third of the angels of heaven, who became wicked spirits or demons, subtly began to gain control of mankind and to manipulate man to do his bidding in an effort to control and to ultimately destroy him. The devil continually endeavors to destroy the image of God in human beings by blinding them spiritually and by deceiving them to believe his religious lies and schemes, since he is the father of lies (John 8:44). He has succeeded in perverting men and women to deny their gender, to engage in same sex relationships to satisfy the lusts of their flesh and to become involved in other degrading behavior. The goal of Satan is to prevent man and woman from fulfilling the command and purpose of God, that is for man and woman to become one in marriage to reproduce offspring to continue the human race and to achieve their mandated responsibility of subduing the devil and destroying his kingdom of darkness.

After only a few generations, Satan had so morally and spiritually corrupted the human race through the power of sin that

The Lord saw that the wickedness of man was great in the earth, and that his heart was evil continually. The Lord was sorry that He had made man on the earth, and He was grieved in His heart. So the Lord decided to destroy man and beast together with creeping things and the birds of the air. (Genesis 6:5-7)

But one man, Noah, found grace in the eyes of the Lord. God said to Noah, *The end of all flesh has come before Me, for the earth is filled with violence through them; and behold, I will destroy them with the earth* (Gen 6:11-13). *And behold, I Myself am bringing floodwaters on the earth, to destroy from under heaven all flesh in which is the breath of life; everything that is on the earth shall die* (Gen 6:17). Satan reached the very brink of success in becoming the eternal ruler over his kingdom of darkness upon planet Earth by destroying the image of God in men and influencing them to defy God.

One man prevented Satan from accomplishing his goal.

Noah was a just man, perfect in his generations. Noah walked with God (Gen 6:8, 9). God commanded Noah to build an ark of gopher wood; to make rooms in the ark and cover the inside and outside with pitch (Gen 6:14). God established His covenant with Noah to save him and his immediate family by sending Noah, his sons, his wife, and his sons' wives into the ark (Gen 6:17, 18). Noah did according to all that God commanded him (Gen 6:22). Then the Lord told Noah to enter the ark together with his household, because the Lord observed that he was righteous before Him in that generation (Gen 7:1). The Bible tells us that *Noah delivered himself by his righteousness* (Ezek 14:14). *By faith Noah, being divinely warned of things not yet seen, moved with godly fear, prepared an ark for the saving of his household, by which he condemned the world and became heir of the righteousness, which is according to faith* (Heb 11:7).

Noah and his wife and his three sons and their wives, together with specimens of animals and fowls, were preserved from the flood that covered the earth because he obeyed God and expressed his faith in God by constructing an ark according to God's command and instructions. God bore witness to mankind for a period of 100 years, during the building of the ark that He was going to destroy the earth and everything on it. Yet man did not repent or turn from his wicked ways. The Lord permitted man to prove his inability to escape the power of sin by which Satan holds him captive. Consequently, God purged the earth of the evil and wickedness of man by water.

One man upon the face of the earth found favor with God, because of his faith in God and his obedience to Him and thereby preserved the human race. One cannot imagine the ridicule and torment Noah endured during the time that he was involved in constructing the ark because of its size, together with the fact that it was built on dry land by him alone. Noah most likely informed the people around him why he was building the ark as well as God's pronouncement of judgment, yet man refused to turn from his wicked ways.

The sinful spiritual nature of man remained unchanged.

Although Noah was a just and righteous man in his obedient relationship to God, his sinful spiritual nature remained unchanged. Upon exiting the ark, Noah immediately

...built an altar to the Lord, and took of every clean animal and of every clean bird, and offered burnt offerings on the altar. And the Lord smelled a soothing aroma. Then the Lord said in His heart, I will never again curse the ground for man's sake, although the imagination of man's heart is evil from his youth; nor will I again destroy every living thing as I have done. (Genesis 8:20, 21)

God acknowledged that "man's heart" or spiritual nature remained unchanged. Therefore, God established a covenant with man to never again destroy the earth with a flood (Gen 9:11-13) for the purpose of purging it of the sin and the wickedness of mankind.

The offering of a burnt sacrifice, which became a soothing aroma to the Lord, is mentioned for the first time in the Bible. If the offering of a substitutionary sacrifice by Noah for the atonement of his sins was sufficient, then why was it necessary to burn the sin-laden carcass of the animal? Scripture reveals that the burning of the sacrifice symbolized the sins of man that it bore were being consumed by the fire of God. Therefore, the purging of man's sins became a sweet aroma to God as well as a foreshadowing of how the sins of all humanity, that God would place upon His only begotten Son in the flesh, would be purged by His consuming fire (Deut 4:24).

Although the earth was cleansed of the wickedness of man by the flood that covered the face of the earth, the sinful nature of man soon manifested itself again (Gen 9:20-22). Within four generations, Satan began to establish his presence and influence over man in the world through Nimrod, the great grandson of Noah and the grandson of Ham. The name Nimrod comes from the Hebrew word *"marad"*, which means to rebel or "we will rebel". It points to his open rebellion against God as demonstrated by his life endeavors. Scripture states that *Nimrod became a mighty one in the earth.* The Hebrew word *"gibbor"*, which is translated "mighty", also means a tyrant or giant or strong one. The word *"gibbor"* is also used for giants, who were known for their wickedness (Gen 6:4, Ps 52:1-3, Ps 120:4, Isa 5:22, Jer 9:23).

Nimrod established the first kingdom upon the earth after the flood as well as the first universal false religion in opposition to God (Gen 10:8-12). He was responsible for the tower of Babel being built to openly exalt his false gods before the only true and living God of the universe (Gen 11:1-9). When the ruins of the tower of Babel were discovered in 1876, the remains indicated that many small shrines, which were dedicated to various gods, were located around the base of the tower. A sanctuary for the false god, Gel-Merodach, and the signs of the Zodiac were located on top of the tower of Babel. Literal Babylon became the site of the first great rebellion against God and will be the site of the last great rebellion of man against Him at the end of the age (Rev 14:8, 16:17-21, 18:1-24). Literal Babylon is always associated with demonic religious and idolatrous activity. We find in the book of Revelation of the Bible that Babylon is the city where demonic activity, including sorceries and enchantments, will be centered in the final days. The tower of Babel was so offensive to God that he destroyed it and confused the language of the people and scattered them over the face of the earth.

Chapter Six

God Seeks the Legal Right to Send His Son into the World

The puzzling question arises: if God so loved the world, why did He delay sending His Son into the world to save it rather than destroying it by flood? Did God not promise Adam that He would send the Seed of woman into the world to destroy the lordship of Satan over man? We have already seen that hundreds of years later the love of God motivated Him to send His Son into the world to save it, rather than to condemn it. Scripture tells us that the Lord does not change (Malachi 3:6, James 1:17, Heb 13:8). If He is a loving and merciful God, why was His wrath vented upon mankind in such a horrendous manner in the time of Noah? Were the people upon the earth at that time more evil or wicked?

We will discover the reason if we perform a quick review. Satan gained Adam's God-given authority to rule over the world, which enabled him to establish his kingdom of darkness over God's domain. As a matter of fact, Jesus during His time on earth confirmed the power of Satan when He described the devil as the ruler of this world (John 12:31, Rev 2:12). Scripture tells us *the whole world lies under the sway of the wicked one* (I John 5:19).

Christ Jesus bore witness to Adam's surrender of his God-given power and authority to Satan when He was being tempted by the devil in the wilderness. Jesus did not question the legitimacy of the devil's offer when he *took Jesus up on an exceedingly high mountain, and showed Him all the kingdoms of the world and their glory,* and told Him, *All these things I will give You if You will fall down and worship me* (Matt 4:8, 9). If the devil did not rule and reign over the kingdoms of the world, then his offer would not have constituted a valid temptation. Jesus further attested to this truth when He instructed man as to how to pray. He said pray: *our Father in heaven, hallowed be Your name. Your kingdom come. Your will be done on earth as it is in heaven* (Matt 6:9, 10). If God's kingdom had existed on earth then the "Lord's prayer" would have been redundant or meaningless.

Satan became the spiritual head of the human race (Rev 2:13) when Adam chose to obey him instead of God. Therefore God could not legally send His Son into Satan's kingdom of darkness upon the earth to redeem man until He could find a man, who by faith, would obey Him and permit God to spiritually deliver him into His Kingdom of Light. After being spiritually set free, that man would be required to offer a sacrifice to God in like manner as God had promised to do for mankind in offering the "Seed of woman". Such an obedient act by that individual would provide God with the authority to reciprocate on behalf of humanity. He could then send His Son into the world as the "Seed of woman" to become the ultimate sin-bearing sacrificial offering once for all mankind by virtue of His obedience to God.

Many have said God can do anything, yet He cannot violate His own holiness or the legal action He exercised in conveying all power and authority to the first man Adam to rule over the earth and to subdue Satan. God could not arbitrarily reverse the adverse effect that Adam's transgression placed upon mankind and the earth since, as a free moral agent, Adam possessed the authority to surrender his rights as ruler over the earth to Satan. Because Satan legally gained the authority to rule over the earth, God could not invade Satan's kingdom of darkness for the purpose of freeing any man from Satan's power. Neither could God allow any man to spiritually enter into His kingdom of Light without the spiritual nature of that individual being changed from unholy to righteous.

Scripture declares that man's only means of escape from Satan's kingdom of darkness is through spiritual rebirth, which can be performed only by God through His Son by His Spirit and not by any man (John 3:3-6). Only God, through his Son, in whose image man was created, can offer new spiritual birth to deliver man by His Spirit from the power of sin out of Satan's kingdom of darkness. Jesus, the Son of Man said: *I have come as a light into the world, that whoever believes in Me should not abide in darkness* (John 12:46).When He mentioned darkness, He obviously referred to the kingdom of Satan. God alone is able to deliver the believer from the power of darkness and convey him into the kingdom of the Son of His love, which is Light.

God chose a man to determine if he would do for Him that which He had promised to do for mankind.

We find in biblical genealogy a man named Abram who dwelled in his native land, the Ur of the Chaldeans. Abram was married to Sarai, but they were childless (Gen 11:27-32). Scripture makes it evident that Abram was chosen and called by God to obey for the purpose of entering into a righteous spiritual relationship with Him.

The Lord instructed Abram, a heathen Gentile who was 75 years old, to leave his country, his family, and his father's house and to go to a land that He would show him. God promised to make Abram a great nation; to bless him and to make his name great if he obeyed. He told him he would become a blessing and that He would bless those who blessed him. God said He would curse those who cursed Abram and in Abram all the families of the earth would be blessed. Abram obeyed the Lord and took Sarai, his wife and Lot, his brother's son, and all their possessions and the people whom they had acquired in Haran, and they departed for the land of Canaan. When they arrived, the Lord appeared to Abram. He told him the land of Canaan would be given to him and his descendants. Abram built an altar to the Lord, which signified that he had accepted the promises of the Lord. In honor of God's promises, Abram moved from there to the mountain east of Bethel and he pitched his tent and built an altar to the Lord and called on the name of the Lord (Gen 12:1-9). The building of an altar further confirmed that a spiritual relationship was developing between Abram and the LORD.

Abram obviously knew that to commune with God required the offering of a sin sacrifice for *without the shedding of blood there is no remission* of sins (Heb 9:22). The "blood" of the innocent animal was accepted by God as a temporal substitute for the death (Ezek. 18:20), which the sinner deserved. The very act of offering a sin sacrifice speaks of man's recognition of his sinful nature in the presence of a holy God and of his need to be spiritually cleansed.

It is of interest to note that as *Abram journeyed on, still going toward the South, a famine occurred in the land. So Abram went down into Egypt to live temporarily because the famine was severe* (Gen 12:9-10). Abram was setting a pattern that was to follow later when his offspring, the Israelites, because of famine, would enter into Egypt and became slaves to Pharaoh during which time God would birth a nation of people unto Himself. Abram, out of fear for his life and because Sarai his wife was very beautiful, begged her to say that she was his sister so it would be well for his sake and his life would be spared because of her. As a result, Sarai was taken into Pharaoh's harem and Abram was treated well for her sake and he became very rich in livestock and in silver and gold during the time she was enslaved to Pharaoh. But the Lord scourged Pharaoh and his household with serious plagues because of the enslavement of Sarai (Gen 12:12-20).

Although Abram was assured of being protected and blessed by God, fear motivated him to allow his wife to become a slave to Pharaoh. Once again Satan attempted to prevent God from achieving His goal of gaining the right to send the "Seed" of woman into the world. Without the intervention of the Lord, Sarai would have remained in bondage, which would have prevented her from ever having children by Abram. God sovereignly delivered both of them by visiting plagues upon Pharaoh and his people as He would later do in delivering Abram's offspring, the nation of Israel, from their bondage of slavery in Egypt.

Strife arose between Lot and Abram as their cattle increased. Abram gave Lot, his nephew who had accompanied him, the choice of the area of land before them. Lot chose the Jordan valley. So they separated and Abram dwelt in the land of Canaan (Gen 13:10-12). Lot chose the land of Sodom, where the men were wicked and sinning greatly against the Lord. Abram looked through the spiritual eyes of faith into the spirit realm and saw the land promised to him, the New Jerusalem, which will come down from above to the earth at the end of the age to become the future eternal dwelling place of God with redeemed mankind (Heb 11:10).

Lot looked through the eyes of the flesh—or his natural eyes—and saw the attractive country of the plains, which appealed to the lusts of his flesh. The Lord told Abram that all the land which he could see and set his foot upon would be given to him and his descendants forever. God promised to make his descendants too numerous to be numbered and Abram again built an altar to the Lord, acknowledging his acceptance of His promised blessings (Gen 13:14-18).

Each time Abram had a personal encounter with the Lord God, he built an altar that also indicated he foresaw God's plan of redemption for mankind (Col 1:14). The building of an altar by Abram for the offering of a sacrifice to the Lord affirmed he understood a substitutionary sacrificial offering was required for man to have a holy spiritual relationship with the living God.

The priest of God Most High offered Abram bread and wine.

Later Lot and his family and their belongings as well as other inhabitants were seized and taken away. Abram and his trained men born in his household recovered all their goods and brought back Lot and his possessions, together with the women and the other people (Gen 14).

Upon Abram's return, a remarkable event occurred which attested to the fact that Abram understood God's plan of redemption for mankind as well as his acceptance of it by faith. *Melchizedek, king of Salem, who was priest of God Most High, brought out bread and wine. He blessed Abram saying, Blessed be Abram by God Most High, Creator of heaven and earth. And blessed be God Most High who delivered your enemies into your hand. Then Abram gave him a tenth of everything* (Gen 14:14-20). Melchizedek is described as *king of righteousness and king of peace,* without father, without mother, without genealogy, without either a beginning of days or an end of life, but made like the Son of God and continues to be a priest eternally (Heb 7:1-3).

Abram, as a Gentile, is the only man in recorded biblical history to partake of bread and wine offered by the priest of the Most High God until the Seed of woman came into the world. He partook of the sacraments hundreds of years before Christ Jesus appeared upon this earth as the Seed of woman, before the Law was given by God to Moses and also before he, Abram, entered into a blood covenant of circumcision with God after which his name was changed to Abraham. Being offered the bread and wine by Melchizedek confirmed that Abram had been delivered out of the kingdom of darkness into the Kingdom of light, since the two elements of bread and wine are to be received only by those who have entered into a spiritual relationship with God.

The next time a similar event occurred, Christ Jesus Himself offered bread and wine to His disciples during the last Passover celebration before His death on the cross. He who was to become the Passover Lamb for all of mankind took bread, blessed and broke it, and gave it to the disciples and said, *Take, eat; this is My body. Then He took the cup, and gave thanks, and gave it to them, saying, Drink from it, all of you. For this is My blood of the new covenant, which is shed for many for the remission of sins* (Matt 26:26-28).

The apostle Paul, after the death of Jesus, explained what the bread and wine represented and that it serves to remind us of the sacrificial sufferings of Jesus for our redemption from bondage to Satan:

For I received from the Lord that which I also delivered to you: that the Lord Jesus on the same night in which He was betrayed took bread; and when He had given thanks, He broke it and said, Take, eat; this is My body which is broken for you; do this in remembrance of Me. In the same manner He also took the cup after supper, saying, This cup is the new covenant in My blood. This do, as often as you drink it, in remembrance of Me. For as often as you eat this bread and drink this cup, you proclaim the Lord's death till He comes. Therefore whoever eats this bread or drinks this cup of the Lord in an unworthy manner will be guilty of the body and blood of the Lord. But let a man examine himself, and so let him eat of the bread and drink of the cup. For he who eats and drinks in an unworthy manner eats and drinks judgment to himself, not discerning the Lord's body. (I Corinthians 11:23-29)

Abram, during each encounter with God, built an altar for the offering of a sacrifice to Him. In performing this act of worship, Abram undoubtedly received revelation enabling him to understand the meaning of the bread and the wine that Melchizedek gave to him while he was still an uncircumcised Gentile. According to Scripture, Abraham was justified by faith while still uncircumcised, inasmuch as the gospel was preached to him by God saying, *In you all the nations shall be blessed* (Gal 3:7, 8). Only the Lord could have revealed to him that the elements represented the body and blood of the sacrifice He would offer for the eternal benefit of mankind.

In partaking of the sacraments Abram was proclaiming his faith in God to provide His Son as the substitutionary sacrificial offering for the remission of the sins of all mankind. Abram, by faith, was looking forward to the Lord's death until He came to offer Himself on the cross at Calvary. He was looking forward to His death through spiritual eyes of faith enlightened by the Holy Spirit, just as the faithful in Christ Jesus today look back to the cross believing the revelation God has given to mankind through His written word, which He confirms by His Holy Spirit. Scripture tells us that those who exercise faith in God in the manner of Abram likewise become heirs of the promises made by God to Abraham (Gal 3:29).

Chapter Seven

Abraham Became the Father of Christianity

Scripture confirms that Abram as a Gentile received revelation of the gospel, or the good news of Christ Jesus, the Messiah. God was fore-telling that the Messiah, when He appeared on Earth, would be received first by the Gentiles. Jesus personally acknowledged during His life on earth that Abraham, through the spiritual eyes of faith, understood the gospel of salvation and accepted Him as the Messiah. He testified that Abraham—as well as his offspring, Isaac and Jacob—entered the kingdom of God: *And I say unto you, that many shall come from the east and west, and shall sit down with Abraham, and Isaac, and Jacob, in the kingdom of heaven* (Matt 8:11). On one occasion during a discourse with the Jews of His day Jesus said: *Your father Abraham rejoiced to see My day, and he saw it and was glad* (John 8:48-58). Scripture confirms that Abraham believed God, and it was accounted to him for righteousness (Gal 3:6-9) and that he was redeemed by the Lord (Isa 29:22).

Jesus proclaimed that Abraham, looking forward to His coming, saw His day and understood the meaning of Jesus offering Himself as the substitutionary sacrifice for the sins of all mankind. He confirmed that the gospel, which is the good news concerning Himself and the kingdom of God, had been revealed to Abraham—a man of faith. Jesus admonished the Israelites, saying: *If you were Abraham's children, you would do the works of Abraham (John 8:39).*

The works of Abraham involved obeying God and believing in the Messiah whom God would send into the world as the Seed of woman. Jesus witnessed to the fact that Abram had been delivered out of Satan's kingdom of darkness into God's Kingdom of Light. Abram was in a position not only to provide the LORD with the legal right to send His Son into the world as the Seed of woman, but also to provide God with legal standing to penetrate the kingdom of darkness for the purpose of restoring His Kingdom of Light upon Earth.

After Abram received the bread and the wine from Melchizedek, the word of the Lord came to him in a vision, saying, *Do not be afraid, Abram. I am your shield, your exceedingly great reward (Gen 15:1).* God's statement confirmed that Abram had entered into an intimate spiritual relationship with God, who promised to protect him and greatly bless him.

Then Abram asked the Lord God what He would give him since he was childless. The Lord told him that he would become the father of an heir. He brought Abram outside and told him to *look now toward heaven and to see if he could count the number of stars.* God assured him that his *descendants would be innumerable. Abram believed in the Lord, and the Lord accounted it to him for righteousness* (Gen 15:1-8).

God enters into an intimate blood covenant relationship with Abram.

Then the Lord told Abram that He was the Lord who brought him out of Ur, the land of the Chaldeans, to give him the land of Canaan as an inheritance.

Abram asked the Lord how he would know with certainty that he would inherit it. So the Lord instructed him to bring Him a three-year-old female cow, a female goat and a ram, together with a turtledove and a young pigeon. Abram presented all of them before the Lord and cut them in half, down the middle, except the birds. He placed each half opposite the other. When the vultures appeared, Abram prevented them from eating the carcasses.

When the sun was about to set, Abram fell into a deep sleep and suddenly horror and great darkness came upon him. Then the Lord spoke to Abram. He said with absolute certainty that the descendants of Abram would become strangers in a foreign land and would serve the people, who would afflict his descendants for 400 years. God said He would judge the nation and afterwards his descendants would come out with great wealth. He told Abram that he would go in peace to his fathers and would live to be a good old age. He said that the people of Abram would return to the land promised to him in the fourth generation because the iniquity of the Amorites was not complete. When the sun set and darkness prevailed, there appeared a smoking oven and a lighted torch that passed between the pieces of the sacrifices. During the same day the Lord entered into a covenant with Abram, assuring him that his descendants would be given the land He had promised to Abram (Gen 15:7-21).

The cutting in halves of the animals signified the end of the existing lives of the sacrifices for the purpose of sealing the new covenant between God and Abram. The shedding of innocent blood also attested to the sacred nature of the new spiritual relationship that existed between the two of them. God passed between the sacrifices as a burning fire to sanctify them and to bear witness that He initiated the covenant between the two of them and therefore it was His responsibility to fulfill its provisions, providing Abram remained faithful in honoring his part of the covenant.

God foretold how He would birth a nation unto Himself through the descendants of Abram and how they would ultimately return to occupy the land that He had promised to him. Abram became the first man after Adam and Eve with whom God personally entered into a blood covenant relationship that was initiated by Him. For the first time in biblical history, after the fall of Adam, God entered into a covenant relationship to give man, Abram and his descendants, land upon the earth for an eternal possession. The land may have included the former location of the original Garden of Eden inasmuch as all subsequent actions of the Lord have been and will be centered in the same area upon Earth as well.

Before Abram entered the kingdom of God, all men were born into the world under Satan's rule. The Lord God could not restore ownership of His land to any man who remained in Satan's kingdom of darkness inasmuch as He could not enter into a relationship with sinful man under Satan's rule. Due to Abram's faith and obedience, he was delivered out of the earthly kingdom of darkness into the Kingdom of Light. He thus became eligible to represent God upon the earth and provided God with the legal right to re-establish His kingdom of righteousness upon Earth as well. Although the Lord gave Adam authority to spiritually rule over the earth, He did not convey ownership to him. For the Bible states, *The earth is the Lord's, and all its fullness* (Ps 24:1).

Satan attempts to thwart God's plan for Abram.

Because Sarai, Abram's wife, had borne him no children, she offered Hagar, her Egyptian maidservant, to him. Abram heeded the voice of Sarai and took Hagar to be his wife, after he had dwelt ten years in the land of Canaan. After Hagar conceived Ishmael (Gen 16:1-8) she fled from Sarai because of her harsh treatment. Then the Angel of the Lord met her and told her He would multiply her descendants exceedingly, so that they could not be counted because of their multitude. God was covenant bound to bless her child despite Sarai's transgression, because he was fathered by Abram and came under the covenant promises that God had made to Abram.

God prophesied that Ishmael, as a child of the will of the flesh, would be rebellious without Godly discipline. He would come under the power of Satan and would oppose God's chosen people. Ishmael would remain in the midst of his brethren to accomplish the will and purpose of the devil to persecute the offspring of Isaac (Gen 16:9-16). Despite the promises of God, as well as having entered into a blood covenant relationship with Him, Abram heeded the advice of Sarai, just as Adam obeyed Eve in the Garden of Eden when she gave to him the forbidden fruit and he did eat. Satan attempted to use Sarai, just as he had used Eve, to prevent God from accomplishing His plan and purpose through Abram.

The devil tried to corrupt God's plan involving Abram to prevent the Lord from sending His son into the world as the Messiah to redeem humanity from the devil's kingdom of darkness. As a result of Sarai's intercession, Ishmael was born into the world according to the flesh, whereas afterwards Isaac was born according to the Spirit (Gal 4:29) as a son of promise. The prophecy declared that Ishmael and his descendants would persecute Isaac and his offspring. The conflict continues unabated in the world today as the nation of Israel is surrounded by the offspring of Ishmael, who are intent on destroying it. Despite his influence and interference, Satan was unable to defeat or destroy the blood covenant that existed between God and Abram.

God entered into a second covenant with Abram and changed his name to Abraham.

When Abram was 99 years old, the Lord appeared to him and said,

I am Almighty God; walk before Me and be blameless and I will make My covenant between Me and you, and will multiply you exceedingly... As for Me, behold, My covenant is with you, and you shall be a father of many nations. No longer shall your name be called Abram, but your name shall be Abraham; for I have made you a father of many nations. I will make you exceedingly fruitful; and I will make nations of you, and kings shall come from you. And I will establish My covenant between Me and you and your descendants after you in their generations, for an everlasting covenant, to be God to you and your descendants after you. Also I give to you and your descendants after you the land in which you are a stranger, all the land of Canaan, as an everlasting possession; and I will be their God... As for you, you shall keep My covenant, you and your descendants after you throughout their generations. (Genesis 17:1-9)

Again God entered into an everlasting covenant with Abraham to be God to him and his descendants, providing he remained obedient and walked blameless before Him. The magnitude of God's promises were amazing in view of the fact that Abraham and his wife were childless and could not produce offspring to occupy the land of Canaan. The consequences following Abraham's fulfillment of his covenant with God would become even more astounding. God literally said that Abraham, by remaining obedient to His commands, would give Him the authority, or standing, to invade Satan's kingdom of darkness upon the earth, to birth a nation, and to ultimately establish His kingdom of righteousness on planet Earth in the land of Canaan where the nation of Israel is presently located.

After the Lord God evicted Adam and Eve from the Garden of Eden, His kingdom on Earth ceased to exist because of Adam's disobedience. The faithfulness of Abram would provide God with the opportunity to re-establish His spiritual kingdom upon Earth so that He could dwell again in the midst of His people to empower them to rule and reign under His authority in His Kingdom of Light.

To become a party to this covenant, Abraham and every male child among his people were required to be circumcised to bear in their flesh the sign of the covenant. Any uncircumcised male child would be cut off from his people for having broken God's covenant (Gen 17:10-14).

God promised Abraham a son by Sarah with whom He would establish an everlasting covenant.

The Lord God changed the name of Sarai to Sarah, which means "queen of princes". He told Abraham that He would bless her and also give him a son by her. Then He would bless her and make her a mother of nations so that kings of peoples would be from her. Abraham fell on his face and laughed, and said in his heart, *Shall a child be born to a man who is one hundred years old? And shall Sarah, who is ninety years old, bear a child?* And Abraham said to God, *Oh, that Ishmael might live before You...* Then God said: *No, Sarah your wife shall bear you a son, and you shall call his name Isaac; I will establish My covenant with him for an everlasting covenant, and with his descendants after him* (Gen 17:15-21). The Lord stated unequivocally that His kingdom on earth would be established only through the lineage of Isaac, as the offspring of Abraham, which would eliminate all other people on earth as they would remain heathen Gentiles, separated from God, under the spiritual rule of Satan.

God went up from Abraham and *that same day Abraham took Ishmael his son, all who were born in his house and all who were bought with his money, every male among the men of Abraham's house, and circumcised them. Abraham was ninety-nine years old when he was circumcised and Ishmael his son was thirteen-years-old* (Gen 17:22-27). The only means by which man can enter into God's kingdom is to walk in the path of faith as demonstrated by Abraham in his obedience to God (Rom 4:1-12). Circumcision in the flesh was a foreshadowing of the believer in Christ Jesus being spiritually circumcised in his heart or spirit by the Holy Spirit, whereby the old sinful nature is removed (Rom 2:29, Col 2:11-14).

Later the Lord appeared to Abraham and told him that He would certainly return to him, and his wife Sarah would have a son despite their advanced age (Gen 18:9-15). This act of God would be symbolic of the Virgin Mary being visited hundreds of years later by the Holy Spirit to conceive a Son of promise. Only by the intervention of God in the natural process of life could Sarah give birth to a miracle child at her age.

The Lord visited Sarah and did for her as He had spoken. Sarah conceived and bore Abraham a son in his old age, at the exact time of which God had spoken to him. And Abraham called the name of his son Isaac. Then Abraham circumcised his son Isaac when he was eight days old, as God had commanded him. Abraham was 100 years old when his son Isaac was born to him (Gen 21:1-8).

Just as Christ Jesus was the only begotten Son of God as well as the Son of Promise, so was Isaac figuratively. God deliberately allowed Abraham and Sarah to reach the age of being unable to naturally produce a child through their physical bodies before He quickened Sarah's womb to conceive the miracle child, who became a gift from God to be offered back to Him as a sacrifice. Later God would send and offer His only begotten Son on behalf of mankind in like manner.

Chapter Eight

God Subjected Abraham to the Ultimate Test

To fulfill his part of the covenant, Abraham had to undergo the testing of his faith to see if he would remain obedient in the offering of his son of promise to God. The Lord had entered into blood covenants with Abram, promising to greatly bless him if he remained faithful in responding to His commands. No doubt Abraham realized that he and Sarah could not produce any more children on their own. One cannot comprehend the impact that the command of God must have had upon Abraham after he had waited for decades to become the father of a child by Sarah only then to be told to offer him as a burnt sacrifice. Yet when God told Abraham to take his only son Isaac, whom he loved and go to the land of Moriah and offer him there as a burnt sacrificial offering on one of the mountains of which the Lord would show to him, he did not hesitate. Only a man fully surrendered in an intimate relationship with God would know His voice and obey such a command.

Abraham rose early in the morning and saddled his donkey, and took two of his young men with him and Isaac his son. He split the wood for the burnt offering and went to the place of which God had told him. On the third day Abraham saw the place at a great distance and instructed his two young men to remain *with the donkey while he and his son went forward to worship. Abraham assured them that he and his son would return to them* (Gen 22:1-5). Abraham considered his obedient response to God's command to be an act of worship.

Abraham travelled three days with his son to the mount designated by God, which some biblical historians believe to be the same place where God would later offer His only begotten Son. In his heart Abraham had offered Isaac, his son of promise, as a living sacrifice to God prior to beginning the three-day journey when he committed his first act of splitting the wood for the purpose of making his son a burnt offering to the Lord. Abraham fully believed that God would raise Isaac from the dead, since he had previously offered assurance to the two young men traveling with him that both he and his son would return to them.

Abraham was a type of God the Father and Isaac was a type of the Son of God.

Abraham placed the wood for the burnt offering on Isaac his son; and he took the fire in his hand, and a knife, and the two of them went together. Isaac pointed out to his father that they carried the fire and the wood, but asked where was the lamb for a burnt offering? Abraham told him God would provide for Himself the lamb for a burnt offering. (Genesis 22:6-8)

Just as Jesus bore the wooden cross to Calvary, Isaac, who was a shadow or type of Jesus, carried the wood for the burnt offering on his back while Abraham, who was representative of God the Father, carried the knife with which to take Isaac's life and the fire with which to purge Isaac's body of sin after his death. Abraham, seeing through the eyes of faith, knew that God would provide His Son as a sacrificial offering in the future and would resurrect Him from the dead afterward. Twice reference is made to them acting in unison, which emphasizes that Abraham was a type of the Father going with the Son and the Son going with the Father up to Mount Calvary to offer His life as the supreme substitutionary sacrifice for sinful humanity.

Upon arriving at the place where God had instructed them to go, Abraham built an altar and placed the wood in order. He bound his son Isaac and laid him on the altar, upon the wood. Abraham stretched out his hand and took the knife to slay his son. But the Angel of the Lord called to him from heaven and said, *Abraham, Abraham! And he said, Here I am. And He said, Do not lay your hand on the lad, or do anything to him; for now I know that you fear God, since you have not withheld your son, your only son, from Me.* Then Abraham lifted his eyes and looked, and there behind him was a ram caught in a thicket by its horns. So Abraham took the ram and offered it up for a burnt offering instead of his son (Gen 22:9-13).

The ram caught in the thicket, which was offered by Abraham in Isaac's stead, was a type of Christ Jesus, the Son of Man, being sent by God and offered by God as the substitute sin-bearer for all of humanity. This served as an example of the revelation of the Passover to man. God provided a substitute sin-bearer and His judgment passed over Isaac and fell upon an innocent animal sparing the life of Isaac. God, by example, was pointing to the cross at Calvary where Christ Jesus, the Son of Man, would become our Passover sacrifice (I Cor 5:7) to satisfy our sin debt to God.

Abraham called the name of the place, THE-LORD-WILL-PROVIDE; as it is said to this day,

On the Mount of The LORD it shall be provided. Then the Angel of the Lord called to Abraham a second time out of heaven, and said: By Myself I have sworn, says the LORD, because you have done this thing, and have not withheld your son, your only son- blessing I will bless you, and in multiplying I will multiply your descendants as the stars of the heaven and as the sand which is on the seashore; and your descendants shall possess the gate of their enemies. In your seed all the nations of the earth shall be blessed, because you have obeyed My voice. (Genesis 22:14-18)

How many people read about Abraham without grasping the astonishing effect his obedience had upon the entire world? Because Abraham obeyed God in offering his *only son* as a living sacrifice, perhaps he became the second most significant man in biblical history aside from Noah, who enabled God to physically preserve the human race. In contrast, Abraham enabled God to provide for the spiritual redemption of all mankind upon becoming the father of Christianity, when he did for God that which God had promised Adam and Eve He would do for mankind. Consequently, Christianity preceded Judaism by over 400 years, during which period of time the offspring of Abraham were birthed in captivity in Egypt to become the nation of Israel.

When Abraham was told that in his seed, singular, all nations of the earth would be blessed because of his obedience, the Lord was referring to the Seed of woman who would enter the world in the lineage of Abraham as the

Son of Man. This is the first mention of "seed" by God subsequent to the eviction of Adam and Eve from the Garden of Eden. The Lord acknowledged that Abraham, by faith, which produced obedience to His command, had given Him the legal right to send His Son into the world as Abraham's "Seed" to bless all nations and all people of the earth. Abraham also provided God with the authority to enter Satan's jurisdiction upon earth to establish His kingdom of righteousness. God had the power, but lacked the authority to enter the kingdom of darkness of Satan upon the earth until Abraham passed the ultimate test of his faith in the offering of his son Isaac as a sacrifice unto Him.

Most people do not grasp the magnitude of Abraham's contribution to the Kingdom of God upon this earth. If he had failed the final test, God would not have been able to restore His government upon Earth or to birth a people unto Himself or build His earthly tabernacle to dwell in the midst of His people. Neither would He have been able to bestow unto His people the land that He had promised to Abraham and his descendants nor, most importantly of all, would He have been able to send His Son into the world to redeem us from the power of Satan.

We concede that we can never duplicate the accomplishments of Abraham. Nevertheless God has placed a call upon each of us to spiritually depart the kingdom of darkness by seeking Him and His Kingdom of Light because He has made irrevocable promises to us as well. Yet, unless we are willing and motivated to seek first His Kingdom, we will not become familiar with His promises or see them fulfilled or know the unique plan He has for each of our lives. Even if we enter His Kingdom of Light, we will fall short of fulfilling His plan for our lives if we refuse to accept His discipline and fail His tests of our faith.

Chapter Nine

God Fulfills His Covenant Promise to Abraham

Rather than sending His Son into the world as the Seed of woman at that time in biblical history, God had already covenanted with Abraham to invade Satan's spiritual domain upon Earth by birthing a nation of people unto Himself in Egypt as the descendants of Abraham. God had promised to shepherd them to the land of Canaan. The Lord reiterated His covenant promises to Isaac and his descendants. His son Jacob was chosen by God to be the one He would bless in the descending order of the lineage of the Messiah, who was to come (Gen 28:3-22). He reaffirmed the blessings of Abraham to Jacob, who lived in the covenanted land of Canaan, and changed his name to Israel (Gen 37:1). Israel had 12 sons, his favorite being Joseph, who was the son of his old age (Gen 35:1-22).

God anointed Joseph to preserve the people of Israel during a seven-year famine that was used to bring all of them together in the land of Goshen in Egypt (Gen 45:10). According to the divine plan of God, Israel's offspring (constituting the nation of Israel) were birthed in Egypt during a 430 year period of captivity. The descendants of Abraham multiplied under harsh labor, but remained together in one place due to their being captive slaves. If the Lord had allowed them to remain free, they undoubtedly would have scattered far and wide, which would have made it virtually impossible to gather them again as one nation or one people unto Himself.

The children of Israel were isolated from God during their captivity and were exposed to various false religions and cultish practices by wise men, sorcerers and Egyptian magicians, all of whom were empowered by Satan (Exo 7:11), who continues to imitate God in this world and seeks to be worshiped as a god. They had become unfamiliar with the Lord and His ways because of His silence during their period of captivity.

After 435 years God chose Moses, an Israelite by birth, to deliver the people of Israel from Egyptian bondage. He told Moses to say to the children of Israel:

I am the LORD; I will bring you out from under the burdens of the Egyptians, I will rescue you from their bondage, and I will redeem you with an outstretched arm and with great judgments. I will take you as My people, and I will be your God. Then you shall know that I am the LORD your God who brings you out from under the burdens of the Egyptians. And I will bring you into the land which I swore to give to Abraham, Isaac, and Jacob; and I will give it to you as a heritage: I am the LORD. (Exodus 6:2-8)

The Lord promised to judge the Egyptians, and to deliver and redeem the descendants of Abraham, and to fulfill his covenant promise to give them the land of Canaan in a manner similar to Adam and Eve being placed in the

Garden of Eden. Even more profound, the Lord announced that He would again manifest Himself to a people on Earth for the first time after Adam and Eve were evicted from His presence. The descendants of Abraham would become His people and He would become their God to deliver, lead, protect and provide for them.

In the book of Exodus we see that only God could deliver the Israelite nation from the bondage of slavery in Egypt by performing ten miracles through Moses, whom He had chosen to lead His people to the land that He had promised to Abraham. The Lord anointed Moses to perform the first three miracles, which were duplicated by the Egyptian magicians who did the same things by their secret arts. Satan was demonstrating his power to perform miracles for the purpose of validating the magicians who led the Egyptians in the worship of false idols to spiritually enslave the people.

During the period of their captivity, the descendants of Abraham were not only exposed to the deceptive practices of Satan, but they had grown accustomed to them. The Egyptian magicians could not duplicate the succeeding miracles that God performed in Egypt. Moses performed the fourth miracle of the plague of the lice. In the performance of the fifth miracle, which was the plague of the flies, the Lord put a division between His people—the Israelites—and the Egyptians. Only the people of Egypt were affected and not the people of Israel. The sixth plague inflicted death to the livestock of the Egyptians, yet not one animal belonging to the Israelites died. The seventh plague of boils broke out on men and animals throughout the land of Egypt, including Pharaoh's magicians. They could not stand before Moses because of the boils, which were upon them and upon all the Egyptians.

God sent hail throughout the land of Egypt as the seventh plague, but it did not hail in the land of Goshen, where the Israelites lived. The eighth plague (or miracle) involved locusts swarming over the land and devouring everything growing in the fields. They covered all the ground until it was black. The ninth plague of darkness spread over Egypt for three days. Yet all the Israelites had light in the places where they lived. After each of the plagues was performed, Pharaoh refused to allow God's people to leave Egypt. The Lord revealed to Pharaoh and the Egyptians that His power and dominion, as the only true and living God, was greater than that of the devil. The plagues were, for the most part, directed against the false gods of Satan to reveal the supreme power and authority of the Living God, which led Pharaoh to finally confess that he had sinned and that God alone was righteous and that he and his people were wicked.

God again emphasized that before sinful man can be delivered out of bondage to enter into a relationship with Him, an atoning blood sacrifice must be made for the remission of sin. The Lord instructed Moses to tell the Israelites that each household was to take a year-old male lamb or goat without defect and to offer it as a sacrifice at twilight. They were instructed to take some of the blood and put it on the sides and tops of the doorframes of the houses where they would eat the lambs roasted over the fire, along with bitter herbs and bread made without yeast.

The blood on the houses was a sign for the Israelites and the Lord did not permit the destroyer to enter their houses and strike down any of them. During the same night at midnight the Lord struck down all the firstborn in Egypt, from the firstborn of Pharaoh to the firstborn of the prisoner who was in the dungeon and the firstborn of all livestock, as well as the firstborn of his officials. In performing the miracles of deliverance, God not only brought judgment upon the rebellious Egyptians, but upon all the false gods of Egypt as well.

The deliverance of the Israelites foreshadowed God delivering us from the power of sin by shedding the innocent blood of His Son, who became our Passover Lamb, and leading us by His Spirit to obey and follow Him until we receive the fullness of our promised salvation.

During that fateful night Pharaoh told Moses to leave Egypt and to take the flocks and herbs that he had requested. In their departure, they plundered the Egyptians of articles of silver and gold and clothing because the Lord had made them favorably disposed toward the Israelites. About 600,000 men on foot, besides women and children, and a mixed multitude went with them also, together with flocks of sheep and goats and herds of cattle, which con-stituted a great number of livestock. All the armies of the Lord went out from the land of Egypt. The Lord by day went before them in a pillar of cloud to guide the Israelites on their way and by night in a pillar of fire to give them light, so that they could travel day or night.

The Lord performed miracle upon miracle as their Protector, Deliverer and Provider as He led them through the wilderness to the land of Canaan. In the middle of the second month after the Israelites had departed from the land of Egypt, the people had exhausted their food supply and the Lord rained Manna from heaven to provide food for them until they reached the land promised to Abraham (Exo 16:1-31). He also provided water for the people to drink when none was available. Despite the presence and provisions of the Lord, they complained to Moses and even expressed their regrets for having left Egypt.

In the third month after the children of Israel had departed from Egypt, they camped in the wilderness before Mount Sinai. The Lord called to Moses from the mountain and told him to remind the people as to the things that He *had done to the Egyptians; how He had provided for them and set them apart unto Himself. Through Moses He assured the people if they would indeed obey His voice and keep His covenant, then they would be a special treasure to Him above all people. Since all the earth was His, they would be to Him a kingdom of priests and a holy nation (Exo 19:3-6).*

The Lord brought the people of Israel out of Egypt to personally shepherd them for the purpose of establishing His Kingdom of righteousness upon Earth in the land of Canaan to fulfill His covenant promise to Abraham. As members of His Kingdom, the Israelites would become a special treasure to Him, separate and apart from all other people on the earth. As faithful members of God's Kingdom, they would become a kingdom of priests and a holy nation unto Him or a forerunner of the Church, the spiritual Body of Christ Jesus, the Messiah. God intended for His chosen people to subdue Satan and to rule the world under His guidance, protection, and power as Adam was originally commanded to do in the Garden of Eden.

The Lord instructed Moses to consecrate the people in order for them to be ready for His appearance on the third day upon Mount Sinai in the sight of all the people. He told Moses to set bounds for the people all around the mountain to prevent them or any animal from even touching the mountain, lest they be put to death by stoning or by arrows. Once a long blast sounded on the trumpet, they were to come near the mountain. After Moses sanctified the people and they had washed their clothes, in the morning on the third day thundering and lightning occurred as a thick cloud appeared on the mountain.

The trumpet of the Lord sounded long and very loudly, causing all the people in the camp to tremble with fear. Moses assembled the people of the camp at the foot of Mount Sinai, which was completely enveloped with smoke as the Lord descended in fire upon it.

The smoke resembled the ascending smoke of a furnace as the entire mountain quaked violently. Moses spoke and God orally answered him from the top of the mountain (Exo 19:10-25). God sanctified the mountain by His holy fire before descending to meet the people of Israel, who were sinful by spiritual nature. As a result of Satan contaminating the earth and all of the people with sin, it was necessary that the mountain be sanctified by Holy Fire before the Lord could appear upon it. For the first time in biblical history, the Lord revealed Himself to a multitude of people at once, rather than to just one or two individuals at a time as He had done in the past.

Because the Lord was silent over a 400-year period, the people of Israel were accustomed only to the deceptive works of the devil being manifested in their midst. God revealed His power and glory to the people to instill fear in their hearts and minds so that they would not disobey His commands that He would give them through His servant Moses. As the Lord had an intimate spiritual relationship only with Moses, to whom He personally spoke, He served notice to all the people that He was more than just a cloud by day and a fire by night, guiding and protecting them. He was also confirming Moses as their anointed leader.

God gave Moses ten commands for the Israelites to obey for the purpose of establishing and maintaining a holy spiritual relationship with Him. His commands were:

I am the Lord your God, who brought you out of the land of Egypt, out of the house of bondage. You shall have no other gods before Me. You shall not make for yourself a carved image—any likeness *of anything* that *is* in heaven above, or that *is* in the earth beneath, or that *is* in the water under the earth; you shall not bow down to them nor serve them. You shall not take the name of the Lord your God in vain, for the Lord will not hold *him* guiltless who takes His name in vain. Remember the Sabbath day, to keep it holy. Six days you shall labor and do all your work, but the seventh day *is* the Sabbath of the Lord your God. Honor your father and your mother, that your days may be long upon the land which the Lord your God is giving you. You shall not murder. You shall not commit adultery. You shall not steal. You shall not bear false witness against your neighbor. You shall not covet. (Exodus 20:1-17)

The commandments are eternal. They were given to serve the same purpose from generation to generation throughout the ages inasmuch as they reveal the righteous nature of God and the need for us to be sanctified or made holy from our sins to experience a spiritual relationship with Him.

The commandments were given to the Israelites, as well as to us, to govern our relationship with the Lord, together with our fellowman according to His holy stature. God also gave the people laws of righteousness, civil laws, and ceremonial laws to govern their relationship with each other as well as with Him (Exo 21-23). The Lord did not mention religion. Instead, He demanded that the Israelites remain obedient in covenant relationship with Him as His chosen people. It became necessary for the people of Israel, who were void of knowledge of the only true and holy God of the universe, to be taught God's standard of righteousness in the same manner as we are to learn and to teach our children today. The Lord, during His appearance on Mount Sinai, again stressed to the people of Israel that they remain obedient to Him and not turn aside to worship and serve false gods, wherein they would be obeying the devil in much the same manner as Adam and Eve did in the Garden of Eden.

Since God repeatedly emphasized to Moses and the people of Israel that they were never to bow down to false gods, it becomes evident that Satan had reestablished his kingdom of darkness upon the Earth after the flood. He continued to deceive and corrupt the human race by inducing and inspiring man to worship his false gods as he does today throughout the world in opposition to God. Since only two principal spiritual forces exercise authority in the supernatural or spirit realm in the world, we have but two choices available to us in deciding whom we will serve and obey. We either serve or worship almighty eternal God or the devil, for there is no middle ground on which we can spiritually stand.

The Israelites, upon being informed of God's laws and commandments, agreed to do all that the Lord commanded. Moses recorded in the Book of the Covenant all the words of the Lord and read them to the people, who again said they would obey. Moses sprinkled sacrificial blood on the people and on the book to seal their covenant with God. Thus the Israelites, who by their spiritual nature were sinful, entered into covenant relationship with the Lord, who is holy, when they agreed to obey His laws and His commandments as His covenant people.

The Lord also chose to personally reveal Himself to the leaders of His covenant people. Moses went up on Mount Sinai with Aaron, Nadab, and Abihu, and 70 of the elders of Israel. The Nobles of the children of Israel not only saw the manifestation of the God of Israel at a distance, but observed Him standing on what appeared to be a paved work of sapphire stone that resembled the very heavens in its clarity. They ate and drank and remained in His manifested presence in a manner similar to Adam and Eve in the Garden of Eden (Exodus 24:9-11). In a sense, God was training His army to obey Him as their General to become capable of defeating the enemy who controls the kingdom of darkness and to destroy his power over mankind.

Chapter Ten

The Rebellion of the Israelites

Aaron, who was to become the high priest of the Levitical priesthood, along with 72 other elders of the Israelites, returned from ascending Mount Sinai with Moses after being in the presence of God (Exo 24:9-11). Moses remained with God on the mountain for many days after Aaron and the others had returned, so they wondered what had become of him. Despite the presence of the Lord in their midst, as manifested by the cloud that covered Mount Sinai, when the people saw that Moses delayed in coming down from the mountain, they gathered together and asked Aaron to make for them gods that would go before them.

At the insistence of the people of Israel, Aaron collected their golden earrings and fashioned the gold with an engraving tool and made a molded calf. Then the people declared the golden calf to be the god of Israel that brought them out of the land of Egypt. When Aaron saw it, he built an altar before it and proclaimed the next day to be a feast to their newly proclaimed lord. The next day they rose early and offered burnt offerings and brought peace offerings; the people sat down to eat and drink, and rose up to play (Exo 32:1-6). Less than 40 days after they had entered into a blood covenant relationship with the Lord, the Israelites had rejected Him and returned to their pagan ways of worship under the influence of Satan because their spiritual nature remained unchanged.

Not only did Aaron and the people sin against God by breaking His commandment in making an idol, worshiping it, and offering sacrifices to it, but they pronounced it to be the new god of Israel, whom they would depend upon to provide for them, protect them, and lead them out of the wilderness. Satan quickly regained authority over them to serve him because of their sinful rebellious nature. Their direct relationship was with the missing Moses and not with God. Only Moses had an intimate spiritual relationship with the Lord, engaging in personal conversation with Him and receiving from Him direct commands for himself and the Israelites. Since Moses was visible to the Israelites as their leader and had given to them all of the words of the Lord, they became totally dependent upon him in their wilderness journey. So in making their idol god they used the gold that God had influenced the Egyptians to give to the people when they were told to leave Egypt. As scripture later reveals, the primary use of the gold was to be for the construction of the Lord's earthly tabernacle and its furnishings according to the explicit instructions that God gave to Moses on Mount Sinai.

Before Moses could return from his 40 days with God on Mount Sinai with the laws of God written on two stone tablets, which the people had already orally agreed to obey, they not only had rejected God, but they had created their own lifeless idol to worship and to serve as their god. Satan was continuing his relentless efforts to prevent God from establishing His Kingdom of Light upon planet Earth and was striving to maintain his authority over the land of Canaan, which God had promised to give to Abraham and his descendants.

The Lord, upon seeing what the people had done, commanded Moses to go down the mountain because his people whom Moses brought out of the land of Egypt had corrupted themselves. God told Moses that they had turned aside quickly from the way, which He had commanded them to obey, and described to Moses what had happened. Then the Lord said to him, *I have seen this people, and indeed it is a stiff-necked people! Now therefore, let Me alone, that My wrath may burn hot against them and I may consume them. And I will make of you a great nation (Exo 32:9, 10).*

But Moses pleaded with the Lord and persuaded Him not to destroy His people whom He had brought out of the land of Egypt with great power and with a mighty hand. He told the Lord that the Egyptians would think that He had brought them out for the purpose of killing them in the mountains and consuming them from the face of the earth. He reminded the Lord of His covenant promises to Abraham, Isaac, and Israel, to whom He swore that He would multiply their descendants as the stars of heaven and would give all the land of Canaan to their descendants as an eternal inheritance. So the Lord relented from the harm that He said He would do to His people. And Moses went down from the mountain with the two tablets of the Testimony in his hand. The commandants were written on both sides of the tablets. The tablets were the work of God and the writing was the writing of God engraved on the tablets.

As soon as Moses approached the camp, he saw the calf and the dancing of the people. His anger became hot and he cast the tablets out of his hands, and broke them at the foot of the mountain. Then he took the calf, which they had made, burned it in the fire, and ground it to powder and he scattered it on the water and made the children of Israel drink it. And Moses said to Aaron, *What did this people do to you that you have brought so great a sin upon them?(Exo 32:21).* Aaron in essence told Moses not to lose his temper because he knew the people, that they were evil by nature. Aaron explained to him what the people had said to him and what they had done.

When Moses saw that the people were unrestrained, he stood in the entrance of the camp and said that whoever was on the Lord's side to come to Him. And all the sons of Levi gathered themselves together to him. He said to them, *Thus says the Lord God of Israel: Let every man put his sword on his side, and go in and out from entrance to entrance throughout the camp, and let every man kill his brother, every man his companion, and every man his neighbor (Exo 32:27).*

The sons of Levi obeyed Moses and about 3,000 men of the Israelites died that day. Then Moses commanded them to consecrate themselves that day to the Lord in order that the Lord might bestow on them a blessing, because every man had opposed his son and his brother (Exo 32:25-29).

The next day Moses told the people that they had committed a great sin and that he was going up to the Lord to see if he could make atonement for them. Moses returned to the Lord and confessed that the people had committed a great sin and had made for themselves a god of gold! He asked the Lord if He would forgive them, but if not, would He blot his name out of His book, which He had written. And the Lord replied that whoever had sinned against Him, He would blot him out of his book. He instructed Moses to go and lead the people to the place of which He had spoken to him about. God said nevertheless, in the day when He visited for punishment, He would visit punishment upon them because of their sin (Exo 32:7-35).

Due to their sinful nature, spiritual ignorance, and hardness of heart, the Israelites failed to recognize that the sacrifice that they made to the golden calf idol, in essence, represented the offering of Christ Jesus the Messiah as a sacrifice to the devil, which was a gross abomination unto the Lord. There is little wonder as to why the anger of Moses and the wrath of God were kindled by their idolatry. Moses was provoked to break the two original stone tablets of the Law and to severely punish the Israelites. God was aroused to punish the people for their rebellious sins of rejecting Him as their redeemer, protector, and provider and then committing themselves to serve and worship a worthless god of the devil.

At various times, in various ways, members of the nation of Israel rebelled against Moses and even challenged his authority to be in charge of them in their journey to the promised land of Canaan, despite the many miraculous acts God performed through him. Their journey lasted for 40 years because of the lack of faith on the part of men who refused to obey the Lord and follow His commands after searching out enemy territory.

After Moses had led the rebellious nation of Israel for 40 years, they came to the Jordan River to cross over into the land promised to Abraham and his descendants. Moses reminded the people of the statutes and judgments that God commanded them to observe and obey with all their heart and with all their soul. He reminded them that day, they had proclaimed the Lord to be their God and that they had agreed they would walk in His ways and keep His statutes, His commandments, and His judgments, and that they would obey His voice. Also that day the Lord proclaimed the Israelites to be His special people, just as He promised them. They were instructed to keep all His commandments, and He would set them high above all nations, which He had made, in praise, in name, and in honor. He said they would be a holy people to Him, just as He had spoken (Deut 26:16-19).

Moses stressed that obedience to God was absolutely necessary on the part of the nation of Israel in order for them to be a holy people to the Lord after entering the land of Canaan. Since God is altogether holy and righteous, He cannot change His nature to allow the practice of sin in His presence. Moses exhorted them to be holy by observing and obeying the Lord's commands to enable Him to dwell in their midst and to bless them.

Moses enumerated the blessings that would come upon them and overtake them if they diligently obeyed the voice of the Lord their God and observed carefully all His commandments. He then gave a list of curses that would come upon them and overtake them if it came to pass that they did not obey the voice of the Lord their God, to observe carefully all His commandments and His statutes which He commanded them to keep (Deut 28:1-68). The same conditions prevail today in the life of each and every individual. Our responses to the Lord and His commandments will bring either blessings or curses upon us as well as upon our nation.

On two occasions during the 40 years, the people wandered in the wilderness, they cried out to Moses for water because there was not any available near their midst. On the first occasion the Lord instructed Moses to strike the rock once with the rod. On the second occasion, the Lord told Moses to take the rod and for him and his brother Aaron to gather the congregation together. Moses was told to speak to the rock before them and it would yield its water for the congregation and their animals. So Moses took the rod from before the Lord and He and Aaron assembled the people before the rock. Because he was angered by the rebellious conduct of the assembly, he struck the rock twice with his rod instead of speaking to it and water came out in great quantity. Then the Lord told Moses and Aaron, because they did not believe Him, to hallow Him in the eyes of the children of Israel, they would be prohibited from bringing the assembly into the land which He had given them (Num 20:7-13, 23-24). For the rock represented the Lord Jesus Christ, the Messiah, who was to be stricken only once by being nailed to a cross as our substitutionary sin sacrifice in order to provide us with the eternal spiritual water of life (John 7:37, 38).

The disobedient act of Moses did not mean that he would be eternally separated from God. But even though Moses served as mediator between God and the Israelite nation for 40 years, under the most demanding conditions, he was denied entry into the land promised to Abraham and his descendants for his disobedient act. His failure to honor God before the nation of Israel by not following His explicit command, prevented Him from completing His ordained mission. We, too should remember that God requires obedience for us to see the fulfillment of His goal in our lives while upon Earth. It is not that we just start and endure the race for a while, but the critical test is whether we finish the race in relationship with the LORD. For the final outcome will determine our eternal future with God.

After the death of Moses, the Lord spoke to Joshua the son of Nun, the assistant to Moses, telling him that Moses was dead. He instructed Joshua to cross over the river Jordan with all the Israelite people to the land, which the Lord was giving to them. The Lord said He was giving to them every place that the soles of their feet would walk upon, just as He had told Abraham. He specifically described the area that would become their territory. The Lord told Joshua that He would be the same with him as He was with Moses and He would not leave him or forsake him. He exhorted him to be strong and of good courage as he would divide as an inheritance the land among the people of Israel, which the Lord swore to their fathers to give them.

The Lord told Joshua to know and obey all the law that was given to Moses. If he obeyed God, he would prosper wherever he went. Joshua was never to speak contrary to The Book of the Law, that contained the commandments of the Lord, and he was to meditate in it day and night and to do according to all that was written in it. Then God would make his way prosperous and he would have good success (Joshua 1:1-9). If we respond to God accordingly, will we not also be blessed?

Joshua admonished the Israelites in accordance with God's instructions after he led them under the miracle-working power of God into the land that was promised to Abraham. He exhorted the people of Israel to fear the LORD, to serve Him in sincerity and in truth, and to put away the gods their fathers had served on the other side of the river Jordan and in Egypt. He strongly emphasized, "Serve the LORD!" Joshua said to them, "If it seems evil to you to serve the LORD, choose this day whom you will serve, whether the gods your fathers served or the gods of the Amorites, in whose land you dwell. But as for me and my house, we will serve God" (Joshua 24:14, 15).

Down through the ages every man has constantly faced the same decision that was set before the Israelites as to whether he will serve God or the devil, for there is no neutral ground between the two of them. The words of Joshua to the people of Israel hold the same truth today for all people as they have down through the centuries. We individually must make the decision as to whom we will obey and serve, for our eternal future depends upon it.

Joshua warned the people of Israel, *If you forsake the LORD and serve foreign gods, then the LORD will turn and do you harm and consume you, after He has done you good.* And the people said to Joshua, *No, but we will serve the LORD!* So he said to the people, *You are witnesses against yourselves that you have chosen the Lord for yourselves, to serve Him. And they said, We are witnesses! Now therefore, he said, put away the foreign gods which are among you, and incline your heart to the LORD God of Israel. And the people said to Joshua, The LORD our God we will serve, and His voice we will obey!* (Joshua 24:20-24).

Chapter Eleven

The Nation of Israel Rejects the Direct Ruler-ship of The Lord God

Scripture reveals that Israel remained faithful to the Lord during the time of Joshua's leadership and as long as the elders lived, who had known all the works of the Lord that were done for Israel. Yet the generation that followed after them did not know the Lord or His work and did evil in the sight of the Lord by serving the Baals, who were the idols of the devil. The children of Israel forsook the Lord God of their fathers and followed other gods that the people who were all around them served and they provoked the Lord to anger (Judges 2:7-12).

How often do we witness the children or grandchildren of parents who are devoted to God turn aside to follow after things or pleasures of the world without realizing they are removing themselves from the blessings of the Lord? Although the open or public worship of idols may not take place, the devil nevertheless gains control of their lives through equally devious means to enslave them and to prevent them from repenting and seeking reconciliation with their Creator. In too many instances the devil either destroys the lives of those who choose to reject God or leads them to encounter much bondage and sufferings as well as premature deaths.

With regard to the children of Israel, Satan continued his spiritual battle to reclaim the land of Canaan and to rule over the Israelite people as their god. When they forsook the Lord and served the idols of Satan, they incurred the wrath of God. He removed His protection and provision and allowed them to come under the control of their enemies all around. Wherever they ventured, the hand of the Lord was against them for calamity, just as He had warned and sworn to them.

Nevertheless, the Lord raised up judges who delivered them from those who plundered them. They still would not listen, but played the role of a harlot with other gods and worshiped them. They turned quickly from the pathway of their fathers—who obeyed the commandments of the Lord—and refused to obey Him. When the Lord was moved to compassion by their groaning because of those who oppressed them and harassed them, He raised up judges. He delivered them from their enemies during the life of a judge (Judges 2:13-18). But upon his death, they reverted to their former ways and acted more corruptly than their fathers by following after other gods, serving them and bowing down to them. They never ceased their rebellious activity, which aroused the anger of the Lord against them (Judges 2:19-23). Even though the Lord removed the Israelites from Egypt, He could not remove the customs and practices of the pagans of Egypt from them because of their sinful nature.

Finally the people of Israel demanded that God give them a king to judge them. The people insisted upon having a king rule over them because they wanted to be like all the nations around them and wanted the king to be their judge and to go before them to fight their battles. The Lord heeded the voice of the people, for they had rejected Him and no longer desired that He should reign over them. Because of all the misdeeds the Israelites had done since the Lord brought them up out of Egypt, which included forsaking Him to serve other gods, the LORD heeded their request to have a worldly king reign over them instead of Himself.

They were warned of the behavior of an earthly king who would take their sons and use them for military purposes to wage war; to plow his ground and reap his harvest. Additionally they were told that the king would take their daughters for his personal use and would take the best of their fields, vineyards, and their olive groves and make them servants. They were warned that because of the oppression of the king, which the people would choose, they would cry out, but the Lord would not hear them (1 Samuel 8:6-22). The people of Israel became even more concerned with worldly customs and practices than they were about their relationship with God. Their relationship with the all-powerful and all-loving God of the universe began to deteriorate more than ever before.

Breaking the law of God and rebelling against His instructions invokes the wrath of a jealous God who visits the iniquity of the fathers on the children to the third and fourth generation of those who hate Him (Exo 20:5). The books of the prophets, as well as in the Psalms and the book of Kings, chronicle the unchanged rebellious nature of the people of Israel. Despite God's presence, provision, and protection, including His love, mercy, and grace being bestowed upon them as His chosen covenant people, they continued to remain spiritually blind and inclined to follow Satan.

The Israelites refused to destroy the idol worshipping people as the Lord had commanded them, but instead they mingled with them and learned their works. They served their idols and were ensnared by them, even sacrificing their sons and their daughters to demons. The innocent blood of their sons and daughters was shed in sacrificing them to the idols of Canaan. As a result, the land was polluted with blood as they defiled themselves by their ungodly works. Thus the wrath of God was aroused against His people, causing Him to abhor His own people. As a consequence He allowed the Gentiles, who hated them, to rule over them and their enemies to oppress them as they became subject to their rule.

Many times the Lord delivered them from their oppression, but they refused His counsel and were again subject to bondage because of their iniquity. Yet, He had compassion on them and when He heard their plea He remembered His covenant for their sake and had mercy upon them. He also caused their rulers who captured them to have pity on them (Ps 106:33-46).

God declared that He would send a righteous Judge for His people, after the lineage of King David. His righteous Judge would be girded with faithfulness and righteousness. The Spirit of God would rest upon Him manifesting wisdom and understanding, counsel and might, knowledge and the fear of the Lord. He would not judge by what He saw or decide by what He heard, but He would judge the poor with righteousness and make equitable decisions on behalf of the meek. He would strike the earth with the all-powerful word of God and with the breath of His lips He would slay the wicked (Isa 11:1-5). The LORD prophesied that He would send His Son into the world and He would become the righteous judge and the minister of His word.

Biblical scholars have identified over 400 prophecies contained in the Old Testament concerning Jesus the Messiah. Prophecy is future revelation from God given through one of His prophets. The prophet Daniel prophesied that

God's first begotten Son in the flesh would regain and restore the dominion and authority over His kingdom on earth and over Satan, which the first man Adam forfeited through his disobedience. God foretold that the spiritual government of His kingdom on earth would rest upon the shoulder of Christ Jesus as the Son of Man and not upon Him as the Second Person of the Trinity. His government and His peace in this world would never end (Dan 7:13, 14).

The prophet Isaiah announced that the "Seed of woman" would be forthcoming in the fullness of time as the Son of Man to establish God's government upon Earth (Isa 9:6, 7). Isaiah emphasized that the zeal of the Lord would perform the miracle of God's Son coming to rule and reign rather than an earthly man doing so. The "Seed of woman" would become the One to eternally rule and reign over the world in righteousness. The Lord was informing the Israelite nation that He no longer believed that His covenant people could fulfill their responsibility of establishing His kingdom of righteousness upon Earth and that His Son would be forthcoming to perform and accomplish that which was impossible for man to do.

Chapter Twelve

The Seed of Abraham Arrives
in the World As The SON of MAN

The plan of God to establish His kingdom upon Earth, in fulfillment of His covenant promises to Abraham, was compromised by the unfaithfulness of His chosen people due to their sinful nature remaining unchanged. The Israelites failed dismally to follow God's decrees and instructions. Even though the Lord manifested Himself to the Israelite nation on numerous occasions in miraculous ways and blessed them beyond measure, they continued to rebel by turning to false gods and worshiping idols. God was legally compelled to send His Son into the world as man to establish His kingdom of Light upon the Earth.

Since the death of Christ Jesus, biblical teachers, ministers, and seminarians have centered their focus upon Christ Jesus fulfilling His appointed mission on Earth as the Son of God and upon His crucifixion and His resurrection as the Son of God. Yet the name Jesus was given to the only begotten Son of God as the Son of Man. During His life on Earth, Jesus never once said He came to fulfill anything as the Son of God, but always as the Son of Man. In the four Gospels of the Bible Jesus clearly voiced His dependence upon God the

Father and professed that He did all things as the Son of Man and all things would be visited upon Him as the Son of Man.

From the beginning, God the Father foretold that the Seed of woman would redeem man and would defeat the devil (Gen 3:15). The Seed of woman could only come forth into the earth realm clothed in humanity to be able to unite with sinful man. The Seed of woman could not have been fathered by an earthly man without him receiving the sinful spiritual blood-line of the first Adam, in whom all die. Scripture clearly states that all offspring of the first Adam are born with a sinful spiritual nature, which alienates and spiritually separates them from God, resulting in spiritual and physical deaths. The sinless spiritual bloodline of the Son of God came from the Holy Spirit and not from carnal man. Jesus, in whose image man was created, was legally required to enter into the world clothed in humanity as the Seed of woman to conform to the image of the first Adam to be able to fulfill the Law as man. Only as man could He destroy the works of the devil and fulfill God's plan and purpose for the redemption of man.

The Second Person of the Trinity had to be clothed in humanity to become the only man begotten by God in the flesh as His Son (John 3:16). As God the Son, He was not begotten, for He is and was the ever existent One. If everything in heaven and on earth was created by Him, through Him, and for Him (Col 1:16, 17), then He obviously existed as the Second Person of the Trinity before time began. If the Son of God had not become incarnate as the Son of Man, the sins of man could not have been removed, since atone-ment—according to God's law—is realized only by the shedding of righteous blood. Only a sinless one of the same nature could qualify to atone for the sins of those who transgressed God's law.

Since by the first man's transgression came death, accordingly only by man could come the resurrection of the dead. The first begotten Son of God had to appear as the Son of Man to be able to unite with sinful humanity and then offer himself as propitiation acceptable to God the Father. As the Second Person of the Godhead, He could not have become one with man as Deity, since the Three in One cannot be broken.

There is one God the Father, one Lord Jesus Christ, and one Holy Spirit who in their perfect unity form the Godhead as One (I Cor 8:6; Eph 4:3, 6; I John 5:7; John 17:11, 21-23). Man can never be elevated above the level in which he was originally created to become a member of the Godhead. Since man was created a little lower than God he can never be exalted to the level of the Trinity. When the Son of Man came to redeem man from bondage in the kingdom of Satan, He, too had to be born into the world a little lower than the Trinity as man in order to unite with man to become his sin bearer. Only two of like nature can become one. Deity cannot unite with one in nature below the Trinity.

To become the Son of Man, the Son of God had to be made a little lower than angels, crowned with glory and honor (Ps 8:5, Heb 2:9). The Hebrew translation for "angels" in the Psalms is *Elohiym*, meaning Gods. The word *Elohiym* is first used in scripture when God said let "us" or "*Elohiym*" make man in our image, referring to the Trinity and not to angels (Gen 1:26). Therefore the Son of Man entered the world a litter lower than the Godhead as the first begotten Son of God in the flesh to identify with man. As sinless man, He had to be given dominion over the works of the Father's hands and to have all things put under His feet (Ps 8:4-6) to enter the world as the last

Adam, endowed as man with the same power and authority that God had originally bestowed upon the first man, Adam.

The genealogy of Jesus in the gospel of Saint Matthew confirms God's promise to Abraham and his offspring to send Abraham's "seed" into the world as the Son of Man. Matthew opens his gospel in this manner, *The book of the genealogy of Jesus Christ, the Son of David, the Son of Abraham.* The genealogy of Christ concludes with Jesus being identified as the seed or "the Son of Abraham" and it does not refer back to Adam, the first man. This serves as further confirmation that Abraham by his faith and obedience, in the offering of his son Isaac to God, became the father of Christianity. Abraham provided God with the legal authority to send His only begotten Son into the world as man to redeem mankind from the power of sin and to defeat the devil and destroy his works in fulfillment of His covenant promises (Gen 22:14-18).

Only God, who is the offended party because of man's rebellious sin against Him, could take the initial step toward satisfying the claims of heavenly justice against man. God foretold through the Prophet Isaiah how He would send His Son into the world (Isa 7:14).

God sent the angel Gabriel to a city of Galilee named Nazareth to a virgin named Mary, who was betrothed to a man whose name was Joseph, of the house or lineage of David. Upon entering the angel said to her, *Rejoice, highly favored one, the Lord is with you; blessed are you among women!* But she was troubled at his saying, and did not understand his word of greeting. Then the angel said to her, *Do not be afraid, Mary, for you have found favor with God. And behold, you will conceive in your womb and bring forth a Son, and shall call His name Jesus. He will be great, and will be called the Son of the Highest; and the Lord God will give Him the throne of His father David. And He will reign over the house of Jacob forever, and of His kingdom there will be no end* (Luke 1:26-33).

Mary asked the angel how this could be, since she had never had relations with a man. The angel told her, that the Holy Spirit would come upon her, and the power of the Highest would overshadow her and she would become pregnant with child. Therefore, since God the Holy Spirit would Father her child, He would be born the Holy One to be called the Son of God. He told her with God nothing would be impossible. Mary responded, as the maidservant of the Lord, to let it be unto her according to His word, whereupon the angel left her (Luke 1:34, 35, 37, 38).

After Mary became engaged to Joseph, before they had relations, she was pregnant with child by the Holy Spirit. Her husband, Joseph, being a just man, did not want to embarrass her, so he decided to put her away secretly. But as he thought about it, an angel of the Lord spoke to him in a dream, saying, "Joseph, son of David, do not be afraid to marry Mary your wife, for she is pregnant by the Holy Spirit. She will birth a Son and you are to name Him Jesus, for He will save His people from their sins."

So all this was done that it might be fulfilled, which was spoken by the Lord through the prophet Isaiah, saying: *Behold, the virgin shall be with child, and bear a Son, and they shall call His name Immanuel (Isa 7:14),* which is translated, "God with us". Then Joseph did as the angel of the Lord commanded him and married Mary and did not have relations with her until after she had delivered her firstborn Son. And Joseph called His name Jesus (Matt 1:18-25). The name Jesus corresponds with the Hebrew name Joshua, which means "Jehovah is salvation".

The Son of God, who being in the form of God, laid aside or emptied Himself of His Divine form and power to be made in the likeness of man in the womb of the Virgin Mary by the Holy Spirit (Luke 1:35) to become the Son of Man or "God manifested in the flesh" (Phil 2:6-8; I Tim 3:16).

Because the Holy Spirit fathered Jesus, He was born with the holy nature of God. His bloodline, or righteous nature, was due to His Divine origin and did not come from His mother, Mary. Christ was born into the earth realm as the Son of Man altogether holy and righteous, completely void of the sinful nature of all offspring of the first man, Adam.

Although Jesus was the Son of God, everything He accomplished on the earth had to be as man and not as deity, since the power and authority given to the first man Adam was voluntarily forfeited to Satan by him and not by a member of the Godhead. Since man gave it away through his disobedience, only by the obedience of a sinless man could it be regained and restored. For this reason God was compelled to send His own Son into the world in the likeness of sinful flesh as the Son of Man (Rom 8:3) rather than as deity.

When *The Son of Man* is used in scripture, preceded by the definite article *the,* reference is always made to the Son of God embodied in the flesh. He came clothed in righteousness to take the place of the first Adam, who surrendered himself and the human race to the kingdom of darkness. Only by having the same human nature as man could the only begotten Son of God spiritually unite with sinful man on the cross at Calvary to become his sin bearing substitute.

By virtue of the sacrificial offering of Himself and His sufferings as the Son of Man for all of humanity, Jesus would become the new spiritual head of redeemed humanity as a life-giving spirit (I John 5:11, 12). In so doing, He would provide man with the opportunity to be spiritually born again from above by the Spirit of God. Carnal man could then be delivered out of Satan's kingdom of darkness into God's Kingdom of Light.

The arrival of the Son of Man upon the Earth did not escape the attention of the wicked adversary of God and man. Unlike man, Satan is acutely aware of spiritual events that occur in the natural as well as in the spirit realm. Upon learning that Jesus was born in Bethlehem of Judea, the devil immediately exercised his influence and power through Herod, the king of Judea, in an attempt to prevent Jesus from accomplishing His mission as the Son of Man. When Herod heard about the birth of Jesus, he made inquiry of the chief priests and scribes to locate Christ. He was told that prophecy identified His birthplace as *Bethlehem of Judea.* Herod secretly called the wise men and sent them to Bethlehem to search for the Child and ordered them to report back to him.

Satan was determined to identify the Christ child and to have Him slain. He deceived King Herod into believing that Christ would replace him as king and therefore motivated him to kill Him. But after finding Jesus, the wise men did not report back to Herod.

Joseph was divinely warned in a dream to beware of Herod, so he and Mary departed with Jesus for their own country another way. After they had departed, an angel of the Lord appeared to Joseph in a dream and told him to take the young Child and His mother and to flee to Egypt. He was instructed to stay there because Herod would seek the young Child to destroy Him. Joseph took Him and His mother by night and departed for Egypt. When Herod realized that he had been deceived by the wise men he became exceedingly angry and had all the male children put to death who were in Bethlehem and in all its districts, from two years old and under, according to the time he had determined from the wise men that Christ was born. Then what the prophet Jeremiah had spoken was fulfilled: *A voice was heard in Ramah, Lamentation, weeping, and great mourning, Rachel weeping for her children, Refusing to be comforted, Because they are no more.* Untold anguish was visited upon the families when the male children were slain in Satan's attempt to prevent the Christ Child from remaining in the world as man to defeat him and to ultimately destroy his kingdom of darkness.

Following the death of Herod, an angel of the Lord appeared in a dream to Joseph in Egypt, saying, *"Arise, take the young Child and His mother, and go to the land of Israel, for those who sought the young Child's life are dead."* Joseph took the young Child and His mother, and they returned to the land of Israel. But when he heard that Archelaus was reigning over Judea instead of his father Herod, he was afraid to go there. And being warned by God in a dream, he turned aside into the region of Galilee. He dwelt in a city called Nazareth so that which was spoken by the prophets might be fulfilled: *He shall be called a Nazarene* (Matt 2:1-23). Figuratively Jesus was called out of Egypt just as Abraham and his offspring were delivered from the same country before they entered into covenant relationship with God.

When Jesus was eight days old, He underwent circumcision according to the Law on the eighth day after His birth (Luke 2:21; Gen 17:12). So after they had performed all things according to the law of the Lord, they returned to Galilee, to their own city, Nazareth *(Luke 2:27). And the child grew and became strong in spirit and filled with wisdom; and the grace of God was upon Him* (Luke 2:39, 40).

The only other biblical reference to Jesus during His childhood occurred when He was 12 years old. His parents went to Jerusalem to attend the Feast of the Passover. After they had finished, they returned and the Boy Jesus lingered behind in Jerusalem. Joseph and His mother were unaware of His absence until after a day's journey and they looked for Him among their relatives and acquaintances. They were unable to find Him and returned to Jerusalem, seeking Him. After three days, they found Him in the temple, sitting in the midst of the teachers, both listening to them and asking them questions. And all who heard Him were astonished at His understanding and answers. So when they saw Him, they were amazed; and His mother said to Him, *Son, why have You done this to us? Look, Your father and I have sought You anxiously.* And He said to them, *Why did you seek Me? Did you not know that I must be about My Father's business*? But they did not understand the statement He spoke to them. He returned to Nazareth with them and obeyed them, but His mother kept all these things in her heart. And *Jesus increased in wisdom and stature, and in favor with God and men* (Luke 2:41-52).

Chapter Thirteen

The Son of Man Received
The Empowerment of The Holy Spirit

From birth, Jesus did not suffer the adverse effects of sin or the curse that God placed upon sinful humanity and the earth after the first Adam's transgression. His spirit, soul and body remained untainted and uncorrupted by sin, which enabled Him to experience unbroken spiritual relationship and fellowship with the Father until He was made to be sin with the sins of all humanity on the cross at Calvary. He was able to communicate with His Father and to hear His voice unlike any mortal man has ever experienced. In a sense, He remained tethered to His Father by His spiritual umbilical cord, which enabled the Son of Man to have uninterrupted spiritual communion and relationship with His Father. He neither experienced the deadly effects of sin nor the power of Satan being exercised over Him during His earthly walk.

Although Jesus was empowered at birth with the same dominion and authority over the earth and over Satan that God originally bestowed upon Adam, He was unable to exercise His authority and dominion as the Son of Man until after He was anointed or empowered by the Holy Spirit. Scripture does not record any ministry activity on the part of the Son of Man until He was about 30 years of age, at which time Jesus came from Galilee to John the Baptist and was baptized by him in the Jordan River. After Jesus was baptized and while He prayed, the heaven was opened. And the Holy Spirit descended upon Him in bodily form like a dove and a voice came from heaven saying, *You are My beloved Son; in You I am well pleased.* (Luke 3:21-23; Matt 3:13-17).

God the Father personally spoke from heaven and acknowledged the Son-ship of Jesus immediately after the Holy Spirit released His anointing to empower the Son of Man to perform His ordained ministry upon Earth. God also prophesied concerning the anointing of the Son of Man hundreds of years beforehand when He spoke through the prophet Isaiah concerning Him. God pronounced that He would put His Spirit upon His chosen Servant with whom He was well pleased, His Elect One in whom His soul delighted. He said His Servant would proclaim and bring forth justice to the nations (Isa 42:1-4, Matt 12:18).

The Son of Man personally acknowledged His anointing as well. Jesus came to Nazareth, where He was reared, and went into the synagogue on the Sabbath day. He read from the book of the prophet Isaiah, who said:

The Spirit of the Lord is upon Me, because He has anointed Me to preach the gospel to the poor; he has sent Me to heal the broken-hearted, to proclaim liberty to the captives and recovery of sight to the blind, to set at liberty those who are oppressed; To proclaim the acceptable year of the Lord. (Luke 4:18, 19)

He said to them, *Today this Scripture is fulfilled in your hearing* (Luke 4:21). Scripture further declares that *God anointed Jesus of Nazareth with the Holy Spirit and with power and He went about doing good and healing all who were oppressed by the devil, for God was with Him (Acts 10:38).* Jesus spoke the words of God with the unlimited anointing of the Holy Spirit and the Father gave Him authority over all things after He was baptized with the Holy Spirit (John 3:34, 35).

Until He was made to be sin on the cross at Calvary with the sins of all mankind, Jesus neither suffered the deadly effects of sin nor experienced the devastating curse that Satan brought upon man and the earth after the first Adam's transgression. His intimate fellowship and communion with God the Father was never adversely affected by the power of His adversary. Since the Son of Man remained faithful to His Father, His spiritual relationship with Him remained unbroken and sin never entered into Him. He was able to communicate with God without experiencing any interference from the devil as carnal man faces. If the first Adam had remained obedient to God and had partaken of the fruit of the "Tree of Life", he would have been empowered by the same Holy Spirit to rule and to reign over the earthly world and to subdue Satan just as the Son of Man demonstrated in His earthly walk.

All scripture concerning the Son of Man's life on earth relates to the exercise of the gifts of the Holy Spirit operating in and through His life as man rather than in and through Him as the Second Person of the Trinity or the exercising of His natural abilities as a human being. Jesus did not claim the attributes of His Father, but only the anointing of the Holy Spirit. During the first 30 years of His life, even though the Son of Man obeyed the Father and lived a sinless life, He did not demonstrate any power or authority different from ordinary man (Luke 3:23). Not one act of ministry or the performance of any miracle or the casting out of any evil spirit on the part of the Son of

Man occurred until after He was baptized with the Holy Spirit immediately following His baptism in water by John the Baptist in the river Jordan.

After receiving the anointing of the Holy Spirit, the Son of Man demonstrated His power and authority over the natural and supernatural realms of the earth when He turned water into wine, walked on water, calmed the storm, fed the multitudes with a few loaves and fish, healed all who touched even the hem of His garments, raised the dead, cast out demons, and performed many other miraculous works. He demonstrated His authority and power over Satan as well as over the material world. Since the Son of Man entered the Earth with the righteous spiritual nature of God the Father, He was not subject to the limitations God had placed upon the Earth as well as over all the sinful offspring of the first Adam.

As soon as the Son of Man was empowered to fulfill His mandated mission upon earth, He was led by the Holy Spirit into the wilderness to be tempted by Satan in body, soul and spirit. God allowed His only begotten Son to be tested just as He did in the life of the first Adam, as well as He does in our lives. Satan immediately pursued the opportunity to seize the power and authority that God had bestowed upon Jesus with the obvious intent and purpose of defeating Him by enticing Him to sin. The devil knew that if he succeeded, he would become the eternal god of this earthly world, since God did not have anyone other than His Son to send into the world as the redeemer of mankind.

Scripture describes the devious temptation of Jesus in the wilderness. After Jesus was filled with the Holy Spirit, He was led by the Spirit into the wilderness and was tempted by the devil for 40 days. During that time He ate nothing and was hungry. The devil said, *If You are the Son of God, command this stone to become bread.* But Jesus responded, *It is written, Man shall not live by bread alone, but He must abide by every word of God.*

Then the devil took Him up on a high mountain and showed Him all the kingdoms of the world. The devil told Him that he would give Him the authority to rule over them for it had been delivered to him and he could give it to whomever he desired. Jesus commanded Satan to get behind Him, for the Word of the Lord commanded Him to worship and serve only the Lord God.

The devil then brought Jesus to Jerusalem and set Him on the pinnacle of the temple and said if He was the Son of God, to throw Himself down to the ground. The devil then quoted scripture to Jesus stating that God would give His angels charge over Him and would prevent Him from being injured. Jesus answered, *You are not to tempt the Lord your God.* After the temptations had ended, the devil departed from Jesus until an opportune time arose to again tempt Him (Luke 4:1-13).

The devil first appealed to the lust of the flesh, attempting to entice Jesus to satisfy His hunger by supernatural intervention to prove that He was the Son of God in the flesh. Satan tried to deceive Jesus by provoking Him to fulfill God's word for egotistical reasons. Jesus remained in the spirit by obeying the word of the Lord. In each instance, the Son of Man quoted the word of God back to the devil as His higher authority and thus overcame Satan's temptations by remaining obedient to God the Father.

If Satan had not possessed the authority to rule over the kingdoms of the world, then his offer to give this power to the Son of Man could not have constituted a genuine temptation. The devil admitted such power had been freely delivered to him, which would have allowed him to give it to whomever he wished. Later during his ministry, Jesus testified that Satan has a kingdom on planet Earth. After He healed a man who was demon-possessed, blind, and mute, He was accused by the Pharisees of casting out demons by Beelzebub, the ruler of the demons. But Jesus knew their thoughts, and said to them: *Every kingdom divided against itself is brought to desolation, and every city or house divided against itself will not stand. If Satan casts out Satan, he is divided against himself. How then will his kingdom stand?* (Matt 12:22-26).

Jesus did not dispute Satan's representation of authority, since it had been voluntarily forfeited to Satan by Adam in the Garden of Eden. The devil tried to entice Jesus to sin by influencing Him to bow down and worship him as the ruler of this world. If Satan did not rule this world, his offer would not have constituted a valid temptation. If the Son of Man had succumbed to any of Satan's temptations, He would have suffered the same spiritual death as the first Adam experienced when he partook of the forbidden fruit in the Garden of Eden. The Son of Man would have forfeited to Satan His power and authority to rule over God's Kingdom of Light on earth as man and would have become a slave to sin. The devil would have aborted God's plan to redeem mankind and to restore the ruler-ship over the Kingdom of Light to Jesus as man. Jesus would have lost His power to subdue the devil and to destroy his works.

As the Second Person of the Trinity, the Son of God was immune to temptation, for God cannot be tempted by evil, nor does He tempt anyone (James 1:12-15). As the Son of Man, He became subject to temptation and had to overcome every temptation known to man. Scripture states, He *was in all points tempted as we are, yet without sin* (Heb 4:15). *In all things He had to be made like His brethren, that He might be a merciful and faithful High Priest in things pertaining to God, to make propitiation for the sins of the people. For in that He Himself has suffered being tempted, He is able to aid those who are tempted* (Heb 2:17, 18).

The Son of Man came to save lives of men and not to destroy them (Luke 9:56). Following His anointing by the Holy Spirit and after being tempted by the devil, Jesus began to preach the good news of the Kingdom of God and to exhort men to repent for the Kingdom of heaven was near (Matt 4:16, 17). Jesus went throughout Galilee and taught in their synagogues, preached to them the gospel of the kingdom, and healed all kinds of sicknesses and diseases among the people. His fame went throughout Syria. All sick people who were afflicted with various diseases and torments, and those who were demon-possessed, epileptics, and paralytics were brought to Him and He healed all of them (Matt 4:23, 24).

Jesus was demonstrating that He had come to establish the Kingdom of God upon Earth and to subdue the devil, as well as to remove the evil effect of sin that is visited upon man in the kingdom of darkness. Jesus was also setting the example that we are to follow as believers in Him, to fulfill God's plan on planet Earth. Jesus was performing the work that God had ordained Him to do, as opposed to practicing empty religious duties and rituals. His word was being fulfilled by the Holy Spirit as He carried out the mission of the Father.

Upon being asked by the Pharisees when the kingdom of God would come, Jesus told them that the kingdom of God does not come so that we can see it, nor can we say here it is or there it is, *because the kingdom* of God *is within us who believe* (Luke 17:20, 21). Jesus explained that He did not come to establish a material kingdom upon earth during His first Advent, but a spiritual kingdom within the hearts of men, which is not apparent to the natural senses.

Jesus used the parable of a sower of seed to describe how man gains entry into the spiritual Kingdom of God. The seed sown represent the living Word of God and the sower represents the Son of Man.

Behold, a sower went out to sow. And as he sowed, some seed fell by the wayside; and the birds came and devoured them. Some fell on stony places, where they did not have much earth; and they immediately sprang up because they had no depth of earth. But when the sun was up they were scorched, and because they had no root they withered away. And some fell among thorns, and the thorns sprang up and choked them. But others fell on good ground and yielded a crop: some a hundredfold, some sixty, some thirty. He who has ears to hear, let him hear! (Matthew 13:3-9)

Jesus used an earthly example to explain how we respond upon hearing the word of God taught or preached, as well as our response when we read and study His word. The condition of our hearts determines how the word of God is received by us, as well as the effect it has upon our lives. We are encouraged to let the word of Christ dwell in us richly in all wisdom (Col 3:16). Did Jesus not say, *If you abide in My word, you are My disciples indeed and you shall know the truth, and the truth shall make you free* (John 8:31, 32)? The word of God *is* alive and powerful, and sharper than any two-edged sword. It is able to divide the soul and spirit of man, piercing even to the division of joints and marrow, and it discerns the thoughts and intents of the heart. No one is hidden from His sight, but all things *are* naked and open to the eyes of Him to whom we *must give* account (Heb 4:12, 13). We are admonished to rid ourselves of all moral filthiness and the evil that is prevalent in our lives and to humbly accept the word of God, which can save us. We are to be doers of God's word, and not just hearers only, deceiving ourselves (Jam 1:21, 22).

Jesus gave many parables or examples of the Kingdom of God, as well as who would be able to enter into it. He commanded us to seek first His Kingdom and His righteousness and then all things needed to sustain life in this world would be provided for us (Matt 6:33). He encouraged man to pray: *Our Father in heaven, Hallowed be Your name. Your kingdom come. Your will be done on earth as it is in heaven* (Matt 6:9).

From the beginning of His ministry, Jesus made it clear that He had come to reestablish the Kingdom of God upon the earth that was lost through the disobedient act of the first man Adam. He also confirmed that God's kingdom is opposed to the kingdom of Satan, the Prince of the power of the air. The Kingdom of God is one of righteousness, peace, light and life, whereas the kingdom of Satan is one of deception, evil, darkness, and death. The kingdom of God can be established only within and upon the territory that belongs to Him. If we are unwilling to surrender our hearts and lives to Him, then we remain under the dominion of the devil and God will not allow His Holy Spirit to dwell in us. If we obey His word and surrender ourselves to Him, then we become His purchased possession and gain entry into His Kingdom of righteousness as a member of His Body spiritually united with Him.

Chapter Fourteen

The Son of Man Was Immortal

J esus came eating and drinking, and the people said, *Look, a glutton and a winebibber, a friend of tax collectors and sinners!* (Matt 11:19). Only as the Son of Man could He have mingled with sinful men without them being slain by His holy presence. If Christ had appeared in his divine or glorified body, no man could have remained in His presence. For example, when the Lord descended upon Mount Sinai during the time of Moses and sanctified the mountain with holy fire, He told the people through Moses that any person or animal that even touched the mountain while He was present would be killed. Only by laying aside His divinity and becoming clothed in humanity was Jesus able to mingle with sinful men without immediate judgment being imposed upon them. Remember the comments that Jesus made to the most religious Jewish people of His time: *You are of your father, the devil* (John 8:44). Yet, as the Son of Man, Jesus was able to mingle with sinful mankind, whether Jew or Gentile, in His day to day activities without the penalty of death being imposed upon those who entered into His presence.

Unlike the offspring of the first Adam, Christ Jesus, as the sinless Son of Man, was immortal when He walked upon the earth. He was not subject to physical or spiritual death at the hands of man, regardless of the measure of severe punishment and abuse that carnal man could inflict upon Him. Physical wounds could not slay the sinless One. No man could take His life against His will. Man did not possess the power or authority to physically overpower Him in His sinless spiritual condition.

Satan could not exert any power or authority over Him, since the devil only derives his lordship over man through the power of sin. For the same reason the curse upon the earth did not adversely affect Jesus due to His sinless spiritual condition. The Son of Man did not have to battle the sins of the flesh as mortal man does, but He continued to experience unbroken communion and fellowship with God the Father until He was made to be sin with the sins of humanity. Because of his sinless obedient life, the Holy Spirit was able to anoint Him with the fullness of the Godhead (Col 2:9).

Jesus declared: *Therefore My Father loves Me, because I lay down My life that I may take it again. No one takes it from Me, but I lay it down of Myself. I have power to lay it down, and I have power to take it again. This command I have received from My Father* (John 10:17, 18). He later said to his disciples: *I will no longer talk much with you, for the ruler of this world* (Satan) *is coming, and he has nothing in Me* (John 14:30).

Jesus literally said that Satan did not have any power to exercise over Him, since He was altogether righteous. Christ proved His authority over Satan as the Son of Man by casting out demons or evil spirits and exerting total command over the devil in His earthly walk and ministry. His unlimited empowerment by the Holy Spirit in His sinless condition set the Son of Man apart from the sinful offspring of the first Adam and served as testimony that no one fathered by natural man could exercise authority over the devil and over the earth as He demonstrated as man during His earthly life.

On several occasions Satan inspired carnal men to attempt to kill the Son of Man. A crowd was angered when Jesus told them that no prophet is accepted in his own country and cited examples to the people. He related how many widows were in Israel in the days of Elijah when there was a great famine throughout all the land for three years and six months, but Elijah was sent only to Zarephath, to a woman who was a widow. And there were many lepers in Israel during the time of Elisha the prophet, but none of them was cleansed except Naaman the Syrian. So when all those in the synagogue heard these things, they were filled with wrath and thrust Him out of the city. They led Him to the edge of the hill on which their city was built, intending to throw Him over the cliff, but He passed through the midst of them and went on His way (Luke 4:24-30).

Members of the synagogue, who were the Jewish people that Christ Jesus came to seek and to save, became so incensed that they thrust Him out of the city and maintained control over Him. When they attempted to kill Him by throwing Him over the cliff, He simply went His way unharmed. Because of His spiritual perfection, mankind could not exert any authority over Him unless He submitted to them.

Another incident occurred during a discourse with the Jews when Jesus told them that their forefather Abraham was very happy to see His day. By faith Abraham saw it and he was glad. The Jews said, "You are not yet 50 years old, how could you have seen Abraham?" Jesus told them that He existed before Abraham. They picked up stones to hurl at Him, but He concealed Himself and left the temple, moving through the midst of them (John 8:56-59). No one was able to so much as touch Him with one stone even though He moved among them and departed. The men of that day were so spiritually blind, as are the majority of people today, that they did not even hold Him in awe or fear Him.

At another time Jesus cried out as He taught in the temple, saying,

You both know Me, and you know where I am from; and I have not come of Myself, but He who sent Me is true, whom you do not know. But I know Him, for I am from Him, and He sent Me. Then they sought to take Him; but no one laid a hand on Him, because His hour had not yet come. (John 7:28-30)

On a different occasion there was a division among the people because of Jesus. Some of them wanted to take Him, but no one laid hands on Him (John 7:43, 44).

Later the Jews took up stones again to stone Him. Jesus asked them to explain why they wanted to do so. The Jews accused Him of committing blasphemy because He was a Man and had made Himself God. Jesus reminded them of what was written in their law. He asked if they were accusing Him, whom the Father had sanctified and sent into the world, of blasphemy because He said He was the Son of God. Jesus said if He was not doing the works of His Father, then they should not believe Him. But if He did His Father's works as a man, even though they refused to believe Him, they should believe in His works, that they might know and believe that the Father was in Him and He was in the Father. They tried to seize Him again, but He delivered Himself out of their hand (John 10:31-39).

When Jesus and His disciples were in the garden of Gethsemane, Judas Iscariot, together with a detachment of troops and officers from the chief priests and Pharisees, came with lanterns, torches, and weapons to seize Him. Jesus knew all things that would happen to Him, so He went forward and asked them who they were seeking. They said, "Jesus of Nazareth." Jesus identified Himself and Judas, who was betraying Him, was in their midst. When He told them who He was, they fell backwards to the ground. He asked them again who they were seeking. They responded, "Jesus of Nazareth." Jesus admitted His identity a second time (John 18:1-8). The Son of Man once again was demonstrating to the mob that mortal man could neither exercise any power or authority over Him, nor could any man even touch Him without His permission due to His unlimited anointing by the Holy Spirit.

Following His voluntarily submission to them, Jesus was later taken before Pilate, who said to Him, *Are You not speaking to me? Do You not know that I have power to crucify You, and power to release You? Jesus answered, You could have no power at all against Me unless it had been given you from above* (John 19:10, 11). Jesus was again emphatic in His response to Pilate that he could do nothing to Him since He was immune to death in His sinless spiritual condition. He stressed that only God the Father held the power to take His life.

Jesus possessed the power to heal, which the Son of Man demonstrated on numerous occasions during His earthly ministry. Wherever He entered into villages, cities, or the country, they laid the sick in the marketplaces and begged Him that they might just touch even the hem of His garment. All who touched Him were made well (Mark 6:56).

Even though the Son of Man voluntarily endured the wrath of man to the degree that His countenance was marred beyond human appearance from the beatings and lashes that He endured (Isa 52:13, 14), He still could not have been slain by man. He remained immune to death in His sinless spiritual condition, for He possessed the power to heal even His own body. Physical death could not overcome the Son of Man so long as He remained obedient and therefore spiritually alive unto God. Only sin could separate Him from His Father and cause His spiritual death. If men were unable to cause Him to sin, accordingly they could not take His life regardless of the physical punishment they inflicted on Him.

Jesus only did what He saw the Father doing and what the Father told Him to do. He said, *I do nothing of Myself; but as My Father taught Me, I speak these things (John 8:28). And He who sent Me is with Me. The Father has not left Me alone, for I always do those things that please Him (John 8:29). The words that I speak to you I do not speak on My own authority; but the Father who dwells in Me does the works* (John 14:10). As the Son of Man, Jesus never acted upon His own volition in thought, will, or deed contrary to His Father's will.

As the Son of Man, He demonstrated His power over death by raising a synagogue ruler's daughter from the dead (Matt 9:18, 19). On another occasion Jesus raised Lazarus, the brother of Mary and Martha, to life after he had been dead for four days (John 11:39-44). Even the people present did not realize that Jesus had to specifically call Lazarus by his name otherwise a multitude of the dead would have been raised to life with him.

The only lethal force that could cause the Son of Man's death was the power of sin, which would result first in His spiritual death, separating Him from God, and then subject Him to physical death as was demonstrated in the life of Adam in the Garden of Eden. Since Christ Jesus was birthed into the world by the power of the Holy Spirit, He was as holy as God, His Father, without any trace of sin in His spiritual or physical being. Due to His obedience to God the Father, sinful man did not have the power to slay Him despite their repeated attempts to do so.

The power and authority of Adam paralleled that of the Son of Man at birth. But Christ Jesus, as the Son of Man, revealed to the world the dominion and authority that the first man Adam could have exercised over the earth and over Satan, as well as his wicked spirits, if he had remained obedient to God and had partaken of the Tree of Life in the Garden of Eden rather than partaking of the Tree of the Knowledge of Good and Evil. Men teach and preach that because Jesus was the Son of God He was able to do all things, rather than Him accomplishing all things during His ministry as the Son of Man under the empowerment of the Holy Spirit. How could this be true if He laid aside His divine attributes to enter the world to be made like His brethren in all things? Does Scripture not clearly state that He was anointed by the Holy Spirit to do all the things as man?

Chapter Fifteen

The Son of Man Came to Fulfill the Law

The Son of Man said He did not come to destroy the Law or the Prophets, but to fulfill. He gave his assurance that until heaven and earth passed away, not one jot or one tittle would by any means pass from the law until all of it was fulfilled (Matt 5:17, 18). The Law included the Ten Commandments together with civil and ceremonial laws that related to the Levitical priesthood and its duties (Exo 20:1-17) under the Mosaic or Old Covenant.

According to scripture, the Law of the Lord is perfect and converts the soul of man (Ps 19:7). So why was it necessary for the Law to be fulfilled by the Son of man? On the other hand, scripture later declared that the Law was annulled by Jesus because it was weak and unprofitable for man, since the Law made nothing perfect (Heb 7:18, 19). Does a contradiction exist as to the Law of God?

Quite to the contrary, the perfect Law of God is spiritual, but man is carnal, sold under sin (Rom 7:14), which *is the transgression of the Law* (I John 3:4, KJV). The Law could not overcome the conflict arising from its holy nature and the unrighteous nature of man because it could not change the spiritual condition of man. Instead, the Law condemned man, since it could not save or deliver him from his bondage to sin (Rom 7:24). As a result, the Law became known as the *Law of sin and death* (Rom 8:2), because by the deeds of the Law no man can be justified in the sight of God, for the Law makes man recognize or become conscious of sin (Rom 3:19, 20).

Since carnal man cannot keep or fulfill the Law because of his sinful spiritual condition, it becomes a curse condemning him to eternal death and punishment as a Law breaker. The Law was given to reveal to man the imperfections of his sinful nature and to govern his relationship with the Law Giver as well as his fellowman. God gave the Law to serve as man's tutor to bring him to Christ, that he might be justified by faith in Christ Jesus and not by the works of the Law (Gal 3:24).

In the fullness of the time it was necessary for God to send His Son, born of a woman, born under the Law, to redeem those who were under the Law, that they might receive the adoption as sons (Gal 4:4, 5). Christ had to be born in human form to come under the Law or He otherwise could not have personally kept the Law in His earthly walk to qualify as man's sin-bearing substitute on the cross. Only as the Son of Man could He fulfill the Law on behalf of mankind and not as deity, during His suffering on the cross and His suffering God's judgment in man's stead. As the second person of the Trinity, He was the Law Giver (John 1:3) and as the Law Giver, the Son of God was not subject to the Law.

As man's surety and substitute, He became the Law Keeper and thus was able to bear the curse of the Law for mankind by taking sinful man's place. He then became subject to the demands of divine justice under the Law (Gal 3:13). The only way Jesus could fulfill His appointed mission was to be born of woman under the Law as the sinless Son of Man. Christ as the Son of Man could then suffer once for the sins of all mankind, the just for the unjust, that He might bring or reconcile man to God (1 Pet 3:18). To be able to unite with earthly man and become his sin bearer, the Son of God had to humble himself as the Divine "Law Giver" to be born into the world as the Son of Man to become the "Law Keeper". Since the triune being of God is altogether holy and cannot sin, only as the Son of Man could Jesus be made sin by God the Father with the sins of corrupted humanity (II Cor 5:21). Thus, He could qualify as man's substitutionary sin sacrifice to destroy the works of the devil (I John 3:8) by satisfying man's sin debt to God through His vicarious sufferings on the cross and in hell.

The fulfillment of the Law on the part of the Son of Man was twofold. First, He had to remain obedient to God the Father in His earthly life to fulfill the Law as man in order to become eligible to be made the sinless sacrificial offering required by God for the sins of all mankind. Secondly, He had to be chosen as the sacrificial sin offering for humanity according to Levitical Law to become eligible to take man's place in judgment and to endure the punishment necessary to fulfill the penalty of the Law on sinful man's behalf. As the Law Keeper, the Son of Man was required to fulfill the Mosaic or Old Covenant ordained by God that was ratified by the nation of Israel. The most critical phase of fulfilling the Law involved the performance of duties by the Levitical priesthood to bring the Old Covenant to a close.

God established the Levitical Priesthood to be able to have a spiritual relationship with sinful man under the Mosaic covenant and to minister mercy and grace to him under the Law. The priesthood was ordained to mediate between God, whose wrath is aroused by sin, and sinful man, who is unable to fulfill the demands of the Law. The priesthood was temporal inasmuch as it was imperfect; the service rendered by it in the sacrificial offering of the blood of animals could not cleanse the spirit and soul of man. The blood only served as a covering to cleanse the flesh of man to permit an outward relationship to exist between man and God. Man's spiritual condition remained unchanged under the Law.

The Levitical priests appeased God on a temporal basis by offering acceptable animal sacrifices whose blood served as atonement for the sins of the people. All of the animal sacrifices pointed to Christ Jesus, who would offer Himself once as the ultimate perfect sacrifice as the Son of Man for all people for the remission of their sins. The Levitical priesthood served as a shadow or representation of the priesthood of Christ, which was to come after the original order of Melchizedek. The Levitical priesthood was purposed by God to only remain in force until the Law was fulfilled and the true priesthood was established and administered by the Son of Man as our eternal Mediator and High Priest.

God ordered the Levitical priesthood and the Israelite nation to observe the "Day of Atonement" once each year as a holy convocation and to make an offering by fire to the Lord (Exo 40:12-15; Lev 23:27-32). The Day of Atonement was designated by God as the day that atonement was to be made before *the Lord your God* by and for the high priest and the people of Israel. The Levitical priesthood was ordained to remain unending until the Law was fulfilled in its entirety by the Supreme Sacrifice of the Son of Man to appease God, whose wrath is aroused by the rebellious nature and unlawful acts of man.

God commanded that atonement be made once each year for the sins of the Israelites and the Levitical priesthood. On that day the high priest chose the sacrifice and made atonement for himself and for the Israelite nation, to cleanse them from all their sins before the Lord (Lev 16:30). On the Day of Atonement only, the Levitical high priest entered the Holy of Holies in the tabernacle of Moses behind the veil that separated it from the Holy Place. He alone approached the atonement cover or the Mercy Seat of the Ark of the Covenant. Since God appeared in the cloud over the atonement seat, the high priest could enter the sanctuary area only with the blood of the sacrificial animal, which he offered as a burnt sin sacrifice to God for himself and for the people of Israel (Lev 16:27-30). After entering the Holy of Holies, the high priest deposited the blood on the mercy seat of the Ark of the Covenant before the Lord in the Holy of Holies in the Tabernacle of Moses as atonement for himself and for the sins of the people.

The only means by which the Law regarding sinful mankind could be fulfilled in its entirety required the Levitical high priest to choose and to offer a sinless sacrifice of like nature, as was the first man Adam before he disobeyed God. The Lord was demonstrating that the Mosaic covenant did not apply to the Godhead, or to angels or to animals, but only to man. Eternal fulfillment of the Law required a sinless man to become the atoning sacrifice once for all mankind. God was further signifying that only the Levitical high priest was ordained to choose that substitutionary sacrifice to offer for Atonement, to symbolically transfer the sins of the people to him and then offer him up to God as a sin sacrifice on behalf of mankind.

Caiaphas, the Levitical high priest, without realizing the significance of what God was speaking through him, prophesied that Jesus would be chosen as the perfect sacrifice. Caiaphas, who was the high priest, told the Jewish people that they did not know anything, nor did they consider that it was expedient for them that one man should die for all the people to prevent the whole nation from perishing. Caiaphas did not say this on his own authority. But as high priest that year, he prophesied that Jesus should die for the entire nation and that Jesus would bring together in one body the children of God who were scattered throughout the nations. From that day on, they plotted to kill Him (John 11:49-53) because their evil nature was offended by the righteous authority of the Son of Man (John 8:44).

In order for God to legally bring the Levitical priesthood and the Old Covenant to a conclusion, it became absolutely necessary for the Levitical high priest to personally choose the Son of Man as the Perfect Sacrifice to be offered as an Atonement for himself and for the sins of the people, since that responsibility was ordained by God under the Law of Moses. Due to his spiritual blindness, Caiaphas chose Jesus, the Son of Man, to become the supreme sacrifice once for all humanity, thus fulfilling the Law on behalf of all mankind. By choosing the Son of Man and charging Him with a capital crime resulting in His death by crucifixion, wherein He was lifted up and presented to God, Caiaphas effectively brought to an end the need for any further offering of animal sacrifices as a temporal atonement for the sins of mankind. An earthly advocate was no longer needed to mediate between man and God, as represented by the Levitical priesthood or any other religion, since it was replaced by a higher eternal priesthood after the original order of Melchizedek.

Jesus confirmed that Caiaphas the High Priest became the one who chose Him to become the sacrificial offering once for all humanity. Jesus said: *Behold, we are going up to Jerusalem, and the Son of Man will be betrayed to the chief priests and to the scribes; and they will condemn Him to death, and deliver Him to the Gentiles to mock and to scourge and to crucify. And the third day He will rise again* (Matt 20:18, 19).

Chapter Sixteen

The Son of Man Endured the Wrath of Man

The most religious leaders of the nation of Israel, because of their spiritual blindness, could not discern the identity of the Son of Man even though the prophets of the Lord down through the ages proclaimed His coming. The prophets had described the purpose of His coming together with His sufferings for the redemption and salvation of man. Nevertheless, they were unable to discern that He was the only begotten Son of God in the flesh. The high priests were jealous and envious of the power and authority Jesus exercised and they judged Him to be their chief competitor in the religious arena. They were violently opposed to the true gospel being proclaimed because it threatened their religious traditions and the empire that they controlled.

The Jewish spiritual leaders were convinced that they were performing their duties to enforce the Law of God, which prohibited blasphemy. They were totally unaware of their required duty under the Law of God to choose the perfect sacrifice to offer as Atonement for the sins of humanity. The Levitical priesthood, together with the Jewish people, interpreted the scriptures to mean that the Messiah would appear to conquer all opposing forces and to establish God's permanent kingdom upon Earth during His initial appearance. Scripture reveals how the chief priests, who were unable to look outside their doctrinal box, executed their plan to arrest, charge, and punish the Son of Man for the perceived offense of blasphemy.

As the celebration of the Passover drew near, the chief priests and the scribes began to develop a plan to kill Jesus, but they were fearful of how the people would react. Then Satan entered Judas Iscariot, who was one of the twelve disciples of Jesus. So Judas conferred with the chief priests and captains regarding how he could help them to safely take Jesus. They were pleased and offered him money. Judas promised to betray Jesus and sought an opportunity to arrange for them to take Him in the absence of the multitude of people. On the Day of Unleavened Bread when the Passover had to be killed, Jesus sent Peter and John, two of His disciples, to prepare the Passover for them to eat (Luke 22:1-8).

During the Passover meal, Jesus told them He had a fervent desire to eat the Passover with them before He suffered. He said He would not eat of it again until the Passover was fulfilled in the kingdom of God. Then He took the cup, and gave thanks, and told them to take the bread and divide it among themselves because He would not drink of the fruit of the vine again until the kingdom of God had come. He took bread, and after giving thanks broke it, and gave it to them. He said the bread represented His body, which He was giving for them and commanded them to observe the Passover in the future in remembrance of Him. In like manner, *After eating the Passover meal, He took the cup and said that it represented the new covenant in His blood, which was shed for them (Luke 22:15-20).*

The fruit of the vine, grape juice, symbolized the blood of Jesus, which was to be shed for the remission of the sins of man, and the unleavened bread, which was broken, represented the brutalized body of Jesus for the healing of man. The Son of Man was forewarning His disciples that He would offer Himself to God as the atoning Passover Lamb to enable the spiritual kingdom of God to be established upon earth. He explained to them that the kingdom of God could come only by Him offering Himself as man's substitutionary sin sacrifice by the shedding His own righteous blood for them. Jesus warned His disciples that they would be offended because of Him being crucified, but after He had risen again, He would go before them into Galilee. Jesus warned Peter that he would deny Him three times and said His disciples would be scattered after His death (Matt 26).

Jesus had previously informed the people that the hour had come for the Son of Man to be glorified. He said to them most assuredly that unless a grain of wheat enters the ground and dies, it remains alone. But if it dies, it will produce much grain (John 12:23, 24). He then told them a parable concerning Himself. He described how He would die. He said the world would be judged and the ruler of this world, Satan, would be cast out. He told them if He were lifted up from the earth, He would draw all peoples to Himself, speaking of His being united with all mankind as their sin bearer on the cross at Calvary. But the people answered Him saying that they had heard from the law that the Messiah would remain forever. So they asked Him how He could He say that the Son of Man must be lifted up and who was this Son of Man (John 12:31-34).

The people were convinced that when their Messiah came, He would set up a permanent kingdom and would remain to rule and reign over it eternally.

The Jewish people probably did not have the biblical scrolls available to them to personally read and therefore depended upon the Levitical priests to read and interpret them. Even though Christ told His 12 disciples during the Passover that He was going to die for them, they could not comprehend the purpose and meaning of His death. The Levitical priests were unable to associate the animal sacrifices that God commanded them to offer once each year on the Day of Atonement with the sacrificial death of Jesus. They did not realize that the Day of Atonement foreshadowed God the Father offering His only begotten Son once for the sins of all people.

Satan, by blinding the minds of men through envy, anger, and hatred, inspired them to seize the Son of Man in the darkness of night. The devil believed that he had reached the pinnacle of success in his efforts to defeat and destroy the One whom God had sent into the world as man, empowered to rule over him. The chief priests, the scribes, and the elders of the people assembled at the palace of the high priest, who was called Caiaphas, and plotted to take Jesus by trickery and kill Him (Matt 26:3, 4).

Judas, with a detachment of troops and officers from the chief priests and Pharisees, went to the garden of Gethsemane with lanterns, torches, and weapons (John 18:3). The troops, together with the captain and the officers of the Jews, arrested Jesus and bound Him. They took Him first to Annas, the father-in-law of Caiaphas, who was the high priest that year. Caiaphas was he who had prophesied to the Jews that it was expedient that one man should die for the people (John 18:12-14), although he did not realize what God was saying through him. Annas then sent Him to Caiaphas the high priest (John 18:24).

The chief priests, the elders, and all the council sought false testimony against Jesus to put Him to death, but found none even though many false witnesses came forward. But finally two false witnesses came forward and testified that Jesus had said He was able to destroy the temple of God and to rebuild it in three days. Caiaphas, the high priest arose and asked if He had anything to say. He was asked to explain what the two witnesses were saying concerning Him. But Jesus did not reply. Then Caiaphas put Him under oath by the living God and asked Him if He were the Christ, the Son of God. Jesus told him that he was and added that later Caiaphas would see the Son of Man sitting at the right hand of the Power or God and His coming on the clouds of heaven. Then the high priest tore his clothes and accused Him of having spoken blasphemy! He said there was no further need to call other witnesses since all had heard Him speak blasphemy! He asked the people for their opinion and they responded that He was deserving of death (Matt 26:59-66).

Previously, when the Son of Man came into the region of Caesarea Philippi, He asked His disciples who they thought He was. Simon Peter responded that He was the Christ, the Son of the living God. Jesus told him that he was blessed, for God His Father in heaven had revealed His true identity to Him (Matt 16:13-16). Christ again acknowledged his dual identity as Son of God and Son of Man when He was brought before the High Priest (Mt. 26:57-64; Mark 14:61, 62). Based upon the response of Caiaphas, when Jesus acknowledged His dual identity, he had not received the revelation from God as Peter had earlier experienced. The people and the high priest remained confused by the Son of God appearing in the form of man as they had expected Him to come to rule and reign as deity.

When morning came, all the chief priests and elders of the people plotted against Jesus to put Him to death. And when they had bound Him, they led Him away and delivered Him to Pontius Pilate the governor (Matt 27:1, 2). Pilate asked whether they wanted him to release to them Barabbas or Jesus who was called Christ, because he knew that they had brought Jesus before Him because of envy. But the chief priests and elders persuaded the multitudes to ask for Barabbas (who was a criminal) and to destroy Jesus. They remained unaware that they were fulfilling the provisions of the Law.

Pilate asked what they desired for Him to do with Jesus, called the Christ. They emphatically responded that they wanted Him to be crucified. The governor asked what evil had He done. Then they screamed even louder, saying that they had a law and according to their law, He should die, because He confessed that He was the Son of God (John 19:6, 7). Pilate saw that they were determined to crucify Him and that a tumult was rising. So he washed his hands before the multitude and declared he was innocent of the blood of Jesus whom he judged to be a just Person. He told them that they were responsible to make the decision concerning Him. The people answered in one accord and declared His blood to be on them and on their children as they would become responsible for His crucifixion (Matt 27:17-25). In the Gospel of John we are told that the chief priests and officers repeatedly screamed, *Crucify Him,* when they saw Jesus. Pilate replied, *You take Him and crucify Him, for I find no fault in Him.*

Caiaphas, the Levitical high priest, as well as sinful men judged the Son of Man to be guilty of blasphemy, the most heinous sin in the eyes of religious men, when He truthfully acknowledged that He was the Son of God. The Levitical Law commanded that whoever blasphemes the name of the Lord shall surely be put to death (Lev 24:16). In their mind they were obeying the law of God in carrying out their duties under the Mosaic covenant to punish Jesus for the unpardonable sin of blasphemy.

Not only did the high priest and the people unknowingly accept full responsibility for choosing Jesus as their substitutionary sin sacrifice, but they also accepted responsibility for His crucifixion and death as well. Verbally, they applied the blood of Jesus to themselves and their offspring, as the high priest physically performed under the Levitical priesthood once each year, according to the Law on the Day of Atonement. The Law governing the Levitical priesthood was fulfilled in its entirety when the high priest, without understanding the spiritual significance of his act, selected Jesus as the substitutionary atoning sin sacrifice for himself and for the people and sentenced Him to be lifted up before God to die on a cross (Lev 16:27-30).

Even though Jesus entered into the world as the sinless Son of Man and remained sinless in His earthly walk, God could not legally set aside the Old Covenant between Himself and man unless and until all provisions of the Law had been fully satisfied by a sinless man. For Jesus Himself said that not one jot or one tittle would by any means pass from the law until all was fulfilled (Matt 5:17, 18).

If Pilate, instead of the Levitical high priest, had sentenced Jesus to death on the cross, the Son of Man would have died in vain because the Law of God would not have been legally fulfilled in its entirety. The old Covenant and the Levitical priesthood could not have been set aside to permit a new covenant and a new priesthood to be established after the original order of Melchizedek. Unknowingly, the Levitical high priest, who alone was ordained by God to offer the Atonement for the remission of the sins of all mankind, chose the Son of Man and offered Him to God as the Passover Lamb according to the provisions of the Law. In essence, the Law pointed to the death of Jesus as its fulfillment on behalf of humanity.

After being condemned to death, the Son of Man was subjected to the wrath of man in the same manner as a common criminal. Scripture in the four gospels of Matthew, Mark, Luke, and John provides an account of the physical suffering of the Son of Man at the hands of carnal men who were incited by Satan. After Jesus had been condemned by the Levitical high priest, Pilate released Barabbas and had Jesus scourged and handed Him over to the governor's soldiers to be crucified (Matt 27:26). A scourge was the Roman method of inflicting severe bodily pain. It consisted of leather cords with jagged pieces of bone or metal affixed to each end to inflict the most brutal punishment. Christ Jesus was given a total of 39 stripes, which was the maximum number allowed by the High Priest under Levitical Law.

If the scourge used on Jesus had the usual nine thongs, then He would have been struck 351 one times. Many would have landed in the same place on His body, cutting deeper and deeper each time as the intense hatred of man, inspired by Satan, was vented upon Him. The entire company of soldiers surrounded Him, stripped Him, put a purple robe on Him, and then twisted a crown of thorns and jammed it on His head. They put a staff in His hand and knelt in front of Him and mocked Him saying *Hail, King of the Jews.* They spit in His face, slapped Him, and struck Him with their fists. They took the staff and struck Him on the head again and again. After they had mocked Him, making sport of Him, they took off His robe and put His own clothes on Him. Then they led Him out of the city to Golgotha to be crucified with two other criminals.

Christ's physical condition after His severe punishment and abuse at the hands of men was foretold by the prophet Isaiah. *His visage was marred more than any man and His form more than the sons of men* (Isa 52:14). Jesus, the very Son of God, was so brutalized and so disfigured by those He came to save that His form was marred beyond human likeness. The prophet Isaiah had also prophesied concerning the suffering of Jesus at the hands of man. *I gave My back to those who struck Me, and My cheeks to those who plucked out the beard; I did not hide My face from shame and spitting. For the LORD GOD will help Me; therefore I will not be disgraced; therefore I have set My face like a flint, and I know that I will not be ashamed* (Isa 50:6, 7).

Jesus, being familiar with the scriptures, realized beforehand that He would be subjected to the wrath of man. But He remained steadfast because He knew God's purpose in permitting Him to suffer the abuse and wrath of man. All too often we see only the benefits that His suffering on the cross provided for us, without realizing that His suffering punishment and shame at the hands of man also provided us as believers with the opportunity to be healed and to be made whole physically. The prophet Isaiah foretold hundreds of years beforehand that he would be despised and rejected by men and that He would be a Man of sorrows and acquainted with grief. Yet, He would be wounded for our transgressions and bruised for our iniquities. He would endure the chastisement for our peace and by His stripes we are healed (Isa 53:1-7).

Chapter Seventeen

The Crucifixion of the Son of Man

The Jewish leaders interpreted the scriptures to mean that the Messiah would first appear to establish a material kingdom on earth rather than coming to restore God's spiritual kingdom in the hearts of men. They expected the Messiah during His first advent to remain forever as their king and ruler upon the earth. They did not realize that the Son of Man had to be lifted up from the earth to be presented as a sacrificial offering to God, as was typified by the sacrificial animals being presented and sacrificed before the Lord, for the atonement of man. The Jewish scholars were totally ignorant of the spiritual battle that Satan wages against God and man, as well as the manner in which the Son of Man would destroy the devil's works and provide for the redemption of mankind.

The four Gospels give an account of His crucifixion. When the Jews and the Roman soldiers arrived with Him at Golgotha ("Calvary" in Latin), which means "the place of a skull" or death, they gave Jesus sour wine mingled with gall to drink. But when He had tasted it, He would not drink it. Christ was stripped of His clothing. At 9:00 AM the Son of Man, *in whom was life, and the life was the light of men* (John 1:4) was nailed to a cross as the true Light

(John 1:9) of the world and placed between two criminals, one on His right and another on His left, who were crucified alongside Him.

Apparently, their purpose was to emphasize that the most reprehensible crime a person could commit, in the eyes of religious men blinded by their religious traditions and doctrines, was blaspheming God. They were totally oblivious as to the identity of the very One that God had sent into the world to deliver them, together with all Gentiles, out of spiritual bondage to Satan to enable them to again experience a personal relationship with Him. They were intent upon carrying out their evil acts. They remained unaware that they were participating in God's plan for the redemption of mankind and were providing the opportunity for man to be restored unto a righteous relationship with Him. None of them realized that the cross had become an altar on which the Son of Man would shed His blood in death for the remission of sins of all mankind.

After crucifying the Son of Man, the Roman soldiers divided his garments, His only possessions, casting lots that it might be fulfilled which was spoken by the prophet David: *They divided My garments among them, and for My clothing they cast lots (Ps 22:18, Jn 19:24).* They kept watch over Him there and they put up a sign over His head with the accusation written against Him: *THIS IS JESUS THE KING OF THE JEWS (Luke 23:38).* Jesus came unto His own people and they did not receive Him, but in their wrath His own condemned Him to death.

Those who passed by blasphemed Him, wagging their heads and saying,

You who destroy the temple and build it in three days, save Yourself! If You are the Son of God, come down from the cross. Likewise the chief priests also, mocking with the scribes and elders, said, He saved others; Himself He cannot save. If He is the King of Israel, let Him now come down from the cross, and we will believe Him. He trusted in God; let Him deliver Him now if He will have Him; for He said, I am the Son of God. (Matt 27:38-40)

Even the robbers who were crucified with Jesus reviled Him in the same manner. Both Jews and Gentiles were unable to comprehend what God was doing in the spirit realm to fulfill the legal requirements of the Law. They did not understand that God was legally required to offer His Son as a living sacrifice to provide for the redemption and salvation of sinful mankind. The majority of the people in the world today are also void of spiritual understanding as to the legal requirements that the Son of Man had to fulfill to become the One and only Redeemer of mankind.

God, who is altogether holy and righteous, cannot violate His own holy nature as well as His own laws governing the universe and mankind. He could not subject sinful man to judgment, sentence, and punishment without first subjecting the Son of Man to all things that carnal man faces in the world as well as to the punishment that follows unrepentant man after his physical death (Heb 2:17). Jesus was required to experience the wrath of man, to the extent that any member of the human race can be exposed, as well as the wrath of God that confronts unrepentant sinful man upon his final death. The Son of Man had to suffer all things that sinful man can experience in his spirit, soul, and body during his life on earth as well as in His spirit and soul after physical death to be able to justify sinful man before God. His suffering after physical death was also necessary to permit God to legally sentence unrepentant man to the same fate for refusing to accept the Son of Man's substitutionary sacrificial offering of Himself for the sins of all humanity.

As Jesus hung on the cross, the ridicule continued as the rulers scoffed and sneered at Him, saying, *He rescued others from death, let Him now rescue Himself, if He is the Christ, the Messiah of God, His chosen One (Luke 23:35).* Since they were spiritually alienated from God, they were unable through their five senses to discern from the writings of the prophets and of Moses as well as in the Psalms what God was doing in the spirit realm to provide mankind the opportunity to be redeemed and restored to a son-ship relationship with Himself. Recognizing this fact, Jesus asked the *Father to forgive them, for they did not know what they were doing* (Luke 23:34).

From the sixth hour until the ninth hour, or from noon to 3:00 P.M. while Jesus was hanging on the cross, extreme darkness enveloped the earth. *And about the ninth hour Jesus cried out with a loud voice, saying, Eli, Eli, lama sabachthani? That is, My God, My God, why have You forsaken Me?* (Matt 27:45-50). And when Jesus had cried out with a loud voice, He committed His spirit into the hands of the Father. After having said this, He breathed His last. And Jesus cried out again with a loud voice, and yielded up His spirit to God (Luke 23:45, 46).

Then the Roman soldiers broke the legs of the two criminals who were crucified with Jesus. When they came near to Jesus, they realized that He had already died and did not break His legs. But one of the soldiers thrust a spear into His side. Immediately blood and water flowed out. The one who witnessed it testified and his testimony is true so that we may believe. All of this was done to fulfill the Scriptures that foretold that not one of His bones would be broken and that they would look upon Him whom they had pierced (John 19:32-37).

To fulfill prophecy, the Law required that Jesus shed His blood in death for the remission of the sins of mankind. If the Roman soldiers had broken His legs, causing Him to die from suffocation, then the spear would not have been thrust into His side to allow His blood and water to flow. As God's Passover Lamb, the Son of Man's blood had to be shed, just as the blood of the Passover lamb that was slain by each Israelite family in Egypt was shed in death before God could deliver His people from the bondage of slavery. God confirmed that the only way that man can be delivered from the bondage of sin is by the shedding of righteous blood in death as atonement for his sins.

At about noon (the sixth hour), Jesus having already hung on the cross for three hours, an impenetrable darkness enveloped the whole land covering the earth until 3:00 P.M. or the ninth hour. The three hours of darkness fore-shadowed the three days and nights that Jesus would spend in hell burdened with the sins of mankind while enduring the wrath of God. When the sunlight was overpowered by darkness, the curtain that separated the Holy of Holies (God's dwelling place in the temple) from the Holy Place was torn in two from top to bottom, which represented a sovereign act of God. This signified that access to the Holy of Holies, or to the presence of God, was no longer restricted to just the Levitical High Priest, but was open to all through the shed blood of the Son of Man (Heb 9:8, 10:19, 20).

Christ offered Himself through the Eternal Spirit to God the Father as the sacrificial lamb for the atonement of the sins of mankind and for man's redemption from the power of sin by which Satan holds sway over him.

Undoubtedly, Satan was convinced that he had succeeded in permanently gaining control over the Earth by spiritually blinding the minds of God's chosen people and leading them not only to reject the Son of Man, but inciting them to condemn Him to be crucified. He mistakenly believed that the slaying of the Messiah would prevent God from destroying his works and from redeeming mankind, which would have enabled him to become the god of the kingdom of darkness upon the Earth and eternal ruler over mankind. Scripture states, *If any of the rulers of this age had known what God was accomplishing through the death of Christ Jesus, they would not have crucified the Lord of glory* (1 Cor 2:8).

As Jesus surrendered His spirit and soul to God, the most religious and learned people of the time, who professed to know God and who represented God to man, stood mute in total ignorance before the cross. They could only stare in wonderment since, through their five senses, they could not spiritually fathom or comprehend the meaning of the brutal death of Jesus or that which was to take place in the supernatural or spirit realm during the next three days and nights. When His body was being taken down and placed in a tomb, most of the people thought, "It's over" since Jesus had said from the cross, *It is finished*. Those present were probably thinking, "We won't have to concern ourselves with this blasphemer anymore," while remaining fully unaware that He had suffered not only for them, but for the sake of all humanity.

The prophet Isaiah, by the inspiration of the Holy Spirit, prophesied concerning the treatment of Jesus hundreds of years before He was crucified:

The fact is, it was our pains He carried—our disfigurements, all the things wrong with us. We thought He brought it on Himself, that God was punishing Him for His own failures. But it was our sins that did that to Him, that ripped and tore and crushed Him—our sins! He took the punishment, and that made us whole. Through His bruises we get healed. We're all like sheep who have wandered off and gotten lost. We've all done our own thing, gone our own way. And God has piled all our sins, everything we've done wrong, on Him, on Him. (Isaiah 53:4-6, MSG)

When sudden darkness enveloped the earth, it signified that Christ Jesus had suffered spiritual death at the sixth hour, which was 12:00 noon. When the One *who said I am the light of the world* (John 8:12) was made to be sin by God the Father for us (2 Cor 5:21), He entered into darkness. The sins of men slew Him spiritually when God united the Son of Man with sinful humanity as the sin-bearing substitutionary sacrifice once for all.

God slew His own Son for the eternal benefit of all mankind when He laid on Him the iniquity of us all. The sins of mankind brought condemnation of death upon the Son of Man spiritually, just as the sin of disobedience by the first Adam in the Garden of Eden resulted in his spiritual death (Rom 5:16). After suffering spiritual death at twelve noon, as signified by the darkness that invaded the earth, the Son of Man became subject to physical death as did the first Adam after he disobeyed God's commandment. Just as Adam was banished from the presence of the Lord, likewise the Son of Man cried, My *God, My God, why have You forsaken Me?*, which confirmed that after the Son of Man was made to be sin with the sins of mankind, He, too became separated and alienated from God. His spiritual condition became the same as that of sinful man, spiritually dead in trespasses and sin (Eph 2:1).

Darkness in the Bible, which is the total absence of light, represents evil, sin, and spiritual death, which separate man from God. The prophet Isaiah told the disobedient people of God in his time: *Behold, the Lord's hand is not shortened, that it cannot save; nor His ear heavy, that it cannot hear. But your iniquities have separated you from your God; and your sins have hidden His face from you, so that He will not hear (Isa 59:1, 2)*. Other scriptures describe the fate of sinners. *The wicked shall be silent in darkness (1 Sam 2:9) and the way of the wicked is like darkness (Prov 4:19)*. Once Jesus was made to be sin with the sins of mankind, He, too suffered the same fate as sinful man. Scripture tells us that because men rebel against the words of God and despise the counsel of the Most High, they sit in darkness and in the shadow of death, bound in affliction and irons (Ps 107:10, 11).

When the Son of Man was made to be sin with the sins of all humanity, He suffered spiritual death, which separated Him from His Father and Jesus entered into darkness. He then became responsible, after facing the judgment of God, for fulfilling the penalty of the Law. Jesus had to endure the punishment that every human being born upon planet earth faces, regardless of the wicked nature or the repulsive type of sin that is committed.

The people were exceedingly satisfied that they had defended God's honor, as if God was unable to sovereignly do so Himself. They were completely blinded to the reality that God had slain His only Begotten Son as the sacrificial Lamb once for all mankind. Although they were the most religious and godly men of their time, they were grossly ignorant of the scriptures, which proclaimed the crucifixion, burial, and resurrection of the Son of Man. They were unaware that the very words that Jesus would speak during each stage of His sufferings were prophesied in the Psalms hundreds of years before He appeared upon Earth.

Contrary to the beliefs and teachings of Christians following the resurrection of Christ Jesus, neither the Jews nor the Roman soldiers killed the Son of Man. In His sinless spiritual condition only God the Father had the power to take His life. When God made Him who knew no sin to be sin with the sins of all humanity, Jesus was slain spiritually. His spiritual death separated Him from God and made Him subject to physical death. Unfortunately, after the death of Christ Jesus, the Jewish people have been persecuted and some have been killed by those who represented themselves to be Christians, because they believed that the Jews were solely responsible for crucifying Him. The deluded Christians were obviously void of spiritual understanding and revelation with regard to what the Law required under the Old Mosaic Covenant.

Scripture states that to be cast into outer darkness results in *weeping and gnashing of teeth* or experiencing torment and punishment (Matt 8:12, 25:30). In order for the Son of Man to deliver us from the power of sin and the kingdom of darkness under the rule of Satan, and convey us into the kingdom of the Son of God (Col 1:13), He had to spiritually unite with every sinful person to be born upon planet earth. Only then could He become our substitutionary sin-bearing sacrifice. He thus became our sin-bearing substitute to be judged by God and to be punished by God for the transgressions of the first Adam together with all of his offspring, including each one of us, to satisfy the demands of the Law.

Hundreds of years before Christ Jesus was crucified, the Holy Spirit spoke through the Prophet David the very words that the Son of Man would utter to the Father from the cross.

My God, my God, why have you abandoned me? Why are you so far away from helping me, so far away from the words of my groaning? My God, I cry out by day, but you do not answer—also at night, but I find no rest. Yet, you are holy, enthroned on the praises of Israel. Our ancestors trusted you. They trusted, and you rescued them. They cried to you and were saved. They trusted you and were never disappointed. Yet, I am a worm and not a man. I am scorned by humanity and despised by people.

All who see me make fun of me. Insults pour from their mouths. They shake their heads and say, put yourself in the Lord's hands. Let the Lord save him! Let God rescue him since he is pleased with him! Indeed, you are the one who brought me out of the womb, the one who made me feel safe at my mother's breasts. I was placed in your care from birth. From my mother's womb you have been my God. Do not be so far away from me. Trouble is near, and there is no one to help.

Many bulls have surrounded me. Strong bulls from Bashan have encircled me. They have opened their mouths to attack me like ferocious, roaring lions. I am poured out like water, and all my bones are out of joint. My heart is like wax. It has melted within me. My strength is dried up like pieces of broken pottery. My tongue sticks to the roof of my mouth. You lay me down in the dust of death. Dogs have surrounded me. A mob has encircled me. They have pierced my hands and feet. I can count all my bones. People stare. They gloat over me. They divide my clothes among themselves. They throw dice for my clothing.

Do not be so far away, O LORD. Come quickly to help me, O my strength. Rescue my soul from the sword, my life from vicious dogs. Save me from the mouth of the lion and from the horns of wild oxen. You have answered me. (Psalms 22:1-21)

During His prayer Christ asked the Father to save him from the power of the dog. The word dog figuratively speaks of the Gentiles. Dog in the singular would refer to Pilate, the Roman governor, the one man who could exercise the power of life and death over Jesus to free Him or to crucify Him. In His plea to be saved from the mouth of the lion, He could only be referring to Satan who was determined to kill Him, for Satan is described as a lion in scripture (2 Tim 4:17; I Peter 5:8). The horns of the wild oxen likely refer to His enemies who were seeking to destroy Him.

The prophet Isaiah continued by stating that it pleased the LORD to allow Jesus to be bruised and to be put to grief. When God made His soul an offering for sin, He looked beyond the cross and saw His seed, those who would be redeemed from the power of sin. Isaiah said God would resurrect Him from the dead to live eternally and the pleasure of the Lord would prosper in His hand because of His absolute obedience. He said God would see the labor of His soul, the sufferings of His Son and He would be satisfied. By His knowledge of that which was required of Him, His righteous Servant would justify many, for He would bear their iniquities. God said He would divide Him a portion with the great, or would empower Him to rule eternally over the Earth as the Son of Man. And He would divide the spoil with the strong, which likely refers to His victory over Satan, because He poured out His soul unto death, and He was numbered with the transgressors, and He bore their sin and made intercession for them *(Isa 53:10-12)*.

According to the gospel of Luke, the last words of Jesus on the cross were: *Father, into Your hands I commit My spirit. Having said this, He breathed His last.* The gospel of John records his final words as being: *It is finished! And bowing His head, He gave up His spirit* (John 19:30). If the words, *Father, into thy hands I commend my spirit* (Luke 23:46) were the last words which the Son of Man uttered before his death, should they not be connected with His other words, *It is finished*, which some believe were the last words He said? Both statements of the Son of Man appear to relate to the earlier words He spoke when He began His ministry upon earth, when He said, *I must be about My Father's business* (Luke 2:49). He had finished the Father's business in the worldly realm during His earthly life and now the conclusion of his days in the flesh had arrived. Nothing was left to be accomplished by Him in the flesh or in the realm of the material world. He could say to his Father, *I have glorified You on the earth. I have finished the work which You have given Me to do* (John 17:4). Yet, was His mission as relating to sinful man and destroying the works of the devil complete when He died on the cross at Calvary as so many Christians contend in their preaching and teaching?

Christ, in His earthly life as the Son of Man, personally fulfilled the perfection of the law of God by remaining obedient to the Father in all His ways. Upon becoming united with sinful man on the cross at Calvary at 12:00 noon, the Son of Man became legally responsible to fulfill the penalty of the law on behalf of all mankind as well. The law demands judgment after the physical death of sinful man. After judgment, according to scripture, the soul and spirit of unrepentant man will be sentenced to the *second death* or the final death. Unrepentant man will be punished by the wrath of God in hell for eternity (Rev 20:13, 14). The sentence for the Son of Man, as man's substitutionary sacrifice, was preset by God to be three days and three nights in hell to satisfy man's sin debt once, for all mankind (Matt 12:40).

Chapter Eighteen

The Son of Man
Endures the Wrath of God in Hell

*T*he Son of Man said He would be three days and three nights in the heart of the earth (Matt 12:40), which would represent hell. He personally said, *for judgment I have come into this world* (John 9:39). In other words, Jesus came as the Son of Man to stand in judgment before God on behalf of all sinners, to be sentenced in their stead to the punishment they deserved.

Jesus came into this world to face the judgment of God the Father in sinful man's stead and not for any sin of His own commission. Upon committing His spirit and soul into the hands of the Father upon His physical death, the judgment of God the Father passed upon Him because *the death that He died, He died to sin once for all (Rom 6:10).* Jesus became a sinner, upon being laden with the sins of mankind, by the Father on the Cross. Thus He became subject to the wrath of God, which comes upon the sons of disobedience (Col 3:6). After the Son of Man faced God's judgment, laden with the sins of humanity, He was sentenced in sinful man's place to be subjected to the punishment that all unrepentant sinners will face. He most certainly did not come under the control or power of Satan to be tormented or humiliated by him or to engage in battle against him for He committed His soul into the hands of the Father.

To legally fulfill the Law, Jesus as the Son of Man was required by God to experience all things to which carnal man can be subjected during His life in the flesh. After suffering spiritual death and surrendering His spirit and soul into the hands of the Father in physical death, Jesus was required under the Law to be fully conformed to sinful man in all things in the spirit realm as well (Heb 2:17). In order to redeem man and destroy the works of the devil, the Son of Man had to follow the same spiritual path of all unrepentant sinners after physical death. When we see the judgment and punishment that awaits impenitent, sinful man, we are able to gain insight into the sufferings that the Son of Man was mandated to endure after his physical death on the cross.

Scripture tells us that it is appointed unto us to die once and afterwards we must face the judgment of God *(Heb 9:27)*. Since we are born into the world spiritually separated from God or spiritually dead, it is appointed for us to die a physical death which results in our inner man, which is our spirit and soul, being separated from our body of dust (James 2:26). Our soul and spirit are immortal and do not go to the grave. They exist in full consciousness throughout eternity (Matt 9:44). If sinful man must face the judgment of God (Exo 12:12) would not the Son of Man laden with our sin have to do likewise?

The soul and spirit of each who dies an unrepentant sinner will be sentenced to eternal punishment in hell (Matt 5:29, 30; 10:28; Luke 16:19-31; 2 Pet 2:9; Rev 20:15; Isa 14:9), which occurs upon the second or final death. Hell is the place of punishment for Satan and his host of evil spirits as well as the souls and spirits of unrepentant men, who will experience the fiery wrath of God throughout eternity. God warns us that *the unrighteous souls of men, the cowardly, unbelieving, abominable, murderers, sexually immoral, sorcerers, idolaters, and all liars, shall have their part in the lake which burns with fire and brimstone, which is the second death* (Rev 21:8). If sinful man is destined to experience the wrath of God in hell, how could our sin bearer escape the same sentence?

Jesus Himself proclaimed alarming words before His death concerning the judgment that a lost or impenitent sinner will face. *The Son of Man will send out His angels, and they will gather out of His kingdom all things that offend and those who practice lawlessness, and will cast them into the furnace of fire. There will be wailing and gnashing of teeth* (Matt 13:41, 42). If the wrath of God will be revealed from heaven against all ungodliness and unrighteousness of men (Rom 1:18-19), would the Son of Man not be subject to the same punishment that He predicted for the unrepentant sinner?

Scripture further declares, *Vengeance is Mine; I will repay, says the Lord. And again, The Lord will judge His people. It is a fearful thing to fall into the hands of the living God* (Heb 10:30, 31). *The Lord is known by the judgment He executes, the wicked is snared in the work of his own hands. The wicked shall be turned into hell, and all the nations that forget God* (Ps 9:16, 17).

Is not the character of God revealed in His judgments that He has visited upon sinful man throughout the ages? To ungodly men God reveals Himself as the judge whose stern severity has visited the doom of physical death upon every man fathered by man and born of woman since the fall of Adam until the present day with two exceptions. The two men who escaped physical death were Enoch, who walked with God and did not suffer death for God took him up to heaven (Gen 5:24) and Elijah, who was taken up by a whirlwind into heaven (II Kings 2:11). Although God is love, He is also a God of justice who hates sin and will not exempt the guilty from eternal punishment upon physical death. So how could the Son of Man, laden with the sins of all humanity, escape the punishment that unrepentant sinful man will experience upon his final death?

Jesus said of the unprofitable servant these dreadful words: *Then shall He say also unto them on the left hand, Depart from me, ye cursed, into everlasting fire, prepared for the devil and his angels* (Matt 25:41). To further emphasize sinful man's fate, Jesus issued this stern warning to impenitent sinners.

Whoever causes one of these little ones who believe in Me to stumble, it would be better for him if a millstone were hung around his neck, and he were thrown into the sea. If your hand causes you to sin, cut it off. It is better for you to enter into life maimed, rather than having two hands, to go to hell, into the fire that shall never be quenched... (Mark 9:42-48)

Jesus emphasized the seriousness of His horrific warning to man by repeating it three times in one discourse. He who spoke these words knew that He would suffer the second or final death for every human being to be born of man upon planet earth. He was not advocating self-mutilation as a means of escaping hell. But the Son of Man was stressing the fact that being subjected to the fiery wrath of God in hell as eternal punishment for sin is exceedingly worse than suffering the loss of a part of the human body that causes man to sin. Jesus warned the people of His time, as well as all of us today, to *Fear Him who, after He has killed, has power to cast into hell; yes, I say to you, fear Him! (Luke 12:4, 5).*

We are admonished not to take blessings of God for granted, allowing our hearts to harden and to remain impenitent. If our hearts remain unchanged, we are storing up for ourselves wrath that will be visited upon us in the day of wrath, when we will stand before the righteous judgment of God. He will render to each one of us according to our deeds. He will reward those who obey Him and seek to glorify and honor Him with eternal life. But to those who seek to satisfy the lusts of the flesh and refuse to obey the truth and obey unrighteousness, He will visit upon them indignation and wrath, tribulation and anguish (Rom 2:4-9).

The Bible makes it crystal clear that sinful, unrepentant men will suffer physical death as well as the second death, resulting in eternal separation from God and punishment by Him (Rev 20:12-14). When the Son of Man bore the sins of mankind in His body on the cross, He became subject to the judgment of God followed by the punishment of God in sinful man's stead. For *just as we shall all stand before the judgment seat of Christ* (Rom 14:10), the Son of Man had to stand before the judgment seat of God the Father in our place to be judged a sinner for having borne our sins in His own body on the tree (I Peter 2:24). As our sin-bearer, He became legally responsible to God to satisfy the divine law of justice for the punishment of sinful mankind. How can a believer in Christ Jesus escape the wrath of God if the Son of Man did not suffer God's wrath in hell in his stead (John 3:36)? Without doubt the suffering of the Son of Man in His soul in hell was far more horrifying than the brutal physical punishment that He endured at the hands of man, including His crucifixion.

Many Christians, including pastors, evangelists and teachers believe and teach that Christ as the Son of God did not go to hell. They erroneously contend that He immediately went to Paradise after His physical death on the cross, based upon His comment to one of the two men who was crucified with Him, *Today you will be with Me in paradise* (Luke 23:43).

Did the Son of Man say that He would enter Paradise the day of His death on the cross? Or did He not clearly state that the thief on the cross upon physical death would enter Paradise that day to be with Him? If the Son of Man went directly to Paradise as man's sin-bearer, then how and when was He purged of the sins of all mankind? If man's sins slew Him spiritually, causing Him to exclaim *My God, my God why have You forsaken Me*, then how were they removed before He arrived in Paradise? Did they just evaporate or did the sins of mankind disappear by osmosis or by some other mysterious means?

If Adam and Eve were cast out of God's presence in the earthly Garden of Eden after they sinned and were not permitted access to His intimate presence, then how could the Son of Man, laden with the sins of all mankind that slew Him, enter into the presence of God in Paradise immediately following His physical death? Likewise, if the Levitical high priest, who was symbolic of Christ the Son of Man, could not enter the Holy of Holies on the Day of Atonement to offer the sacrificial blood of the sin-bearing animals for himself and the Israelite people until after he had been ceremonially cleansed, then how could the sin-laden Son of Man enter into God's presence? Is the Bible void of revelation as to what happened to the Son of Man after His physical death?

Scripture states that *Jonah prayed unto the Lord his God out of the fish's belly, And said, I cried by reason of mine affliction unto the Lord, and he heard me; out of the belly of hell cried I, and thou heardest my voice* (Jonah 2:1, 2; KJV). Jesus Himself said, *For as Jonah was three days and three nights in the belly of the great fish, so will the Son of Man be three days and three nights in the heart of the earth* (Matt 12:40). The heart of the earth represents the innermost fiery part of the earth or hell.

The prophet David spoke these words concerning Him hundreds of years beforehand, *I foresaw the Lord always before my face, for he is on my right hand, that I should not be moved: Therefore did my heart rejoice, and my tongue was glad; moreover also my flesh shall rest in hope: Because thou wilt not leave my soul in hell, neither wilt thou suffer thine Holy One to see corruption* (Ps 16:8-11, Acts 2:25-27, KJV). The prophet David, *seeing this before spoke of the resurrection of Christ, that his soul was not left in hell, neither his flesh did see corruption* (Acts 2:31, KJV). If the Son of Man never entered hell to endure the wrath of God in sinful man's stead, then how could His soul be subject to abandonment in hell?

Scripture also informs us that Jesus first descended into the lower parts of the earth or hell. But after being made alive by the Holy Spirit (Rom 8:11), He ascended from hell to become seated at the right hand of God in heaven, thus He was positioned to accomplish all things under the authority of the Father (Eph 4:8-10). How could Christ Jesus have freed the captives who were bound by the power of sin in hell, without their sin-debt being fully satisfied according to God's standard of judgment and punishment for unrepentant sinners?

After His resurrection Jesus said to his disciples, *How foolish you are! You're so slow to believe everything the prophets said! Didn't the Messiah have to suffer these things and enter into his glory? Then he began with Moses' Teachings and the Prophets to explain to them what was said about him throughout the Scriptures* (Luke 24:25-27, GWT). Jesus reminded them that He had previously spoken these words to them before He was crucified.

He had told them all things had to be fulfilled which were written concerning Him in the Law of Moses and the Prophets and the Psalms. Then He enabled them to comprehend the Scriptures where He pointed out that it was written, and therefore necessary, for Him to suffer and to rise from the dead the third day (Luke 24:44-46).

When the Son of Man surrendered His soul and His spirit into the hands of the Father on the cross at Calvary, obedience was no longer an issue. God had become legally bound to judge and punish Him in the same manner as He would judge and punish any wicked sinner after his physical death, according to the penalty of the law of sin and death (Rom 8:2). Scripture tells us that Jesus did not commit any sin. But He committed Himself to the Father, who judges righteously, and bore our sins in His own body on the tree (I Pet 2:22-24).

Jesus entered the world a little lower than God, for the suffering of death as man, crowned with glory and honor, that He, by the grace of God, might experience death for every individual. For it was fitting for Jesus, for whom all things were created and by whom all things are held together, in bringing many sons into the glory of God, to be made perfect through sufferings as the captain of their salvation. For both Jesus who sanctifies and those who are being sanctified are united as one and for that reason He is not ashamed to call them brethren (Heb 2:9-11).

If He who sanctifies and those who are being sanctified are all of one, does this not mean that He was united with every sinner to become one with them? If the Son of Man tasted death for everyone and it was fitting for Him to be perfected through sufferings in order to sanctify them, would He not also have to suffer the "second death" for them (Heb 5:8, 9)? Before Jesus was arrested He told the Pharisees, *Behold I cast out demons and perform cures today and tomorrow, and the third day I shall be perfected* (Luke 13:31-33). Strong's Concordance gives the following Greek meaning for "perfected": to complete, i.e. consecrate, finish, fulfill, make or perfect.

If the Son of Man remained sinless by obeying His Father, to which the scripture attests, then why would He need to be perfected through suffering? The scripture clearly states that both He who sanctifies and those who are being sanctified were all united as one (Heb 2:9-11). When He was made to be sin with the sins of all humanity, He became spiritually united with sinful mankind, including each one of us. All of this occurred in the supernatural realm, which makes it difficult for us to grasp how this could have taken place.

Only after the Son of Man was made to be sin with our sins did it become necessary for Him to be perfected or purged of sin. Upon paying man's sin debt to God by enduring His fiery wrath in hell for the preordained period of three days and three nights, the Son of Man then could be legally purged of the sins of mankind by the consuming fire of God (Heb 12:29), which would perfect Him and make Him eligible to be raised from the dead. His sufferings not only encompassed the physical suffering in His body at the hands of man before and during His crucifixion, but also the suffering of His soul for three days and nights in hell after experiencing the second death on sinful man's behalf.

Christ, as the Son of Man, had to dethrone the principalities and powers of the rulers of darkness of this age and the spiritual hosts of wickedness in heavenly places (Eph 6:12) to free sinful man from the bondage of Satan and his evil spirits. Sinful man could be set free only if his sin debt to God had been fully satisfied. Otherwise Jesus would have been unable to reclaim and restore the dominion and authority that the first Adam forfeited to Satan through his disobedience. In the same manner, as by Adam's disobedience many were made sinners, so also by the Son of Man's obedience many are being made righteous (Rom 5:19).

The Son of Man is the only One who, by His sinless submissive obedience to the Father, could become our sin-bearing sacrificial offering upon the cross. He then could face the judgment of God in our place and be sentenced to the second death to endure the wrath of God in hell for three days and three nights. His victory over hell and death was not achieved by conquest or combat with Satan as many believe, but by submission to the Father's plan and will.

For this reason scripture declares: *There is no salvation in any other, for there is no other name under heaven given among men by which we must be saved (Acts 4:12).* Scripture further states that God did not appoint us to endure His wrath. But He planned and purposed for us to obtain salvation through our Lord Jesus Christ (1 Thes 5:9). Accordingly the Son of Man could declare that He is the only Way and the only Truth and the only Life and that no one can come to the Father, except through Him (John 14:6). His sinless sacrificial offering of Himself and His vicarious sufferings in the flesh, and in hell, on behalf of man set Him apart from all others who attempt to deceive man into believing otherwise.

As a result of man's sin debt being paid in full to God, and after the Son of Man had regained the dominion and authority over the earth that the first Adam forfeited to Satan, the works of Satan were destroyed and the devil was eternally defeated by the Son of God as man and not as deity. As previously noted, scripture emphasizes: *In all things Jesus had to be made like His brethren, that He might become a merciful and faithful High Priest in things pertaining to God, to make propitiation for the sins of the people (Heb 2:17).*

If Christ had to be made like His brethren in all things, how could He escape the punishment that God has ordained for unrepentant sinful mankind? If He became the sin-bearing substitute for man on the cross, then He most assuredly had to follow the same spiritual course as sinful man after physical death. Scripture states that Christ Jesus, the Son of Man as the last Adam, *upholding all things by the word of His power, by Himself purged our sins* (Heb 1:3). How could He have had our sins purged by the consuming fire of God if He did not serve His preordained three day and three night sentence in hell, which He personally acknowledged and pronounced would happen to Him as the Son of Man?

God, who is altogether holy and righteous, cannot violate His own holy nature and laws governing the universe and mankind. If the Son of Man had to be made like His brethren in all things, then He most certainly had to experience everything that an impenitent sinner will face, including suffering the punishment for sin, to be able to justify sinful man. Otherwise how could God be able to legally sentence an unrepentant man to eternal punishment in hell if he refuses to accept as his Lord and Savior the Son of Man who suffered in his stead?

Over 400 years before the Son of Man actually endured the punishment by God the Father for the sins of all mankind, the Spirit of God spoke through the prophet David the words that Jesus would utter to the Father during the three days and three nights He suffered His wrath in hell.

O LORD, the God of my salvation, I have cried out day and night before You. Let my prayer come before You; incline Your ear to my cry. For my soul is full of troubles, and my life draws near to the grave. I am counted with those who go down to the pit; I am like a man who has no strength, Adrift among the dead, like the slain who lie in the grave, whom You remember no more, and who are cut off from Your hand. You have laid me in the lowest pit, in darkness, in the depths. Your wrath lies heavy upon me, and You have afflicted me with all Your waves.

You have put away my acquaintances far from me; you have made me an abomination to them; I am shut up, and I cannot get out; My eye wastes away because of affliction. Lord, I have called daily upon You; I have stretched out my hands to You. Will You work wonders for the dead? Shall the dead arise and praise You? Selah Shall Your loving kindness be declared in the grave? Or Your faithfulness in the place of destruction? Shall Your wonders be known in the dark? And Your righteousness in the land of forgetfulness?

But to You I have cried out, O LORD, and in the morning my prayer comes before You. Lord, why do You cast off my soul? Why do You hide Your face from me? I have been afflicted and ready to die from my youth; I suffer Your terrors; I am distraught. Your fierce wrath has gone over me; your terrors have cut me off. They came around me all day long like water; they engulfed me altogether. Loved one and friend You have put far from me, and my acquaintances into darkness. (Psalm 88:1-18)

The Son of Man proclaimed that He had been laid in the lowest pit, in darkness, in the depths, which is representative of hell. He acknowledged that the Father's wrath was like a heavy weight upon Him and afflicted Him like violent ocean waves pounding the rocks along the seashore (Ps 88:7, 16, 17). He was alone, separated from the Father and the Holy Spirit. Being afflicted with the sins of all humanity, the Son of Man became an abomination to the Father and the Holy Spirit because of the sins He bore for us. Jesus was confined to hell under the Father's sentence and He could not escape. His two greatest enemies were death and the sins of mankind that held Him captive.

The Son of Man expressed His anguish in trying to gain a response from God the Father while in hell. He questioned the Father as to whether He would hear His cries and raise Him from the dead. He wondered why He remained cut off and isolated from Him. He acknowledged that He constantly suffered the terrors of the Father's fierce wrath that engulfed Him like angry waves of the sea, making Him desperate to be heard.

The Son of Man became the One and only member of the kingdom of God who will ever suffer the *second death*. We, who are born again from above by the Spirit of God, are united with Christ Jesus in His death, including His sufferings, and have been raised in newness of life in Him. If we remain faithful to Him, we will escape the second death because He took our place as our substitute (John 3:36).

The second death is the final death that unrepentant sinners will face after physical death when they appear before the judgment seat of Christ Jesus. The cowardly, unbelieving, abominable, murderers, sexually immoral, sorcerers, idolaters and all liars shall have their part in the lake of fire and brimstone, which is the second death that Jesus suffered for us (Rev 21:7, 8).

Not until the Son of Man returns to put down all rebellion and to rule and reign over the world as King of Kings and Lord of Lords will Satan and his followers be sentenced to the second death and confined to hell. Although

Satan is destined to be sentenced to hell for eternity, He has not been confined to Hell nor was He in hell during the time the Son of Man was there. Jesus did not come under the power of Satan in hell or have any contact with him since He committed Himself into the hands of the Father upon His physical death. The Son of Man is the first and only one to date who has experienced the second death that confronts unrepentant man and Satan, together with his followers.

The mind of carnal man cannot begin to comprehend the suffering that the Son of Man endured in His soul at the hands of the Father on behalf of sinful man. Not only was God angered by man's rebellious sins, but even more so for having to punish His innocent Son in His soul and spirit for three days and three nights in sinful man's stead. Salvation has become so cheap to so many individuals who call themselves Christians because they ignore the word of God and disregard the sufferings that the Son of Man endured to provide for our salvation and to become our Mediator and High Priest.

Seldom if ever do we hear anyone mention the intense suffering that the Son of Man endured following His sentence to the *second death* for the purpose of justifying us. For the most part focus has centered upon His death upon the cross and His resurrection. How often do we hear any warning of the impending doom that an unrepentant sinner will encounter after physical death? If God punished His own Son in our stead, for our sins, how will we escape His wrath if we refuse to accept Him, to honor Him, and to obey His commands and teachings?

Little do we, Christian or non-Christian, realize that Jesus, the very One who was crucified and who suffered the wrath of God in our stead, will be the One before whom we will stand in judgment after physical death overtakes us.

Accordingly all the lame excuses that an unrepentant sinner will offer to the Son of Man on judgment day for going his sinful way will be to no avail. The majority of people today refuse to acknowledge and accept God's provision for their salvation. They continue to engage in the sinful acts of their rebellious lifestyles. They seem to be void of any fear of punishment or of being held accountable by God for their behavior. The majority of the ministers of the Word of God are reluctant to even mention the judgment and punishment that awaits the unsaved, upon facing the *second death*, for fear of offending or losing parishioners or their followers. The fear of the Lord is like a lofty fleecy cloud floating somewhere in the sky, far away and non-threatening, and of little concern to those who do not know the Lord.

Chapter Nineteen

The Resurrection of the Son of Man

G od the Father was legally bound to punish the Son of Man for the preordained period of three days and three nights. The sins of man not only slew Him, but they were also responsible for intense suffering being visited upon Him since He could not free Himself of the sins of man that He accepted in His body while on the cross. As demonstrated in Old Testament times, sin can be purged only by the consuming fire of God (Deut 4:24). For instance, the sinful people as well as the corrupt cities of Sodom and Gomorrah were consumed by the fire of God, which came down from heaven in the time of Abraham. On another occasion, Mount Sinai was purged of sin by His holy fire and all the people of Israel were warned not to so much as set foot on it or touch it, lest they die. Not even an animal could do so without the penalty of death being imposed (Exodus 19). After it was sanctified by the fire of God for three days, the Lord descended upon the top of Mount Sinai and met with Moses.

A vivid and meaningful example of God's consuming fire purging the sins of man occurred in the days of Elijah, a prophet of God. During the reign of Ahab as king over Israel, Ahab did evil in the sight of the Lord more than all who were before him. Ahab and his father had forsaken the commandments of the Lord and followed the prophets of Baal. Elijah commanded Ahab to gather all Israel before him on Mount Carmel, including the 450 prophets of Baal and the 400 prophets of Asherah. He asked the people how long would they falter between the Lord and Baal. He told them if they believed the Lord was God to follow Him, but if they thought Baal to be, then to follow him. Then Elijah told the people that he alone was the remaining prophet of the Lord. But he pointed out that Baal's prophets numbered 450 men.

Elijah told the people to give him one bull and to give one bull to the prophets. He instructed that the bulls be cut in pieces and be placed on the wood on separate altars. No fire was to be put under the altars. Then Elijah told the prophets of Baal to call on the name of their gods and he would call on the name of the Lord. He said that the God who answered by fire would be the true God. Elijah explained to the prophets of Baal how to prepare and offer their sacrifice to their god on their altar, but he instructed them not to put any fire under it.

So the prophets complied and called on their gods to consume their sacrifice by fire from morning until noon, pleading for Baal to hear them. But there was no answer. Despite their cries, as well as their religious and physical efforts, they could not get a response. After midday was past, they prophesied until the time for offering the evening sacrifice, but there was no answer or response from the god of the prophets.

Then Elijah prepared the altar of the Lord and took 12 stones, equal to the number of the tribes of the sons of Israel, to whom the word of the Lord had come. He built an altar in the name of the Lord with the stones and made a large trench around it. Elijah put the wood in order on the altar, then cut the bull in pieces and laid them on the wood. He ordered four pots to be filled with water and to be poured on the burnt sacrifice and on the wood. He commanded it to be repeated and then he had the water poured on the sacrifice and the wood a third time. The water ran all around the altar and Elijah also filled the trench with water.

At the time for the offering of the evening sacrifice, Elijah the prophet asked the Lord God of Abraham, Isaac and Israel to make it known to the people that He was God in Israel and that Elijah was His servant. He also asked the Lord to confirm that he had done all things according to His word. He pleaded with the Lord to hear him so that the people would know that He was the Lord God and that He had turned their hearts back to Himself again.

Then the fire of the Lord came down and consumed the burnt sacrifice as well as the wood and the stones and the dust. The fire even licked up the water that was in the trench. Now when all the people saw what happened, they fell on their faces and confessed *The LORD, He is God! The LORD, He is God!* (I Kings 18:17-40).

The central issue was not in the offering of the sacrifices, but the purging of sins that the sacrifices symbolically bore for man. Despite the fruitless efforts of the false prophets of Satan, who is the author of sin and death, they could not duplicate the fire of God to purge the sacrifices of their sins. God was demonstrating that He is the consuming fire (Deut. 4:24) and only He is able to purge the sins of man. He was further emphasizing that Satan exercises his power over man by influencing him to transgress God's laws. But Satan is unable to purge man of his sins of disobedience that separate him from God, thus leaving man in the same condemned state of being as is he.

Commencing with Noah, the burning of animal sacrifices symbolized the purging of man's sins from the animals offered to God as atonement for sin. Even when God tested Abraham, He instructed him to offer his son Isaac as a burnt sacrifice. When the carcass of the sacrificial animal was burned, it symbolized that the sins it bore for guilty man were consumed by fire. Thus a sweet aroma or savor arose to God because the sins of man were consumed from His presence.

Jesus taught His disciples that *the Son of Man must suffer many things, and be rejected by the elders and chief priests and scribes, and be killed, and after three days rise again* (Mark 8:31). He told the Pharisees that He would be perfected the third day (Luke 13:32). Only the sins of man which slew Him and not any sin of His own commission made it necessary for Him to be perfected by the fire of God. At the conclusion of His suffering the wrath of God for three days and three nights the fire of God consumed the sins that He bore in His body on the cross, thereby sanctifying Him. Once the sins of man were purged by the fire of God, He was made spiritually alive by the Holy Spirit (Rom 8:11) to become the first begotten Son of God raised from the dead.

The LORD God foretold of the resurrection of the Son of Man through the Prophet David in the book of Psalms. The Spirit of Christ said,

The pangs of death surrounded me, and the floods of ungodliness made me afraid. The sorrows of Sheol surrounded me; the snares of death confronted me. In my distress I called upon the Lord, and I cried out to my God; He heard my voice from His temple, and my cry came before Him, even to His ears. Then the earth shook and trembled; the foundations of the hills also quaked and were shaken, because He was angry. Smoke went up from His nostrils, and devouring fire from His mouth; coals were kindled by it. He bowed the heavens also, and came down with darkness under His feet. And He rode upon a cherub, and flew; He flew upon the wings of the wind. He made darkness His secret place; His canopy around Him was dark waters and thick clouds of the skies. From the brightness before Him, His thick clouds passed with hailstones and coals of fire. The Lord thundered from heaven, and the Most High uttered His voice, hailstones and coals of fire. He sent out His arrows and scattered the foe, lightning in abundance, and He vanquished them. Then the channels of the sea were seen, the foundations of the world were uncovered at Your rebuke, O Lord, at the blast of the breath of Your nostrils.

He sent from above, He took me; He drew me out of many waters. He delivered me from my strong enemy, from those who hated me, for they were too strong for me. They confronted me in the day of my calamity, but the Lord was my support. He also brought me out into a broad place; He delivered me because He delighted in me. The Lord rewarded me according to my righteousness; according to the cleanness of my hands He has recompensed me. For I have kept the ways of the Lord, and have not wickedly departed from my God. For all His judgments were before me, and I did not put away His statutes from me. I was also blameless before Him, and I kept myself from my iniquity. Therefore the Lord has recompensed me according to my righteousness, according to the cleanness of my hands in His sight. With the merciful You will show Yourself merciful; with a blameless man You will show Yourself blameless; With the pure You will show

Yourself pure; And with the devious You will show Yourself shrewd. For You will save the humble people, but will bring down haughty looks. For You will light my lamp; the Lord my God will enlighten my darkness (Psalm 18:4-28).

The prophet David foretold of the Holy Spirit quickening the Son of Man in hell. Death surrounded Him and the ungodliness or sins of mankind made Him afraid inasmuch as He was powerless to free Himself from them. The sorrows of Sheol or hell, which were the waves of the wrath of God, engulfed Him and constituted snares of death that bound Him. While suffering the wrath of God in hell, He petitioned the Lord, who heard Him from His temple. A violent earthquake shook the earth, as confirmed in the Gospel of Matthew (Matt 28:2) and even the foundations of heaven quaked in the same manner as during the Lord's appearance on Mount Sinai when He sanctified it before meeting with Moses. The devouring fire of God came forth and consumed the sins of humanity that God the Father had laid on Him on the cross at Calvary.

The most High God answered the cries of the Son of Man. He sent the fire and vanquished the sins of man, thereby delivering Him from His strong enemy, which was eternal death (Rom 8:11). God the Father rewarded Him because of His righteousness as the sinless Son of Man. Only Jesus could be recompensed according to the cleanness of His hands, since all men have sinned and fall short of the glory of God (Rom 3:23). Only Jesus could truthfully say that He had kept the ways of the LORD and had not wickedly departed from His God. The Son of Man himself fulfilled the Law in its entirety. Only Jesus could declare that He was blameless before Him and had kept Himself from iniquity. Although David was a man after God's own heart, he was an adulterous murderer and could not have said this about himself (Ps 51:5). These verses could only apply to the sinless Son of Man rather than to David, whose sins were ever before him, bringing anguish both to him and to his offspring as well.

The Son of Man concluded that God will be merciful to the merciful and with a blameless man He will show Himself blameless just as the Father did with Him. Also the Lord will save the humble as proven by God lighting the Son of Man's lamp to become the firstborn Son of God raised from the dead, when He quickened Him by the Holy Spirit (Rom 8:11).

The Son of man could only be made alive by the Holy Spirit after He was purged of the sins of mankind by the consuming fire of God. *For Christ also suffered once for sins, the just for the unjust, that He might bring us to God, being put to death in the flesh but made alive by the Spirit* (I Pet 3:18). Scripture informs us that God raised Jesus from the dead. It is also written in the second Psalm: *You are My Son, today I have begotten You. He raised Him from the dead, no more to return to corruption* (Ps 2:7, Acts 13:33, 34). "Corruption" undoubtedly refers to the sins of mankind.

Jesus was conformed to man to enable Him to become the new Spiritual Head of redeemed humanity. As the resurrected Son of Man, He became the One and only Man in whom mankind finds its unity with God. His absolute relation to mankind was derived from an absolute relationship with God the Father. He not only became the first born Son of God in the flesh, but as the Son of Man, He also became the firstborn Son of God from the dead. He will rule and reign over the Kingdom of God on the earth upon His second and final appearance as the Son of Man. Until that day, Satan continues to roam about like a roaring lion, seeking whom he may devour (1 Peter 5:8). Why would any man choose to live his life under the influence of Satan and refuse to seek an eternal relationship with the Son of Man, who gave Himself for us?

Before he was nailed to the cross Jesus said, *In this manner, therefore, pray: Our Father in heaven, hallowed be Your name. Your kingdom come. Your will be done on earth as it is in heaven* (Matt 6:9,10). He instructed men to pray that God's kingdom on earth, which was forfeited to Satan by the first Adam's disobedience, be restored—knowing that He had come as man to regain and restore God's dominion and authority over the earth and over Satan. After His resurrection from the dead the Son of Man declared, *All authority has been given to Me in heaven and on earth* (Matt 28:18).

As the Son of God, He exercised power and authority under the Father over heaven and earth, including Satan before He came to earth. As the Son of Man, the last Adam, (I Cor 15:45) through His sufferings as well as His obedience to the Father, He regained and restored all power and authority over the earth and over Satan as man and not as deity. He rules over the earth as the Son of Man, the new spiritual Head of all of us who have been redeemed from the power of Satan. Scripture assures us the Son of Man will return to rule and reign as the King of Kings and Lord of Lords (Rev 17:14). After He has put down all rebellion and has confined Satan and all evil doers to the lake of fire for eternity, He will establish the kingdom of God upon earth as God originally purposed and planned for man to accomplish.

The Gospel of Matthew gives this account of His resurrection from the dead.

Now after the Sabbath, as the first day of the week began to dawn, Mary Magdalene and the other Mary came to see the tomb. And behold, there was a great earthquake; for an angel of the Lord descended from heaven, and came and rolled back the stone from the door, and sat on it. His countenance was like lightning and his clothing as white as snow. And the guards shook for fear of him, and became like dead men. But the angel answered and said to the women, Do not be afraid, for I know that you seek Jesus who was crucified. He is not here; for He is risen as He said. Come, see the place where the Lord lay. And go quickly and tell His disciples that He is risen from the dead, and indeed He is going before you into Galilee; there you will see Him. Behold, I have told you. (Matthew 28:1-7)

According to the Gospel of John, Mary Magdalene went to the tomb of Jesus after His resurrection and met Him. Jesus said to her,

Woman, why are you weeping? Whom are you seeking? She, supposing Him to be the gardener, said to Him, Sir, if You have carried Him away, tell me where You have laid Him, and I will take Him away. Jesus said to her, Mary! She turned and said to Him, Rabboni! (which is to say, Teacher). Jesus said to her, Do not cling to Me, for I have not yet ascended to My Father; but go to My brethren and say to them, I am ascending to My Father and your Father, and to My God and your God. (John 20:14-17)

Songs and hymns have been written and sung and messages preached glorifying the cross. Yet if Christ had not risen from the dead, our faith in His death alone would be empty or in vain. We would remain in our sins. But

Christ rose from the dead. He became the firstfruits of redeemed humanity or the new spiritual head of those who have been saved from sin. For since by man's disobedience *came* death, by Man's obedience also *came* the resurrection of the dead. For as in Adam all die, even so in Christ we are made alive, if we believe in Him and obey Him (I Cor 15:14-22).

Chapter Twenty

The Son of Man Seals
the New Covenant Between God and Man

Although Christ Jesus accomplished His Father's plan and purpose on earth as man, yet a most crucial act remained to be performed by Him as the Son of Man during His first advent. The eternal benefits of His sacrifice and sufferings could not be imparted to mankind until after a new covenant between God and man had been sealed with the blood of the Son of Man. Atonement for the sins of man could not be finalized until the blood of the Son of Man was applied to the Mercy Seat of the Ark of the Covenant in heaven. Not until the first covenant between God and the Israelites was ratified or sealed with the blood of animals did it take effect. Likewise, the New Covenant could not become a reality to supersede the old covenant until after the Son of Man had deposited His blood on the mercy seat of the Ark of the Covenant in the most Holy Place in the true Tabernacle of God in heaven. As the Lord has said, *the life of the flesh is in the blood, and the blood placed upon the altar makes atonement for the souls of men* (Lev 17:11).

The blood of Jesus represented the very life of the Son of Man that was placed upon the heavenly altar to make eternal atonement for the souls of all men. His life constituted the ransom that God paid at a cost to Himself by offering His only begotten Son in payment for the sins man committed against Him. God satisfied His own demand for justice by punishing the Son of Man for the transgressions of all mankind. Jesus not only satisfied the demands of justice under the Law, which condemned sinful man, but He destroyed Satan's power over man by being judged in man's stead before the holy God of the universe and by His vicarious sufferings. God provided the opportunity for man's judicial status to be changed from an enemy, under condemnation to death and punishment, to one of justification in Christ Jesus. No one of less stature than Jesus, who is equally God (being altogether holy and righteous), but also equally man, could qualify to suffer for sinful man's ransom to satisfy God's demand for justice.

Immediately after His resurrection, the Son of Man ascended into the heavens and entered the sanctuary of the true tabernacle, which the Lord erected to deposit His blood on the mercy seat of the Ark of the Covenant in the Holy of Holies (Heb 8:2; 9:11, 12). He sealed the New Covenant between Himself as man—the spiritual head or Cornerstone of redeemed humanity— and God the Father. Prior to His departure to enter the Holy of Holies, upon meeting Mary at the tomb, Jesus told her not to touch or cling to Him since His departure to the true heavenly tabernacle was imminent. Scripture confirms that Jesus as the Son of Man entered once with His own blood into the most Holy Place to do away with sin by depositing His blood that He shed in the offering of Himself as our sacrifice (Heb 9:23-26). Upon sealing the New Covenant with His blood, He provided sinful man the opportunity to be restored to a covenant relationship with God the Father, Who created all things.

Jesus returned to earth and told His followers to examine His hands and His feet and to touch Him so they would know without a doubt He was the Christ *(Luke 24:39, 40)*. Thomas, who was one of His disciples, was not present when Jesus appeared. The other disciples of Jesus told him later that they had seen the Lord. Thomas refused to believe them unless he saw the nail prints in His hands and put his finger into them, and put his hand into the spear wound in His side. Eight days later, Thomas was inside with His disciples when Jesus arrived and the doors were closed, but Jesus entered and stood in their midst. He pronounced peace to them and told Thomas to put his finger into the prints in His hands and to put His hand into His side. He asked Thomas to believe and Thomas exclaimed that Jesus was his Lord and his God (John 20:24-28).

Jesus appeared unto many after His resurrection. Christ died for our sins according to the Scriptures; He was buried, and He rose again the third day according to the Scriptures, and He was seen by Cephas, then by the twelve. After that He was seen by over 500 brethren at once. After that He was seen by James, then by all the apostles. (1 Corinthians 15:4-7)

The Son of Man was raised from the dead for our justification. The Greek word for justification is *"dikaiosis"*, which means the act of God declaring man free from the guilt of sin and being made acceptable to Him as righteous. If Christ had not risen, the faith of man in his death alone would be futile; for man would still be dead in his sins (1Cor 15:17). Yet, for the most part, the principal focus in Christendom has remained centered upon the Son of God's death on the cross. Very little mention is made by ministers concerning His suffering in hell to pay man's sin debt to God, being purged of the sins of mankind by the consuming fire of God, and being raised from the dead for our justification to become the new spiritual head or the cornerstone (Eph 2:20) of redeemed humanity.

Justification is a divine act of God that makes sinful man to be righteous and acceptable before Him through the substitutionary sacrificial sufferings of His only begotten Son in the flesh on the cross at Calvary and in hell as man's sin-and-guilt-bearer. Christ Jesus becomes to us our "righteousness" when we surrender our life to Him to become spiritually united with Him and obey His commands (1 Cor. 1:30; Rom. 3:24). Only through Christ can sinful man gain access by faith into God's grace or unmerited favor (Rom 5:2) and not through religious or pagan practices. The righteous act of Jesus, in offering Himself to God as Man's substitutionary sin-bearer, is the justification that provides the eternal holy life of God to all men who will receive it. Through the obedience of Jesus, carnal man is made righteous upon accepting and receiving Him as Savoir and LORD. As Scripture testifies, *as many as receive Him, to them He gives the right to become children of God, to those who believe in His name: who are born, not of blood, nor of the will of the flesh, nor of the will of man, but of God* (John 1:12, 13).

By Adam came spiritual death, but by Christ Jesus we are resurrected from the dead. For as in Adam all suffer death, even so in Christ we shall all be made alive (1 Cor 15:21, 22). Righteousness is imputed to us who believe in God who raised up Jesus our Lord from the dead after He suffered because of our offenses and was raised to justify us (Rom 4:24, 25).

Justification is an act of God and not by works of righteousness we have done. It is according to His mercy He saves us, through the washing of regeneration and renewing of the Holy Spirit, whom He pours out on us abundantly through Jesus Christ our Savior (Titus 3:5, 6; Rom 4:5; Gal 2:16). We need to recognize and understand that God through Christ reconciled the world to Himself and does not impute our trespasses unto us, if we have been united with Him (2 Cor. 5:19). For by the one offering of Himself, Jesus has forever perfected those of us who are being sanctified or set apart to God (Heb.10:14). Justification is based upon what Christ accomplished as the Son of Man through the shedding of His righteous blood and His suffering the wrath of God in our stead that delivers us from the wrath of God to come (Rom. 5:9), which no other god or religion or teaching of man can offer.

Our justification was fulfilled in Christ Jesus after He experienced the *second death* (Rev 20:14) in everyone's stead by suffering the fiery wrath of God for three days and three nights in hell as punishment for our sins. The Son of Man was not raised from the dead for self-justification, but for our justification before God by fulfilling the penalty of the law on our behalf. There is no other name under heaven given among men by which man must be saved from eternal judgment and punishment by the only Holy God of the universe, who hates sin (Acts 4:12).

Jesus proclaimed before His death,

I am the door of the sheep. All who ever came before Me are thieves and robbers, but the sheep did not hear them. I am the door. If anyone enters by Me, he will be saved, and will go in and out and find pasture.

The thief does not come except to steal, and to kill, and to destroy. I have come that they may have life, and that they may have it more abundantly. (John 10:7-10)

For us to receive and experience the benefit of Christ's sacrificial sufferings under the New Covenant, by faith we must surrender our life to God and accept the finished work of His Son who came into the world as the Son of Man to identify and unite with us to become our sacrificial sin-bearer and Savoir.

If we have entered into a righteous relationship with Christ Jesus, we are assured there is now no condemnation to us who refuse to obey the desires of the flesh, but remain obedient to the Holy Spirit. The law of the Spirit of life in Christ Jesus, under the New Covenant, has set us free from the condemnation of law of sin and death under the Old Covenant. For what the law could not perform because of our weakness through the flesh, God performed by sending His own Son in the likeness of our sinful flesh to become an offering for our sins.

Jesus condemned or overcame sin in the flesh on our behalf so that the righteous requirement of the law might be fulfilled in us who walk in obedience to the Spirit and not according to the sinful desires of our flesh. For we who obey the desires of the flesh set our minds on the things that satisfy our carnal nature, whereas we who live in obedience to the Spirit focus on the things that are pleasing to the Spirit.

We are told if we remain under the control of our carnal mind we face eternal death, but if our minds are fixed upon the Spirit of God we have life and peace. Because the carnal mind is hostile towards God, it does not and cannot submit to the law of God. We who are responding to the appetites and impulses of our carnal nature cannot please God. We are not to submit to the flesh, but to the leading and control of the Spirit, if indeed the Spirit of God dwells in us.

If we do not have the Spirit of Christ dwelling in us, we do not belong to Him and we are not a member of His body. But if Christ lives in us by His Spirit, then our body is dead by reason of its sinful nature, but our spirit is alive because of the righteousness the Holy Spirit imputes to us. And if the Spirit of Him who raised Jesus from the dead dwells in us, He will also restore life to our mortal bodies through His Spirit who lives in us (Rom 8:1-11). No religion on the face of the earth, devised by man or by Satan, can offer the righteous eternal life of God to man because it is void of the vicarious sufferings of the Son of Man and the work of the Holy Spirit.

Holy Scripture states that we who believe in the Son have everlasting life and we who do not believe the Son shall not see life, but the wrath of God abides on us (John 3:36). The Gospel or the good news of Christ is the power of God to give salvation to everyone who believes and personally trusts in Jesus, to the Jew first and also to the Gentile. For the gospel reveals the righteousness of God through faith and it produces more faith in us as a believer. The righteous shall live by faith in the word of God and not by the natural senses alone. The wrath of God is revealed from heaven against all ungodliness and unrighteousness of men, who in their sinful doings suppress the truth in their unrighteousness (Rom 1:16-18).

God has demonstrated His love toward us,

...in that while we were still sinners, Christ died for us. Much more then, having now been justified by His blood, we shall be saved from wrath through Him. For if when we were enemies we were reconciled to God through the death of His Son, how much more, having been reconciled, we shall be saved by His life. And not only that, but we also rejoice in God through our Lord Jesus Christ, through whom we have now received the reconciliation. (Romans 5:8-11)

For God did not appoint us to wrath, but to obtain salvation through our Lord Jesus Christ, who died for us, that whether we wake or sleep, we should live together with Him (1 Thes 5:9, 10).

Seldom, if ever, do we hear about the intense suffering the Son of Man endured following His sentence to the *second death* in order to justify us, or regarding the impending doom the unrepentant sinner will encounter after physical death. If God punished His own Son for our sins, how will we escape His wrath if we refuse to accept Him, to honor Him, and to obey His commands and teachings? Only Jesus is able to deliver us from the wrath of God to come (1 Thes 1:10), therefore He is our salvation.

The wrath of God to come is described by John in the book of Revelation.

Now I saw heaven opened, and behold, a white horse. And He who sat on him was called Faithful and True, and in righteousness He judges and makes war. His eyes were like a flame of fire, and on His head were many crowns. He had a name written that no one knew except Himself. He was clothed with a robe dipped in blood, and His name is called The Word of God. And the armies in heaven, clothed in fine linen, white and clean, followed Him on white horses. Now out of His mouth goes a sharp sword, that with it He should strike the nations.

And He Himself will rule them with a rod of iron. He Himself treads the winepress of the fierceness and wrath of Almighty God. And He has on His robe and on His thigh a name written: KING OF KINGS AND LORD OF LORDS. (Revelation 19:11-16)

Chapter Twenty One

The Son of Man Our Mediator and High Priest

The Son of Man did not ascend into heaven and abandon us to face the trials and tribulations in this world alone. He ascended into heaven to become our Mediator and High Priest to intercede for us before the throne of God. For us to receive His representation before God, we must become a member of His body by entering into a covenant relationship with Him. Only God can justify us by the blood of Jesus to make us righteous and reconcile us to Himself through the death of His Son. We are saved from the wrath of God by the life of the Son of Man who sits on the right hand of God, interceding on our behalf.

Jesus obtained a more excellent ministry as our High Priest than was provided to Israelites through the Levitical priesthood, inasmuch as He became the Mediator of a better covenant, which was established on better promises. Because the first covenant was not faultless, the Lord entered into a new covenant with us. Under the New Covenant, He puts His laws in our minds and writes them on our hearts. If we will receive Him as our God, we become His people. The Lord said that all of us who receive Him will know Him from the least of us to the greatest of us. He covenanted with us, as believers in Christ Jesus, to be merciful to our unrighteousness, and our sins and our lawless deeds will not be recalled. In ushering in the New Covenant, He made the first one obsolete (Heb 8:6-13). Therefore all people who have become righteous believers are able to enter into a more intimate spiritual relationship with God than the Israelites were able to do under the first covenant.

As our eternal great High Priest, Jesus ascended into the heavens to personally serve as mediator between God and us, whereas the Levitical priest only served upon the earth. Since He is the Son of God as well as the Son of Man, Christ is able to divinely represent God to us and us to God unlike the Levitical priesthood was able to do. Therefore, we have access to mercy and grace through the Son of Man to help us in the time of need (Heb 4:14-16), instead of being condemned by the Law of God, which governed the Israelites' relationship with God under the first covenant.

No man is able to appoint himself priest or take this honor upon himself, but he must be called and appointed by God. Christ did not appoint Himself to become High Priest, but God told Him He was His begotten Son and appointed Him a priest forever, according to the original order of Melchizedek. The old covenant was annulled because it was weak and did not profit man, since under it the law was unable to make anything perfect. On the other hand, the new covenant provides us with a better hope through which we are able to draw near to God. Jesus became not only our Mediator, but also the surety of a better covenant between God and us. As our High Priest, He became the author of eternal salvation to all of us who obey Him (Heb 7:11-22).

Because He lives forever, Jesus has an unchangeable priesthood that enables Him to save to the uttermost all who come to the Father through Him, since He always lives to make intercession for them as Mediator before God. Such a High Priest is appropriate for us, for He is holy, harmless, undefiled, separate from sinners, and is higher than the heavens. Jesus does not need daily to offer up sacrifices for Himself and for us as the Levitical high priests were required to do. Christ did this once for all humanity when He offered up Himself as our sin-bearing sacrifice on the cross at Calvary. The law appointed as high priests sinful men who had weaknesses, but God appointed His Son who has been perfected forever (Heb 7:23-28).

How much more then shall the blood of Christ, who offered Himself as an unblemished sacrifice to God, cleanse our conscience from sin-contaminated works to serve the living God than the blood of the animal sacrifices that were offered by the Levitical priesthood. For this reason, Jesus is the Mediator of the new covenant so that those who are called may receive the eternal inheritance promised to us as the children of God (Heb 9:11-15).

This is the main point: we as Christians have a High Priest who is seated at the right hand of the throne of the Majesty in the heavens. He serves as Minister of the sanctuary in the original heavenly tabernacle, that the Lord erected (Heb 8:1-5).

When Jesus came into the world, God said He did not desire sacrifice and offering, but instead He prepared a body for Christ because He did not derive any pleasure in burnt offerings and sacrifices. Jesus said he came to do God the Father's will as it was written of Him in scripture. He thus said He came to take away the first covenant in order that He could establish the second, or the new, covenant. Christ Jesus performed the will of God without sinning so that those who believe in and obey Him are sanctified and set apart unto God through Him (Heb 10:1-10).

By the offering of Himself, He has perfected forever those who are being sanctified or made holy. Those who have been perfected by Him are able to boldly enter into the presence of God in His Holy sanctuary by the life of Jesus, in whom we live and move and exist. Because we have a High Priest over the house of God, we can spiritually draw near to God with a true heart in full assurance of faith. That is, once we have had our hearts cleansed by His blood from an evil conscience and our bodies washed with pure water of the Holy Spirit to make us presentable and acceptable to Him (Heb 10:14-22, Acts 17:28).

The old covenant was temporal, since it was only a shadow or type of the new eternal covenant, which was made between God and the Son of Man, as the representative head of redeemed humanity. There is one God and one Mediator between God and men, the Man Christ Jesus (I Tim 2:5). He is the reason no other man who came before Him or after Him can save or deliver us from the wrath of God to come, regardless of the claims that have been made by those who have fathered various false religious beliefs and practices.

Chapter Twenty Two

The Dispensation of the Holy Spirit

Before His death, the Son of Man said the hour was coming, and had arrived, when the true worshipers of God would worship the Father in spirit and truth, for the Father seeks such individuals to worship Him. *God is Spirit, and those who worship Him must worship in spirit and truth* (John 4:23, 24). God is spirit and is not physically confined to any one place at any given time, thus we are able to worship Him anywhere at any time if we do so with a pure heart under the anointing and leading of the Holy Spirit. We can only experience communion with God spirit to Spirit and not flesh to Spirit or soul to Spirit.

Shortly before His crucifixion, Jesus acknowledged that the hour had come for Him to be crucified. He prayed that God would glorify Him as His Son so that He could glorify His Father. He said God had given Him authority over all flesh so that He could give eternal life to as many as the Father had given Him. Jesus explained the meaning of eternal life as knowing the only true God, and Himself, whom God had sent. Jesus proclaimed He had glorified God the Father on the earth by obeying Him in all His ways and had finished the work the Father had given Him to do. Jesus asked the Father to glorify Him together with Himself, and to restore Him to the position of honor in His presence that He had before the world was created (John 17:1-5).

Jesus assured His disciples, as well as each one of us today, that those who believe in Him will do the works that He did, and greater works will we do, because He was returning to His Father. He instructed us to make requests of the Father in His name, and whatever we ask He will do, that the Father may be glorified in Him. Again, Jesus emphasized that if we ask anything in His name, He will do it. Consequently the answer to our prayers or petitions depends upon whether God will be glorified (John 14:12-14).

Jesus continued by stating that if we love Him, we will keep His commandments. And He will ask the Father who will give us another Helper that He may abide with us forever. He is the Spirit of truth, whom the world cannot receive, because we can neither see Him nor know Him, since the Holy Spirit cannot be observed or detected by our natural senses. The Spirit has been likened to the wind; even though we cannot see either the wind or the Spirit, we can discern the presence and effects of both upon people and the earth. Jesus said His disciples were acquainted with the Holy Spirit, for He lived with them and would be in them. The Holy Spirit lived with them because He dwelt in Jesus. The Lord promised not leave His disciples or us His children as orphans, but said He would return to us by His Spirit (John 14:15-18).

The Son of Man emphasized that those who really love Him will obey His commands. To them the Father will give the Holy Spirit so that He may remain with them forever. Jesus gave many commands, so how can we remember all of them, especially if we are in the initial stages of our walk with the Lord? Jesus answered our question when He said that the first of all the commandments is: *the Lord our God is one. And you shall love the Lord your God with all your heart, with all your soul, with all your mind, and with all your strength. And the second, like it, is this: You shall love your neighbor as yourself. There is no other commandment greater than these* (Mark 12:29-31, Deut 4:29). The commands of Jesus become a stumbling block to those who are unwilling to surrender their lives to Him and refuse to seek first the kingdom of God and His righteousness (Matt 6:33).

The Holy Spirit was not recognized by the religious people of His day because they could not see the Spirit or understand who He was. But the disciples of Jesus recognized the presence of the Holy Spirit, for Christ Jesus was filled with the Spirit without measure (John 3:34). The Holy Spirit performed the works of the Father in and through Christ Jesus, who stressed that the Spirit would dwell in them after He was sent by the Father. Jesus promised that He would not abandon them, leaving them desolate and helpless, but that He would return to them or be manifested to them by His Spirit. The same promise is made to each one of us who believe in Jesus and obey Him.

Jesus explained to his disciples that in a little while the world would not see Him in the flesh anymore, but His disciples would see Him and once He was resurrected, they would be spiritually resurrected in Him and would live eternally. After being made alive by the Holy Spirit, they would become keenly aware of the reality that they were spiritually united with the Father and Jesus by virtue of the Holy Spirit dwelling in them as believers, bearing witness that they were the children of God (John 14:19, 20). How many Christians today are acquainted with the Holy Spirit and are keenly aware of His indwelling presence, as described by Jesus?

Jesus proclaimed that he who has His commandments and keeps them is he who loves Him. And he who loves Him will be loved by the Father and Jesus will love him also and will manifest Himself to him. Jesus was asked how He would manifest Himself to the believers and not to the world. Jesus told His disciples that we who love Him will keep His word and His Father will love us. Then He and His Father will come to us and reside with us. But he who does not love the Lord does not keep His words. Jesus said that He was speaking the words of the Father who sent Him (John 14:21-24). He was emphasizing that relationship with God is founded upon love and obedience.

If we make an unreserved commitment to Christ, He not only promises to reveal or make Himself real to us, but He assures us that He and the Father will be present with us together with the Holy Spirit. If we do not love Him and will not obey His words, neither can we receive the revelation of Christ nor will we receive the Holy Spirit to bear witness in our innermost being that we belong to Him. Love and obedience, through the exercise of our faith in God, are the prerequisite for us to enter into and to remain in an intimate spiritual relationship with both the Father and the Son.

At the time Jesus appeared upon earth as the Son of Man, the most religious and learned men of the Jewish nation, including the Sadducees and Pharisees who were the leaders of religious sects and who professed to know the Law of God and to be able to interpret the scriptures, were unable to discern or apprehend that Jesus was the Son of God incarnate. They even accused Him of being in league with the devil (Matt 9:34). So it does not seem strange in today's world that many professing Christians remain in the same unfamiliar spiritual position with regards to the identity of the Holy Spirit.

Many Christian, who profess to know Jesus, suffer from a lack of knowledge and understanding concerning the person and works of the Holy Spirit as well as His ordained role in the lives of individual believers and in the body of Christ, the Church. Some Christian denominations even consider one or more of the gifts of the Holy Spirit to be of the devil. Consequently, the devil succeeds in blinding and deceiving far too many individuals who profess to be followers of Jesus. He prevents as many of the body of Christ as He can from receiving full revelation concerning the Way and the Truth and the Life, as well as from being able to experience the empowerment of the Holy Spirit. Due to the devil's works, the Church has been splintered into many factions and robbed of its power and authority to rule over the earth as God had originally planned.

Satan has been successful in dividing the Body of Christ into thousands of different segments or denominations by deceiving and misleading men to believe and to receive only a portion of the gospel rather than the whole of it. His actions have caused the Body of Christ to resemble a large clay pot, which has been dropped on cement and broken into thousands of pieces. Each fragment represents a part of the whole of Christianity, but not the fullness of the gospel. Since some shards would be larger than others, the larger the broken piece the more of the truth of the gospel it would represent. Each individual piece of the pot would also be representative of the religious box that each denomination establishes with its doctrines and dogmas of belief.

For example: the Israelites refused to acknowledge and accept Jesus and His teachings despite the validation of His words by God who performed miracles, including even the raising of the dead. Yet, as in the case of the Pharaoh of Egypt, their hearts were hardened because they were not willing to accept and receive the things of God, which were not within their religious parameters. Much the same pattern of belief exists in the various denominations of Christianity today. For example, if a believer receives the baptism with the

Holy Spirit while attending a Christian church which does not recognize or accept it, the believer for the most part is shunned or rejected or requested to leave the church. Despite the Lord, who is unchanging, watching over His word and fulfilling it in the life of the seeking believer, some of the Christian denominations will not recognize or admit that the baptism by Christ Jesus happens today. They are bound by their doctrinal beliefs based upon the interpretation of men and not on the revealed word of God. Other activities also take place in some churches that misinterpret or misapply or violate the word of God in order to maintain the parameters of their religious boxes. These churches for the most part have a form of religion, but deny the power of God. As Hosea the prophet said, *My people are destroyed for lack of knowledge* (Hosea 4:6).

The Holy Spirit, whom Jesus said God the Father would send in His name, became our Helper. He is the One who teaches us all things and brings to our remembrance all things that Jesus said and did. Nevertheless, we have ignored Him for the most part and have attempted to interpret and understand the Scriptures based upon our earthly wisdom and intellect. Jesus promised that He would leave His peace with us as a gift and not as the world gives it. He urged us to not let our hearts be troubled or be afraid because He promised to return to us by His Spirit.

Jesus said if we loved Him we would rejoice because He said He was returning to His Father who is the greater. He told us ahead of time so we would believe (John 14:25-29). Christ explained that the Holy Spirit would be He who teaches us all things and reminds us of all that He taught as the Son of Man while also imparting unto us His peace that passes all understanding. He emphasized that the Holy Spirit would become as real to us as He was when He came into the world in the flesh as the Son of Man.

The Holy Spirit is the *paraclete*. The word *paraclete* is derived from the Greek word *parakletos* and it can be translated into English as Helper, Counselor, Comforter, Advocate, or Intercessor. When one of the words such as Helper is used, reference is made to The Holy Spirit who is the third Person of the Trinity. The Holy Spirit, as the *Paraclete,* is the *Spirit of truth,* who proceeds from the Father and reveals and testifies of Christ Jesus (John 15:26).

The word *paraclete* is so comprehensive in meaning that one English word cannot convey its fullness. The word *paraclete* encompasses more in meaning than the individual words Helper or Advocate or Comforter or Counselor. The one word *paraclete* conveys the meaning for all of these as well as *called to.* This means that the Holy Spirit is He who is called to come to our aid as a believer in Christ Jesus, to help us in our weaknesses, to guide us, to lead us, to empower us, and to serve as our advocate. The Holy Spirit is not an "it", for He is the third person of the Trinity, who teaches and comforts the believer. He alone is able to reveal the truth and the meaning of the Gospel to all men. Accordingly, the Holy Spirit, who anointed and inspired man to write the Bible, is the same Spirit who dwells in each one of us as a child of God interpreting and revealing the truth and meaning of God's word to us. As has often been said, the Bible interprets itself, in the sense that the Holy Spirit uses His word to explain the truth and meaning of His word.

The critical question arises: do we as Christians honor and obey the Holy Spirit as we would the LORD Jesus if He was physically among us? If the Holy Spirit was sent by the Father, as was Jesus, should we not love Him, seek to hear His voice, respond to Him and obey Him as we would Christ Jesus if He was here in the flesh? We are clearly told that the Spirit alone does what the Father and Jesus advises Him to do. Should we not only seek to become fully acquainted with the Holy Spirit, but to also devote the dedicated effort to be empowered by Him and to be led by Him? As a member of the body of Christ, how can we do the works that Jesus did or live a victorious life over the power of Satan that will glorify God without the Holy Spirit leading and directing us in all the things of God?

He, as the *Paraclete*, is also a very present help to the believer in time of need. He convicts the believer of wrongdoing and admonishes him. He anoints the believer and exercises the gifts of the Holy Spirit in him and through him to empower him to accomplish God's plan and purpose in and through his surrendered life, as well as in the Body of Christ, the Church. The Holy Spirit also imparts God's wisdom and strength to each of us as members of the body of Christ and bears witness by His indwelling presence that we are the children of God. His indwelling presence sets true Christianity apart from all other religions and sects that man or Satan devises to enslave man and to glorify himself.

The Holy Spirit was sent as the *Paraclete* to become to the believer, all that Christ Jesus was to his disciples while He was present on earth in the flesh. When Jesus promised that the Father would send His disciples another Helper or Comforter, who would abide with them forever, in essence He was saying that He is the first *Paraclete* and that the Holy Spirit would take His place as the second *Paraclete*. The Holy Spirit came in the supernatural realm rather than in the natural realm as Christ did when He appeared upon the earth.

The Holy Spirit, as the second *Paraclete*, became spiritually to man that which the incarnate Christ Jesus was to man when He was on earth as the Son of Man. But the Holy Spirit is not confined to one person in one place at any given time as when He indwelt the Son of Man. He, as the *Paraclete*, is accessible to all men at any time and dwells in each believer whose body becomes God's temple on earth (I Cor 6:19), as opposed to God's presence being manifested in a chosen few or in a manmade structure such as in the Tabernacle of Moses. The indwelling Holy Spirit is He who unites all believers in Christ to form one body, the Church, which men by their own fleshly efforts cannot accomplish regardless of their good works or the earthly methods they employ. Nevertheless, the Holy Spirit is virtually unknown to the world, including many Christian churches, as was Christ Jesus to the world and to the Jewish people when He reigned upon the earth.

Chapter Twenty Three

The Holy Spirit is the Reigning Member of the Trinity in the World Today

Jesus revealed that after the Holy Spirit became the reigning representative of the Trinity upon the earth, He would act on behalf of the Father and the Son in the redemption of man and in uniting man with the Son of Man. The primary function of the Holy Spirit is to manifest the person and works of the Lord Jesus Christ in and through His body of believers. In so doing, the Holy Spirit glorifies His person, brings to fruition His teachings, and works in the life of the individual believer, as well as in the Body of Christ to accomplish the will and purpose of God. The will and purpose of God was clearly defined in the day of Adam. He was commanded to subdue Satan and to establish the kingdom of God upon the earth.

Only by the person and works of the Holy Spirit, who gives us the mind of Christ (I Cor 2:16), can we be empowered to accomplish God's plan and purpose individually as well as corporately. He is the only One capable of fulfilling the Father's and the Son's promises to the believers, who remain faithful to the Lord Jesus Christ.

According to Scripture, unbelievers or the unrighteous cannot know or receive the Holy Spirit or the things of God because they neither can be seen nor heard, nor do they enter into the hearts of unrighteous men. The things of God are revealed only to those who love Him and to those who reverence Him and promptly obey Him. To those who surrender their lives to Christ Jesus, God unveils and reveals His things to them by and through His Spirit. For the Holy Spirit diligently searches, explores, and examines everything of God, including His divine counsels and things that are concealed and beyond natural man's scrutiny. What person knows or understands what passes through a man's thoughts except the man's own spirit within him? Accordingly, no one can discern or know or comprehend the thoughts of God except by the Spirit of God.

A believer has not been given the spirit of the devil that belongs to the world, but he has been given the Holy Spirit, Who is from God, that he might realize and comprehend and appreciate the gifts of divine favor and the blessing that God so freely bestows upon righteous believers. God's truths are set forth in words not taught by human wisdom, but taught by the Holy Spirit. The Spirit combines and interprets spiritual truths with spiritual language for the spiritually born again believer in whom He dwells. The natural or unspiritual man does not accept or admit into his heart the gifts or the teachings or the revelation of the Spirit of God, for they are folly or meaningless nonsense to him. He is incapable of knowing or understanding them because they can be spiritually discerned only by those who have been made spiritually alive in Christ Jesus (I Cor 2:9-14, AMP). But the believers have the mind of Christ (1 Cor 2:16), for we who are joined to the Lord have become one spirit with Him since our body is the temple of the Holy Spirit (I Cor 6:17, 19), the very One who spiritually unites us with the Son of Man.

All religions inspired by man and by Satan are void of the Holy Spirit and His works. Regardless of the works or beliefs or the teachings of men contrary to the word of God, they cannot offer the revelation of God or the eternal life of God to anyone. Only the Holy Spirit has the power to open the spiritual eyes of man and to change his sinful spiritual nature with which he is physically born into the world. As the Word of the Lord declares, it is not by might or the power of man that all things are accomplished in the kingdom of God, but by the Spirit of God (Zech 4:6). The mere practice of religious doctrines or traditions, or rituals or following the false or misleading teachings of men will not enable anyone to enter into a spiritual relationship with God.

The Holy Spirit has been present and active in the world since the beginning of time, although His role as the Third Person of the Trinity has been different during the three stages of the development of God's plan and purpose for man as recorded in the Bible. When the earth was without form and void, and darkness was on the face of the deep, the Spirit of God was hovering over the face of the waters (Gen 1:1-2, 26). The Holy Spirit was active with God the Father and God the Son in the creation of the earth and all things in the world, including man.

God the Father holds the Headship in His plan of creation and in the redemption of all things. In the first stage or dispensation of His plan, as recorded in the Old Testament, God as the First Person of the Trinity initiated and directed all things upon earth as the reigning member of the Trinity. All things were performed through the Second Person of the Trinity, God the Son. By the Son, all things were created that are in heaven and that are on earth, visible and invisible, whether thrones or dominions or principalities or powers. All things were created through Him and for Him. And He is before all things and in Him all things are sustained (Col 1:16, 17).

God the Holy Spirit, the Third Person of the Trinity, was involved in executing all of the Father's works as well. Each Member of the Trinity is as much God as are the other two members of the Trinity. However, each of their divine roles differs in each stage of God's plan. During the dispensation of the first Person of the Trinity, many specific examples of the Holy Spirit's involvement in the lives of men, as well as in the miraculous acts of God the Father, are recorded in the Bible. In each instance, a specific purpose of God was served or achieved. For example: in the building of the Tabernacle of Moses, the Holy Spirit empowered the workers to build the tabernacle and make its furnishings according to God's exact standards. Bezalel, who was one of the principal workers, was filled with the Spirit of God in wisdom, in understanding, in knowledge, and in all manner of workmanship (Exo 31:2-5). During the time of Moses, the Lord took of the Spirit that was upon him and put the Spirit upon 70 men of the elders of Israel to enable them to help bear the burden of the people that was upon Moses alone (Num 11:16, 17, 25).

Later, the Lord anointed Saul as the first king of Israel when the Spirit of the Lord came upon him (I Sam 10:6-12). The Spirit of the Lord came upon Othniel, the son of Kenaz and he judged Israel and successfully led Israel in war (Judg 3:9, 10). In a similar manner, the Spirit of the Lord came upon Gideon (Judg 6:34) and Samson (Judg 13:24, 25; 15:10-15) and others to empower them to fulfill God's purpose and plan in and through their lives.

The Spirit of God came upon the various prophets of God and spoke through them the words of God while they performed many miraculous deeds. The prophet Ezekiel, under the anointing of the Holy Spirit, foretold things God would perform in men during the dispensation of the Holy Spirit. *I will give you a new heart and put a new spirit in you; I will remove from you your heart of stone and give you a heart of flesh. And I will put my Spirit in you and move you to follow my decrees and be careful to keep my laws* (Ezek 36:26, 27). The Spirit of the Lord came upon David when he was anointed by the prophet Samuel (I Sam 16:13) and the Spirit of the Lord spoke by him (I Sam 23:1, 2). Old Testament Scripture discloses many other instances of the Holy Spirit's involvement during God's dispensation as the First Person of the Trinity.

In the second stage or dispensation of God's plan the Second Person of the Trinity, God the Son became the reigning member of the Trinity upon the earth as the Son of Man. He became the head of the body, the Church as the firstborn from the dead, that in all things He would have the preeminence. It pleased *the Father that* in Him all the fullness of the Godhead should dwell. All things were reconciled to the Father by the Son, including all things on earth and in heaven, when He made peace through the blood of His cross (Colossians 1:18-20).

Christ Jesus came into the world as the Son of Man acting on behalf and at the direction of the Father, under the anointing of the Holy Spirit, to accomplish God's plan and purpose of redeeming and restoring man to a righteous relationship with his Creator, as well as defeating the devil and destroying his works. The Holy Spirit was also active during the dispensation of Christ Jesus. He not only anointed Christ, but He also manifested and exercised the gifts of the Holy Spirit in and through Him, which enabled Christ to have the mind and wisdom of the Father in all things and to perform many miracles and wonders.

In the third and present stage or dispensation of God's plan, the Holy Spirit is the reigning member of the Trinity, who is at work in the world today, acting on behalf of the Father and the Son. From the very beginning, God's plan and purpose for creating man and placing him upon planet earth involved all three members of the Trinity. God's plan has materialized in three distinct phases, with each member of the Trinity in their order being involved in fulfilling His part according to His person.

The Holy Spirit's role under the Father's dispensation was different from that which was manifested during the dispensation of Christ Jesus. The ministry and work of the Holy Spirit in the third phase of God's plan became much more personal and comprehensive in our lives than it was during the Son of Man's reign. The Holy Spirit performs unique spiritual work in every believer, which begins the moment the individual surrenders his life to Christ Jesus and submits unto Him. Only the Holy Spirit can impart God's spiritual life to us through new spiritual birth and empower us to respond to God's call upon our lives.

God has warned us not to blaspheme the Holy Spirit, not to resist Him, not to quench the Holy Spirit, and not to grieve the Holy Spirit of God, by whom we as believers are sealed for the day of redemption (Matt 12:31-32; Acts 7:51; Eph 4:30; I Thes 5:19). The sin of blasphemy against the Holy Spirit is unforgivable by God, whereas sin against the Son of Man is pardonable. Sin against the Spirit is opposed to the only One who can reveal Jesus to man. No man can confess that Jesus is the Lord, but by the Holy Spirit (Gal 5:25). No one can come to Jesus unless the Father who sent Him draws him by His Spirit (John 6:44). So why has the teaching and ministry regarding the person and works of the Holy Spirit become such a clouded and empty issue in the majority of Christian churches?

Chapter Twenty Four

The Holy Spirit Is He
Who Unites the Believer with Christ Jesus

Since we enter into the world with the sinful spiritual nature of Adam, we must be spiritually born again from above by the Holy Spirit to become united with the Son of Man. Otherwise we cannot be delivered out of the kingdom of Satan into the Kingdom of God. Only in this way can we become a new spiritual creation of God (John 3:5, 6). *It is the Spirit who gives life* (John 6:63) and not any religion or the teachings or the works of man.

Through the work of the Holy Spirit, we are re-created spiritually when we accept the Lord Jesus and His finished work and surrender our lives to Him. The Holy Spirit baptizes us into one body, the body of Christ Jesus the Son of Man—whether we are Jew or Gentile, slave or free—and we are made to drink of one Spirit, the Holy Spirit. The body of Christ is not one member, but it is made up of all of the many born again believers who are united in Christ Jesus. Despite the fact there are many members, there is only one body of Christ (1 Cor 12:13, 14, 20) in the world today.

In a similar manner, upon physical birth each individual enters the world as one of the many spiritual members of the body of the first man Adam, in whom all die. When we are spiritually born again from above by the Holy Spirit, we are delivered out of the spiritual body of Adam into the spiritual body of Jesus. The Holy Spirit unites us spiritually with Christ Jesus, who remains alive forever and we become a child of God and an heir of God, and joint heirs with Christ, if indeed we suffer with Him, that we may be glorified together with Him (Rom 8:16, 17). This transforming work of the Holy Spirit occurs in the spirit realm undetectable by the senses of man except for the visible changes that appear in a believer's demeanor and response to God.

Scripture explains how the Holy Spirit spiritually unites the believer with the Son of Man. All who are spiritually baptized into Christ Jesus are baptized into His death. We are buried with Christ when the Holy Spirit unites our spirit with the spirit of Christ in His death. Just as Christ was spiritually slain by our sins when He was united with us, we likewise have our sinful spiritual nature circumcised or slain when the Holy Spirit unites our sinful spirit with Him in His death. After we have been united with Christ in newness of life by the same Spirit, we are then raised from the dead by the glory of the Father by the same Holy Spirit who made Christ Jesus alive from the dead (Rom 8:11). If we as believers have been united together in the likeness of His death, certainly we also shall be united with Him in the likeness of His resurrection. For we know that Christ having been raised from the dead will never die again, because death no longer has dominion over Him. We should realize that our old, sinful nature was crucified with Him that the body of sin with which we are physically born might be done away with, that we should no longer remain slaves to sin. For upon being spiritually united with Him in His death, we are freed from the enslavement to sin.

For the death that Jesus died, He died to sin once for all, but the life that He now lives, He lives to God. We who have been baptized into the body of Christ are to consider ourselves to have died to sin as well and to have been made alive to God in Christ Jesus our Lord (Rom 6:3-11).

Sinful man cannot be delivered from the power of sin under Satan's rule except through spiritual death and spiritual rebirth, which occurs when a believer is born again from above by the Holy Spirit (John 3:3-8). The old sinful nature, with which we are physically born into this world, must be put to death through spiritual circumcision, which only the Holy Spirit can perform, before God's holy spiritual nature can be imparted to us who believe in Christ. The Holy Spirit then can recreate in us the Spirit of Christ and raise us up from spiritual death united in newness of life with Christ, the Son of Man (Rom 8:9-11).

Thus Christ Jesus supersedes the first man Adam and becomes our new spiritual Head or the chief cornerstone of His body, the Church (Eph 2:20). The spiritual nature of God is imparted to the born again believer when he is delivered out of the kingdom of darkness into God's Kingdom of Light. He is set free from the condemnation and the wrath of God. Although this sequence of events is hidden from the eye of man, the spiritual transformation must happen before anyone can enter into a righteous spiritual relationship with the living God of the universe.

Scripture explains the actual events that take place during our new birth after we believe and accept Christ Jesus and His finished work. We are washed; we are sanctified; we are justified in the name of the Lord Jesus and by the Spirit of our God (I Cor 6:11). Notice all things are performed by God and not by man. All the fullness of the deity lives in bodily form in Christ and we are given fullness in Christ, who is the head over every power and authority. In Him we were also circumcised, in the removing of our sinful nature with the circumcision done by Christ, when we were buried with Him in baptism and raised with Him through our faith in the power of God, who raised Him from the dead. When we were dead in our sins and in the uncircumcision of our sinful nature, God made us alive with Christ. He forgave us all our sins, having cancelled the written Law with its regulations that condemned us as sinners. He took the Law away by nailing the One who bore our sins to the cross to suffer God's punishment in our stead (Col 2:9-14, NIV).

The Word of God tells us that we as believers are all sons of God through faith in Jesus. All of us who have been baptized into Christ have put on Christ. There is neither Jew nor Gentile, slave nor free, male nor female, for we have all become one in Christ Jesus. And if we are Christ's, then we are Abraham's seed and have become heirs according to the promise made to Abraham by God (Gal 3:26-29). The promises of God were made to Abraham and his Seed. *He did not say His promises were made to many seeds, but to just one Seed, who is Christ (Gal 3:16).* If we are united with Christ Jesus, then we have become one with the Seed of Abraham.

If we are in Christ, we are a new spiritual creation; our old nature has passed away and all things have become new. Now our spiritual nature is of God, who has reconciled us to Himself through Jesus Christ. God was in Christ, reconciling the world to Himself through Him (2 Cor 5:17-19).

The Holy Spirit performs a spiritual transformation of each believer the moment he surrenders his life to Christ. He resurrects the human spirit and soul from spiritual death by uniting the believer with the living Christ (I Cor 12:13). The spiritual recreation of man is a sovereign work of God inasmuch as only God, who is holy, can justify the ungodly (Rom 4:5). For us to enter into the kingdom of God, we must be conformed to the image of God's Son by the Holy Spirit as Christ Jesus was conformed to the sinless image of man by the Holy Spirit enabling Him to enter the world on our behalf to unite with us on the cross to become our sin-bearing substitute.

We are told in scripture that when one turns to the Lord, the veil of spiritual blindness is taken away. The Lord is the Spirit and His Spirit dwells in us, therefore liberty from the bondage to sin prevails in our lives if we remain obedient to the Lord. All believers in Christ Jesus are being transformed into His image from glory to glory by the Spirit of the Lord (2 Cor 3:14-18). For whom God foreknew—that is those who would believe in and accept the Gospel of Christ Jesus—He also predestined to be conformed to the spiritual image of His Son. Thus Christ Jesus, as the firstborn from the dead, became the Head of all born again believers who constitute His body, the Church (Rom 8:29).

When we are born again from above by the Holy Spirit, God sends the Spirit of His Son into our hearts as His adopted sons, testifying that we are His children (Gal 4:6; Rom 8:15-17) and that we have become a new spiritual creation in Christ Jesus. Both the Word of God and the Holy Spirit bear witness to our spiritual transformation, as well as our son-ship relationship with the LORD. After we have believed in and accepted Christ Jesus as our Savior and Lord, we are sealed individually with the Holy Spirit of promise, which is the earnest of our spiritual inheritance or God's earnest money deposit in us, a guaranty of His promise until our final redemption as His purchased possession (Eph 1:13, 14; 2 Cor 1:21, 22). We must remain united in spiritual relationship with the Son of Man to receive the fullness of salvation that is promised to us upon physical death or upon His return to Earth. Salvation is not just an emotional experience, for Jesus is our salvation. He is not only the author, but He is also the finisher or the very essence of our salvation, therefore we must remain in a righteous relationship with Him to the very end to receive our promised inheritance.

The Holy Spirit also sanctifies the believer in Christ (2 Thes 2:13; 1 Pet 1:2). One might ask, what is the meaning of sanctification? The Hebrew word "*qadash*" in the Old Testament and the Greek word "*haglazo*" used in the New Testament are translated as "sanctify", which means to make holy or to make free from sin, or to purify or to consecrate or be separated unto God. The Holy Spirit performs sanctification of the believer in Christ Jesus by revealing the truth of the gospel and using the word of God to admonish, correct, and impart to the believer the reality of God. Faith is released in us when we hear and act on the word of God (Rom 10:17, Jam 1:22). When we receive Christ as our Savior, the holiness of God is readily available to us in the same manner that salvation is available to all people. But we are not saved until we accept the Lord and commit our life to Him. Every born again believer in Christ Jesus can sin again, but he remains in a position to be sanctified by the Holy Spirit throughout his life if he repents, confesses his sin to God, and remains faithful to Him.

God is light and if we as believers in Christ Jesus say that we have fellowship with Him and walk in darkness, we lie and do not practice the truth. But if we walk with Him who is the light, we have fellowship with one another and His blood cleanses us from all sin. If we say that we are without sin, we are deceiving ourselves and the truth does not abide in us. If we confess our sins, God is faithful and just to forgive us of our sins and to cleanse us from all unrighteousness. We make Him a liar if we say that we have not sinned and His word is not in us (1 John 1:5-10).

Progressive sanctification by the Holy Spirit is necessary for us to live a holy life unto God and to grow in spiritual maturity in our relationship with Him. Since the body of a true believer is the temple or the very sanctuary of the Holy Spirit who resides in him, he has been purchased at a great price. He is to honor God and bring glory to Him in his body. This requires more than words, but also works or deeds of faith that are acceptable and pleasing to Him as was demonstrated in the lives of the faithful men and women of biblical history (Heb chapter 11).

God by His Spirit delivers us from the power of darkness under Satan's rule and conveys us into the kingdom of the Son of His love, in whom we have redemption through His blood, the forgiveness of sins. Christ is the image of the invisible God, the firstborn over all creation or the spiritual head over all born again believers (Col 1:13-15). Just as Christ Jesus is the firstborn Son of God in the flesh, the first Adam was the first creation of God as man. Christ as man, the firstborn Son of God from the dead, became the new spiritual head of the human race in whom all who submit unto Him and accept Him are made eternally alive as contrasted with the first Adam, in whom all die.

When we are spiritually born again from above by the Holy Spirit, we can declare that we have been crucified with Christ and that we no longer live, but Christ lives in us. The life we now live in the flesh, we live by faith in the Son of God, who loved us and gave Himself for us (Gal 2:20). We can further declare that our bodies are the temple of the Holy Spirit who dwells in us, whom we have received from God, and we are no longer our own. For we have been purchased at a price, and we are to glorify God in our body and in our spirits, which belong to Him (1 Cor 6:19, 20).

The prayer of Jesus that we all become one, as the Father was in Him and He was in the Father and that we would be in both the Father and the Son, is fulfilled by the Spirit of God. Thus evidence is presented to the world that God sent His Son and has bestowed His glory upon us, making us one with Him, confirming His love for us as He did for His Son (John 17:21-23).

Only in the Son of Man, as the last Adam, can we be reconciled to God in the body of His flesh through death, to be presented holy, and blameless, and above reproach in His sight—if indeed we continue in the faith, grounded and steadfast, and are not moved away from the hope of the gospel which we have heard (Col 1:21-23). We enter into God's spiritual Kingdom of Light by being spiritually united with the Son of Man as a member of His body, flesh of His flesh and bone of His bones (Eph 5:28-30). Upon being united with the Son of Man, we become a spiritual member of His body as the only begotten Son of God in the flesh as well as the first born Son of Man from the dead. We do not become a member of the Son of God as the Second Person of the Trinity, for we cannot be elevated above the level of our original creation, which is a little lower than God. Jesus was required to become man to enable us to unite with Him as the Son of Man, the only begotten Son of God in the flesh and not as deity.

The apostle Paul contrasts a believer's spiritual position and condition prior to and after being resurrected spiritually by the Holy Spirit. We were without Christ, being aliens from the commonwealth of Israel and strangers from the covenants of promise, having no hope and without God in the world. Now in Christ Jesus we who once were far off have been brought near by the blood of Christ. Christ is our peace and has made both Jew and Gentile one in Himself. Under the Law, the Gentiles were excluded from God's grace. But now the wall separating them from God has been removed by Christ and both Jew and Gentile, which includes all members of the human race, are invited to come to God through Him.

He abolished in His flesh, through His death and His resurrection, the hostility that the law of commandments imparted because of the exclusion of the Gentiles from the Old Covenant. Thus Christ created in Himself one new man from the two, making peace by reconciling both Jew and Gentile to God in His body through the cross, thereby putting to death the enmity that separated them. He preached peace to all of those who were excluded from the covenant promises of God as well as those who were included under the Old Covenant.

Through Christ, whether Jew or Gentile, we have access by one Spirit to the Father. Gentiles, who are righteous believers, are no longer strangers and foreigners, but fellow citizens with the saints and members of the household of God. We have been built on the foundation of the apostles and prophets with Christ Jesus being the chief Cornerstone, in whom the whole spiritual building is joined together and grows into a holy temple in the Lord. In Christ we also are being built together for a dwelling place of God in the Spirit (Eph 2:12-22).

God and not man unites the believer in Christ Jesus, who becomes for us wisdom from God and righteousness and sanctification and redemption (1Cor 1:30). To each one of us who receives Him, He gives the right to become a child of God, to all of us who believe in His name: who are born, not of blood, nor of the will of the flesh, nor of the will of man, but of God (John 1:12, 13).

Satan has filled the world with false religions, false gods, and lifeless idols, which he devises and employs to keep us divided in our beliefs and to enslave us through the power of sin. He preys upon our spiritual blindness by offering us a form of religion mixed with a small portion of the Gospel of Christ Jesus. Satan attempts to deceive and mislead us to worship and serve him or to prevent us from remaining obedient to Christ Jesus and fulfilling God's plan for our lives.

A typical example occurred in the life of Jesus when He was tempted by the devil in the wilderness. Satan even quoted the word of God to Him, but misapplied the word in his effort to induce Jesus to sin. In the same manner He perverts the word of God and attempts to visit his deception upon us to believe a lie or wrongfully interpret the word of God. One of his primary goals is to subtly rob the Church of its power, leaving it to embrace only a form of religion, making it unable to fulfill the plan and purpose of God in this world.

The primary evidence that determines whether the religion or cult is of the devil centers upon the absence of the person and works of the Holy Spirit, who cannot and will not align Himself with the devil or evil. All false religions, cults, and idol worship are void of the presence of the Holy Spirit, who alone is empowered by God to impart new spiritual birth to man by uniting him with the Son of Man.

The responsibility remains upon our shoulders to seek the Lord while He may be found and to study to show ourselves approved, becoming able to rightly divide the word of truth (2 Tim 2:15). If we learn the truth of God's word, we will be able to discern whether that which is being taught or preached deviates from or perverts the word of God. With the revelation knowledge and understanding of God's word, we will able to immediately recognize biblical error when it arises. We will also learn how to apply the word of God in our lives and to resist the Devil and His temptations.

God has given us the Holy Spirit in our hearts to guarantee His promise of our salvation (2 Cor 1:21, 22). Only God can produce spiritual fruit, in and through us as believers, that is pleasing to Him. Think of a fruit-bearing tree. The sap flowing through its branches empowers it to produce fruit. Accordingly, as a born-again believer abiding in Christ Jesus and His word, we are able to produce spiritual fruit acceptable to God by virtue of the Holy Spirit flowing through us.

The Son of Man issued a stern warning to all men who knowingly or unknowingly sin against God and serve the adversary of the Lord and man. Jesus commanded us to repent, for the kingdom of heaven is at hand (Matt 4:17) and unless we repent, we will all perish (Luke 13:3, 5). Jesus did not come to call the righteous, but sinners, to repentance (Luke 5:32). After His resurrection, Jesus told His followers it was written and thus it became necessary for Him to suffer and to be raised from the dead the third day, and for repentance and remission of sins to be preached in His name to all nations, beginning at Jerusalem (Luke 24:46-48).

Webster defines repent as "to feel so contrite over one's sins as to change one's ways or be penitent". Scripture tells us, *For godly sorrow produces repentance leading to salvation, not to be regretted; but the sorrow of the world produces death* (2 Cor 7:10). The prophet Ezekiel said the LORD will judge every one according to his ways. He commanded that we repent and turn from all our transgressions so that iniquity will not be our ruin. We are commanded to cast away all our transgressions and to get ourselves a new heart and a new spirit. He questioned, why should we die? The LORD God has no pleasure in the death of he who dies. He urges us to turn from our evil ways and live (Ezek 18:30-32)!

We are exhorted to lay aside all malice, all deceit, hypocrisy, envy, and all evil speaking and to desire the pure milk of the Word, so that we may grow spiritually once we have tasted that the Lord *is* gracious. Coming to Christ Jesus, who is the living stone that was rejected by men, but was chosen by God and considered to be precious, we as living stones are being united into a spiritual house to become a holy priesthood unto God for the purpose of offering up spiritual sacrifices that are acceptable to God through Him.

We as believers are told in Scripture that God has laid in Zion a Chief Cornerstone. He is elect and precious. We who believe on Him will never be put to shame by Him. For the believer, Jesus is precious. But to those who are rebellious, as the stone which His own people rejected, He has become the Chief Cornerstone and a stone of stumbling and a rock of offense because He provides the only access to God. The unrighteous stumble because they are disobedient to the Word. We as believers have become a chosen generation, a royal priesthood, a holy nation, His own special people. Thus we are able to proclaim the praises of Him who called us out of darkness into His marvelous light. We were once not His people and had not obtained mercy, but we are now the people of God and have now obtained His mercy (1 Pet 2:1-10).

The Word of God offers assurance that we will be saved if we confess with our mouth Jesus as our Lord and believe in our heart that God raised Him from the dead. For with our heart we believe the Gospel, the good news concerning Him, which is accepted by the Lord to make us righteous. With our mouth confession is made unto salvation and all who believe on Him will never be put to shame (Rom 10:9-11).

Jesus Himself proclaimed, *I am the resurrection and the life. He who believes in Me, though he may die* [physically] *yet shall he live. And whoever lives and believes in Me shall never die* [spiritually] (John 11:25, 26).

He also said that whoever confesses Him before men, the Son of Man also will confess him before His angels. But we who deny God before men will be denied before His angels. Whoever speaks a word against the Son of Man will be forgiven, but he who blasphemes against the Holy Spirit will not be forgiven (Luke 12:8-10). This warning serves as even more reason to become intimately acquainted or familiar with the Holy Spirit.

The apostle John said the evidence that we abide in Him and that He abides in us is the presence of the Holy Spirit that He has given to dwell in us as believers. The Father sent the Son to become Savior of the world. Whoever confesses Jesus is the Son of God, then God abides in him and he abides in God (I John 4:13-15). His indwelling presence constitutes the testimony of God that He has given unto us eternal life and this life is in His Son, Christ Jesus. He who is spiritually united with the Son has eternal life with God, but he who is not united with the Son of God does not have life with Him (I John 5:11, 12). Consequently, Jesus becomes salvation for each one of us who is united with Him and endures to the end and does not leave the narrow pathway of righteousness to return again to the sins that so easily beset us in Satan's kingdom of darkness.

But the question arises concerning the born again believers in Christ Jesus: how will we who are spiritually united with Christ be raised up after physical death and what body will be given to us? For example, when a grain of wheat is sown, it must die to produce a life in a different form as a plant. Each seed of different grains produces a body that differs from each of the other grains. God gives all flesh a body that differs according to its nature, whether human, animal, or fish or for that matter heavenly bodies as compared to celestial bodies.

In like manner, the dead in Christ are resurrected in a different body. The physical body is sown or buried in a corrupt and decaying state and it is raised an incorruptible immortal body. It is sown in the dishonor of death and it is raised in the glory of eternal life. The body is sown in weakness, but it is raised in strength and empowered. It is sown a natural or physical body in death and it is raised a supernatural or spiritual body. We are born with a natural body, which must be put off in order for us to receive a spiritual body.

As it is written, the first man Adam was created a living being, whereas the last Adam was resurrected from the dead to become a life-giving spirit. The natural man came first and afterward came the spiritual man. The first man was made of dust of the earth, as compared to the second Man, who is the Lord from heaven. We were made of dust, as was the first man Adam. As is the heavenly Man, so also are we who are united with the Son of Man in the newness of life. Just as we have borne the image of the man of dust, we shall also bear the image of the heavenly Man.

The Lord tells us that flesh and blood (or carnal man) cannot inherit the kingdom of God, nor does corruption inherit incorruption…We shall not all sleep, but we shall all be changed—in a moment, in the twinkling of an eye, at the last trumpet. For the trumpet will sound, and the dead will be raised incorruptible and immortal—then shall come to pass the written saying:

Death is swallowed up in victory. O Death, where is your sting? O Hades, where is your victory? The sting of death is sin, and the strength of sin is the law. But thanks be to God, who gives us the victory through our Lord Jesus Christ. Therefore, my beloved brethren, be steadfast, immovable, always abounding in the work of the Lord, knowing that your labor is not in vain in the Lord. (1 Corinthians 15:35-58)

Chapter Twenty Five

The Son of Man Revealed the Spiritual Path That Man Must Follow to Be Empowered By the Holy Spirit

During His earthly life, Jesus revealed the spiritual path that carnal man must follow to receive salvation and be empowered by the Holy Spirit. Although Jesus was born into the world with the holy nature of God the Father and remained sinless in all of His ways, He nevertheless came from Galilee to John the Baptist at the Jordan River to be baptized in water by him. John had earlier pronounced that he baptized with water, but One mightier than he was coming, referring to Christ Jesus, who would baptize the believer with the Holy Spirit and fire (Luke 3:16).

John tried to persuade Jesus to baptize him with the Holy Spirit and fire, but Jesus responded that it was fitting for them to fulfill all righteousness. So Jesus allowed him to baptize Him in the water of the Jordan River. Jesus came up immediately from the water and the heavens were opened to Him. The Spirit of God descended upon Jesus like a dove and alighted upon Him. Suddenly a voice came from heaven, declaring that Jesus was His beloved Son, in whom He was well pleased (Matt 3:13-17).

When Jesus explained to John that He must fulfill all righteousness required for entry into the Kingdom of God, He was revealing to mankind that salvation, a work of the Holy Spirit, must come first, which is symbolized by water baptism. Following water baptism, Jesus was immediately baptized with the Holy Spirit to receive the anointed power of God to perform the works of God that He had been sent to do.

As we have already seen in scripture, baptism in water is symbolic of sinful man being spiritually born again from above by the Holy Spirit when he is baptized into the death of Christ Jesus and is united with Him in His resurrection to become a spiritual member of His body. As Jesus was begotten by the Holy Spirit to become the Son of Man, likewise sinful man must be spiritually begotten by the same Holy Spirit to enter into a relationship with God as a son, and if a son, then an heir of God through Christ (Gal 4:7).

Jesus was demonstrating that two separate events must take place spiritually in a particular order in the life of every believer for him to enter the Kingdom of Light and to then receive the anointing of the Holy Spirit to be empowered for service unto God. First we must be baptized by the Holy Spirit into the body of the Son of Man before we can be anointed for power. As demonstrated in the life of the Son of Man, He was born into the world as the sinless begotten Son of God and remained obedient to the Father in all things. Yet His ministry of reconciliation did not begin until He was empowered by the Holy Spirit at about 30 years of age.

Not until after Jesus was baptized by the Holy Spirit were the gifts of the Holy Spirit manifested in and through Him during His ministry, including the working of miracles with signs and wonders following. He established the order that sinful man is to follow by showing that salvation precedes the empowerment by the Holy Spirit. Accordingly, once man is baptized by the Holy Spirit into the body of Christ Jesus, he becomes eligible to receive the baptism with the Holy Spirit, which only Christ Jesus can perform. Upon being empowered by the Holy Spirit, we become equipped for service unto God, as was the Son of Man in His earthly life.

The apostle Paul prayed for us, as the faithful in Christ Jesus. He requested that the God of our Lord Jesus Christ, the Father of Glory, would give unto us the spirit of wisdom and revelation in the intimate knowledge of Him so that we can know and understand the hope to which He has called us. Only the Holy Spirit is able to open the eyes of our understanding through the word of God to enable us to know the hope of His calling upon our lives and to know the value that He has placed upon us who have been set apart unto Him. Only by being enlightened can we know and understand the exceeding greatness of His power toward us who believe. He demonstrated the working of His mighty power through the Holy Spirit when He resurrected Christ from the dead and seated Him at His right hand in the heavenly places, far above all principality and power and might and dominion, and every name that is named, not only in this age, but also throughout eternity (Eph 1:15-21).

Paul points out that God has a great inheritance in the believers. If we fail to respond to Him and His calling upon our lives and to yield ourselves for His glory, then He is being defrauded of the inheritance that rightfully belongs to Him. He stressed the importance of each believer recognizing and experiencing the power of the Holy Spirit, who raised Jesus from the dead. Every act performed in the believer's body should be in obedience to the leading and prompting of the Holy Spirit. When a person surrenders himself—including his spirit, soul, and body—to the Holy Spirit and responds to His prompting and leading, then his acts are responsive and agreeable to God's purpose and will.

The opposite is true when we fail to yield ourselves to the Holy Spirit. Our deeds become a work of the flesh, which do not glorify God and fail to accomplish the Lord's plan and purpose in and through our lives to establish His kingdom upon the earth. Since the Holy Spirit indwells the body of the believer, only when we obey the prompting and leading of the Holy Spirit are we able to glorify the Father and the Son. We as believers are exhorted to glorify God in our bodies and in our spirits because we have been purchased at a great cost through the sufferings of the Son of Man and we belong to God (I Cor 6:19, 20).

Jesus baptizes the born again believer with the Holy Spirit.

Jesus presented Himself alive to His followers by many infallible proofs. He was seen by them during 40 days and He spoke of the things pertaining to the kingdom of God. Once they were assembled together, He commanded them not to depart from Jerusalem, but to wait for the Promise of the Father, *which, He said, you have heard from Me; for John truly baptized with water, but you shall be baptized with the Holy Spirit not many days from now (Acts 1:3-5).*

As we have already seen, before Jesus was baptized with the Holy Spirit to receive the anointing for His earthly ministry, John the Baptist announced that Jesus would be He who baptizes the believer with the Holy Spirit and fire (Matt 3:11, 12). Jesus told His followers they would receive power when the Holy Spirit had come upon them and they *would be witnesses to Him in Jerusalem, and in all Judea and Samaria, and to the end of the earth (Acts 1:8).*

Scripture differentiates between the role of the Holy Spirit in the salvation of the believer and that of Jesus as the baptizer with the Holy Spirit, to empower the believer to serve God. Scripture clearly states that the Holy Spirit is He who baptizes the believer into the body of Christ Jesus (I Cor 12:13), making him to be a new spiritual creation. Whereas Jesus is specifically identified as He who baptizes the believer with the Holy Spirit and fire to sanctify and to anoint him with power to become His witness and to do the things that He did as the Son of Man. Scripture declares that Jesus will thoroughly remove the wheat from the chaff, speaking of the obedient believers as wheat and those who reject Him as chaff, whom He will burn with unquenchable fire (Luke 3:17).

If Jesus required the anointing of the Holy Spirit to perform the works of God, would not every believer be in the same position of need? Did He not say if we love Him we will do the things that He did? Yet in most churches today very little, if any, emphasis is devoted to teaching and preaching the truth of God's word as relating to the person and works of the Holy Spirit. How can we please God by being told what to do, if we never receive instructions telling us how to receive the anointing that Jesus promised to all believers? If He did not perform any ministry of reconciliation until after He was baptized with the Holy Spirit, then how can we do so without the same empowerment?

After His resurrection, Jesus told His disciples and followers they would receive power when the Holy Spirit had come (Acts 1:8-11). Jesus fulfilled His promise to His followers.

When the Day of Pentecost had fully come, they were all with one accord in one place. And suddenly there came a sound from heaven, as of a rushing mighty wind, and it filled the whole house where they were sitting. Then there appeared to them divided tongues, as of fire, and one sat upon each of them. And they were all filled with the Holy Spirit and began to speak with other tongues, as the Spirit gave them utterance. (Acts 2:1-4)

Jesus sent the Holy Spirit to take His place upon planet Earth. He baptized His followers with the Holy Spirit to empower them to do the works that He had performed as the Son of Man. Immediately after being empowered by the Holy Spirit, they began preaching and teaching with signs and wonders following their ministry confirming the word of God.

Peter, one of the disciples of Jesus, explained to those present that what they had experienced was the fulfillment of the prophecy spoken by the prophet Joel. Joel foretold that which God said would come to pass in the last days. He said God would pour out of His Spirit on all flesh. Their sons and their daughters would prophesy, their young men would see visions, and the old men would dream dreams. God said He would pour out His Spirit on His menservants and on His maidservants in those days. He said they would prophesy and He would show them wonders in heaven above and signs in the earth, such as blood and fire and vapor of smoke. He predicted that the sun would be turned into darkness, and the moon into blood, before the coming of the great and awesome day of the Lord when Jesus will return to Earth. He said it would come to pass that whoever calls on the name of the Lord will be saved *(Acts 2:16-21, Joel 2:26-32).*

In the four Gospels and in the book of Acts we see the contrast in the lives of the apostles and followers of Jesus, before and after they were empowered with the baptism of the Holy Spirit. His disciples experienced difficulty in understanding many of His teachings and could not comprehend why He had to suffer the wrath of man and die on the cross. During Christ's crucifixion, Peter vehemently denied Him three times and afterward His disciples scattered. Some of them returned to their former occupations. After being empowered with the Holy Spirit, they immediately began to do the miraculous works that Jesus performed while He was on the earth. They taught the people and preached in Jesus the resurrection from the dead. Many of those who heard the word believed and thousands were saved upon hearing the gospel preached to them under the anointing of the Holy Spirit.

The persecution of Christians began by some of the same individuals who were involved in the crucifixion of the Son of Man, including Annas, the high priest, as well as Caiaphas, the high priest, together with many members of the families of the high priests. They were violently opposed to the preaching of the gospel by the apostles because it did not agree with their theology under the Old Covenant. The preaching of the gospel, accompanied by the miracle working power of the Holy Spirit, not only challenged their religious customs, but also their positions as the spiritual rulers over the people. They were concerned that the Gentiles were being blessed by the Lord in such miraculous ways. People were being healed and were delivered of tormenting unclean spirits and were being restored to a righteous relationship with God.

The high priest and those who were with him of the sect of the Sadducees were filled with indignation. They laid hold of the apostles and imprisoned them, but the Lord set them free (Acts 5:12-15). Due to their rigid religious traditions and doctrines, the Levitical leaders remained spiritually blinded to the truth and meaning of the death and resurrection of Jesus. They even forbade the followers of Christ to mention His name despite the miraculous works they saw being performed, which they were unable to duplicate.

Thus Satan, as the enemy of man and God, continued to exercise his influence and power over the religious men of that time in an effort to prevent God from spiritually establishing His kingdom of Light on the earth in opposition to the devil's kingdom of darkness.

The mistreatment and persecution of the apostles and Christian leaders increased to the point that some were martyred for speaking and ministering in the name of Jesus, but the believers remained unswerving in their commitment to God. The devil has remained unrelenting in his efforts to weaken, to pervert and to destroy the Gospel. Down through the years he has been successful in splintering the Body of Christ into many separate factions and denominations by introducing heresies, false doctrines, and by mixing various idolatrous practices with the gospel to form different patterns of religious worship. His efforts have been unrelenting to the point that thousands of spiritually blind individuals have suffered death following their religious cult leaders. Sovereign moves of God, from time to time, have resulted in the outpouring of the Holy Spirit, resulting in powerful revivals of the Church around the world. Some lasted only a short period of time while others lasted for generations. The Lord, rather than man, is able to manifest the power and authority of the Holy Spirit in the Body of Christ to perform and to validate the person and works of Jesus and to fulfill His word.

Chapter Twenty Six

Gifts of the Holy Spirit

The Holy Spirit baptism by Christ Jesus empowers the born-again believers to be His witnesses and to fulfill His plan and purpose in and through their lives. The baptism is received by the believer who seeks the Lord with all of His heart and surrenders his life to Him. Spiritual gifts are then manifested by the Holy Spirit in the life of a believer who yields to the Spirit. In Apostle Paul's first letter to the Corinthians, he addressed how the gifts of the Holy Spirit are to be exercised by believers in the corporate setting of the body of Christ, the Church.

Paul reminded the people that when they were Gentiles they were carried away by dumb idols, so he wanted to inform them about spiritual gifts. He said that no one could speak by the Holy Spirit and curse Jesus, nor could they confess Jesus is Lord except by revelation of the Holy Spirit. He explained there are diversities of gifts, but all of them are manifested by the same Spirit and there are different ministries, but all are of the same Lord. Even though there are diversities of activities, the same God works all in all.

He described each gift that the Holy Spirit can impart to the body of Christ.

For to one is given the word of wisdom through the Spirit, to another the word of knowledge through the same Spirit, to another faith by the same Spirit, to another gifts of healings by the same Spirit, to another the working of miracles, to another prophecy, to another discerning of spirits, to another different kinds of tongues, to another the interpretation of tongues. But one and the same Spirit works all these things, distributing to each one individually as He wills. For as the body is one and has many members, but all the members of that one body, being many, are one body, so also is Christ. (1 Corinthians 12:1-12)

The Gifts of the Holy Spirit fall into three natural divisions of three gifts each. In the Bible the number three is representative of the unity of the Trinity: the Father, the Son, and the Holy Spirit (I John 5:7, 8), who operate in unison. The first group includes the Gifts of Revelation by the Holy Spirit. These gifts are the word of wisdom, the word of knowledge, and the discerning of spirits. The next three gifts are the Gifts of Inspiration: prophecy, diverse kinds of tongues, and the interpretation of tongues. These are often referred to as vocal gifts, since they are orally expressed by the empowered believer. In the last group, the Gifts of Power or the working gifts are identified as the gift of faith, the gift of healing, and the working of miracles. All of the gifts of the Spirit operate in unison in the body of Christ upon His prompting and leading.

Whenever one gift is operating, often times other gifts may also be manifested to accomplish God's will and purpose in a given situation in our personal lives or in the lives of others or in the Church. The Holy Spirit will manifest the gifts required to meet the needs of an individual or others present or to edify the Church. Any or all nine gifts could be operating in one group of believers at any given time. The Holy Spirit works through the body of believers to produce the spiritual life and power of Christ Jesus as if He were present.

The gifts of the Holy Spirit usually function more frequently when a critical need exists. The operation of the gifts of the Spirit are necessary to enable the Lord to divinely minister to the needs of His people and to serve as witness to the world that Christ Jesus is alive and is the same yesterday, today, and forever (Heb 13:8). The manifestation of the gifts of the Spirit also confirm the word of God being taught or preached, bearing witness to His presence in the midst of His body as well.

The Holy Spirit exercises guidance in the ministries of the church. He is the One who calls, equips and anoints believers with the spiritual gifts that enable them to function in the positions in which they serve in the body of Christ (Acts 13:2-4; I Cor 12:4-11). Paul explained how the Holy Spirit would move upon different members of the Body of Christ in a public setting to manifest the same spiritual gifts that were active in the Son of Man's work and ministry. When the gifts of the Holy Spirit are operating pursuant to the Spirit's leading and anointing in the body of Christ, then the Spirit of Christ is manifested in the same manner as if He was present in the flesh.

Needless to say, many born-again believers, due to their lack of spiritual understanding and biblical teaching, as well as false and misleading teachings, are reluctant to seek the baptism with the Holy Spirit. Some Christians, after experiencing the baptism with the Spirit, exercise the vocal gifts of the Spirit under the influence or control of the flesh as opposed to being prompted and led by the Holy Spirit. Thus doubt, fear, and confusion can arise in the body of Christ as they focus attention upon themselves instead of the Lord. Questions arise in the minds of other believers, as well as in nonbelievers, concerning the authenticity of various gifts and their operation if the gifts of the Spirit are being imitated or misused.

One of the devil's favorite ploys involves the false teachings of the Word of God that are contrary to scriptural truth. Believers are either misguided or led to believe that the gifts were only given to empower the apostles to get the early church started, even though evidence to the contrary exists today in the body of Christ. Such deception has prevented believers from seeking and experiencing the anointing of the Holy Spirit. One of the devil's most effective strategies is to visit the spirit of condemnation upon born-again believers who have not received the baptism with the Holy Spirit or to make them feel that they are a second-class Christian. He visits many other deceptions upon us by convincing us that we are not worthy to receive the baptism or that we have committed sins that God will not forgive. The devil convinces others that they must earn or merit the special blessing of empowerment, which only the Lord Jesus can offer to members of His body, the Church, as a gift.

Thus, Satan has been successful in preventing most churches from experiencing the divine power needed to accomplish the mission and work of God. Few congregations are able to witness the word of God being confirmed with signs, wonders, and miracles following as was evident in the ministry of the Son of Man. Individual believers are being deprived of the anointing of the Holy Spirit that equips them to live an obedient life unto the Lord and to fulfill His call upon their lives. Far too many Christian ministers and pastors, out of fear that the gifts of the Holy Spirit will be falsely manifested or misused by individuals under the influence of the flesh, have quenched the Spirit to the point that the role of the Holy Spirit has become practically nonexistent in the

Body of Christ. As a result, the works of the flesh are manifested more than the work of the Holy Spirit.

When misused and abused in a public setting, gifts of the spirit elicit fleshly responses rather than achieving the intended spiritual results that glorify Christ Jesus and testify of Him. Rather than exalting the Lord and bringing his work to fruition, self is exalted. Consequently, Satan's tactics have succeeded in preventing the majority of born-again believers from seeking and receiving the baptism with the Holy Spirit by Christ Jesus to equip them for God's service and victorious living.

Teachers and ministers of God's Word, because of their lack of revelation, understanding or experience involving the Holy Spirit and His ministry-gifts, have become fearful of the spiritual gifts operating within their churches or in their presence. They are concerned that they may lose control over the congregation or disorder will prevail. Perhaps because of the lack of teaching or spiritual understanding, they are reluctant to respond to the leading of the Holy Spirit when His gifts are manifested in their assembly. A quenching of the Holy Spirit occurs. The power and effectiveness of the only One who is able to manifest the person and works of the Lord Jesus in His body is limited or non-existent. Some fail to realize that it is the work of the Holy Spirit to perform the spiritual transformation of sinful man and to correct the born-again believers who transgress God's word. As a result, various church leaders depend upon works of the flesh to attract and minister to those who assemble, even though no man can understand the things of God or perform the works of Christ Jesus without the Holy Spirit's involvement (I Cor 2:10).

Just as Satan attempted to thwart the appointed mission of the Son of Man, he remains unrelenting in his efforts to prevent us from receiving the fullness of revelation of the gospel and the anointing to equip us to understand and proclaim it. When the devil is unsuccessful in preventing us from being born again from above, he redoubles his efforts to prevent the believer in Christ Jesus from receiving the empowerment of the Holy Spirit. Thus the effectiveness of the believer is limited in performing the works of Christ. He also suffers a disadvantage in his efforts to live a righteous life before God and to conduct spiritual warfare against the master deceiver of this world. As apostle Paul said, *no one speaking by the Spirit of God calls Jesus accursed, and no one can say that Jesus is Lord except by the Holy Spirit* (1 Cor 12:3).

The gift of tongues is the most misunderstood and maligned gift of the nine gifts of the Holy Spirit. Some professing Christians have said the gift of tongues is of the devil. Some believe only special members of the body of Christ are blessed with the empowerment of the Spirit. Why does so much controversy arise over this particular gift that is given by the Spirit? As those who have received this spiritual gift know, it is different from anything a person has ever experienced as a human being. Normal speech originates in the mind of man and is released vocally under his control. The tongue has been described as a fire, a world of wickedness that is so situated as a bodily member that it contaminates the entire body and sets on fire the course of man's nature and it is set on fire by hell or the devil. No man can tame the tongue. *It is* an undisciplined evil, full of death-producing poison. What we fail to understand is that with it we bless the Lord God and we curse men, who have been made in the likeness of God (Jam 3:5-10).

The gift of tongues is supernatural speech, which originates in the spirit of man and not in his mind or heart. The Holy Spirit, who dwells in the born-again believer, speaks through the spirit of man in a supernatural language that bypasses his mind. In other words it is He, the Holy Spirit, who uses the yielded tongue of the believer to speak the message of God from spirit to Spirit. The one speaking the supernatural message does not understand the meaning of the words or of the message given unless the Spirit provides an interpretation of the message. Some Christians have said the devil cannot interpret what the Spirit has said in unknown tongues until an interpretation is given.

The tongue of man is the most vulnerable part of his body for Satan to influence and control. When speaking in the supernatural language of the Holy Spirit, Satan is robbed of his power and influence over the believer when the Spirit speaks through him. The Spirit will never speak evil or blasphemous words. The most troubling issue for Satan is that he cannot interfere with our prayer in the Spirit or prevent God from hearing it. A simple analogy is that of a person using a phone to talk directly to God. We who speak in a unknown tongue do not speak to men, but to God, for no one understands what is being said because in the spirit we speak mysteries that cannot be discerned by the natural mind.(1 Cor 14:2).

On occasions, when we pray in unknown tongues the Holy Spirit will intercede on our behalf and respond by manifesting the gift of wisdom or the gift of knowledge or one of the other gifts of the Spirit. Wherever we are, whether at work or in church or at home or elsewhere, the Holy Spirit is resident in us and is able to manifest the gift that is needed on any given occasion. If we are engaged in difficult undertakings, or in the ministry of the word of God, or in need of an answer from God, the Holy Spirit is the ultimate help in time of need, not for the purpose of glorifying us, but to enable us to glorify the Father and His Son.

Some believers convey the impression by their actions that they worship the gifts of the Spirit more than the "Giver". In the corporate setting of the Church, all things are to be done decently and in order. Only when the Holy Spirit prompts, leads, and directs is a believer to respond by orally delivering a message in tongues from God that must be followed by an interpretation in the native tongue of those present in the assembly. In the private and personal life of a believer who has been baptized with the Holy Spirit, he can speak in tongues or pray in tongues at will without an interpretation and still be edified. Often believers do not realize that the gift of tongues is associated with or involved in the operation of other gifts of the Spirit as well. The Holy Spirit will never act or speak in violation of the Word of God or His holy nature or against the will of the person through whom He manifests the gifts. The Spirit will always glorify God. Man, as a free moral agent, can quench the Spirit by refusing to respond to His leading or urging. Because of spiritual blindness man can condemn the works or the gifts of the Holy Spirit.

In his first letter to the Church in Corinth, Paul addressed the issue of the vocal gift of unknown tongues being misused by members of the body of Christ in public assembly. The apostle Paul said he prayed in tongues privately during the time of his ministry more than all believers. Paul exhorted all believers to pursue love and desire spiritual gifts. But he emphasized that we are to preach or teach in the native language of those who are present, so they will be edified. For we who prophesy or speak in the native tongue speak edification and exhortation and comfort to those present. We who speak in an unknown tongue in a public assembly edify only ourselves unless an interpretation is given. Paul wished all members of the body of Christ spoke with tongues privately, but that they spoke in the language of the people in a public gathering unless an interpretation of tongues was forthcoming, so that the Church could understand that which was being spoken (I Cor 14:1-18). If the one who brings the message in tongues to the Body of Christ is unable to interpret and no one is present who is able to do so, then he should remain silent.

Paul made it clear that he was writing to the Church in Corinth and not merely to an individual member of it. He reminded the believers that they were the body of Christ and members individually. And that God had appointed those in the church in a certain order: first came the apostles, second the prophets, third the teachers, after that the gifts of the Spirit including miracles, then gifts of healings, helps, administrations and a variety of tongues. Paul pointed out that all were not apostles or prophets or teachers. Neither did all work miracles, nor did all have gifts of healings or all speak with tongues, nor did all interpret. He encouraged each to earnestly desire the best gifts and to learn a more excellent way of functioning in the body of Christ (I Cor 12:27-31).

Paul emphasized that the Holy Spirit is He who calls and equips each one of us for service in the Church and each member is not necessarily blessed with all the gifts to function in a public assembly. He also pointed out that the Holy Spirit will manifest the gifts that are needed through the yielded person that He chooses. The Spirit does not limit the body of Christ to the gift of speaking in tongues. The gifts most beneficial in meeting the needs of those present at any given time will be manifested according to the will of the Spirit and not the will of man, if the anointing of the Holy Spirit is present in the Church. If we are a member of the Body of Christ, we may be like the toe, or finger, or heart or some other part of the physical body. But each one of us is to function in the Body according to the anointing of the Holy Spirit, when He moves upon us and prompts us to respond to Him. We are not to be responsive to the desires of the flesh to glorify self.

Paul explained to the Corinthian Church that God's order should be followed rather than each member attempting, on his own initiative, to publically demonstrate his ability to exercise the gift of tongues for self-edification or self-glorification. He again emphasized that the Holy Spirit is He who leads, directs, and anoints for ministry. Only the Spirit is to manifest the gifts in a corporate setting as He wills or chooses and not man according to the will of the flesh. Otherwise disorder and confusion result in the Church when the fleshly inspirations and undertakings of man prevail in the body of Christ.

Paul also explained to the believers in Ephesus how God functions through Christ Jesus by the Holy Spirit in gifting those He chooses and calls. He appoints some to the position of apostle, prophet, evangelist, pastor, and teacher for the purpose of equipping the saints for the work of the ministry of reconciliation. Also, their work is to edify the members of the Body of Christ, so that all believers will become unified in the faith and will attain unto the fullness of the knowledge of the Son of God.

The ultimate goal is to enable those chosen and called by God to become spiritually mature in the likeness of Christ. Then we will no longer be like children, being swayed with every wind of doctrine of man, or by their deceptive teachings or by the deceitful plotting of men. We are to speak the truth in love, maturing in all things to become like Christ Jesus. He is the head with whom we, the body of believers, are joined and knit together by the Holy Spirit to form one body connected and functioning in a manner similar to our physical body. If each one of us performs effective work as a member of His body, then that work will cause us as a body to grow to full maturity, built up in love.

Paul continued his exhortation to us as believers in Christ Jesus. He testified in the Lord that we should no longer walk or live as the unbelievers live. They are unable to understand and to receive the things of God. They remain separated from the life of God, because of their spiritual blindness and their hardness of heart. We are not to be like those who have surrendered themselves to unrestrained sensuality, eager to indulge in every type of impurity that they may desire.

As believers we have learned that Christ is not of that nature, if we have heard Him and have been taught by Him. We know the truth is in Jesus and that we are to put off the habits of our former nature that were corrupt according to the deceitful lusts of the flesh. We are to be renewed in the spirit of our minds and to put on the new man that was created according to God, in true righteousness and holiness (Eph 4:11-32).

We have been commanded to walk in the Spirit and not to fulfill the desires of the flesh. The lusts of the flesh are opposed to the Spirit and the Spirit is contrary to the flesh. *The fruit of the Spirit is love, joy, peace, longsuffering, kindness, goodness, faithfulness, gentleness, self-control. Against such there is no law. And those who are Christ's have crucified the flesh with its passions and desires. If we live in the Spirit, let us also walk in the Spirit (Gal 5:16-25).*

One may ask: how does a believer in Christ Jesus receive the baptism with the Holy Spirit after he has been born again from above by the Spirit of God? We are instructed to cleanse our hands as sinners and to purify our hearts and not to remain double-minded (Jam 4:8). If any believer harbors unforgiveness, bitterness, resentment, or is involved in ungodly deeds or practices, he can be prevented from receiving the baptism with the Holy Spirit. If the Holy Spirit quickens us to forgive or to seek forgiveness or to repent of any activity in our life that may block us from receiving, then we must respond first in obedience to Him.

Remember the Lord emphasized that the first of all the commandments exhorts us to love the Lord our God with all our heart, with all our soul, with all our mind, and with all our strength (Mark 12:29-31). We must have faith in order to please God and when we come to Him in prayer, we must believe that He will reward us if we diligently seek Him (Heb 11:6). As a believer in Christ, do not allow man or the devil to deceive you or condemn you to prevent you from earnestly seeking the empowerment of the Holy Spirit. The key is to keep seeking the LORD Jesus and to keep asking until you receive, remaining ever mindful of our need to respond to Him as He speaks to us. Our free will is involved. God will not force Himself or His gifts upon us, even as Christians. The gifts of the Spirit are available to all Christians who will abide in God's word and seek Him.

For Jesus promised that if we will ask, it will be given unto us. If we will seek, we will find. If we knock, it will be opened to us, for we who ask will receive and we who seek will find. He said, "If a son were to ask his father for bread, would he give him a stone? Or if he asked for a fish, would his father give him a serpent instead? Or if he asked for an egg, would he offer him a scorpion?" If we then, being evil, know how to give good gifts to our children, how much more will our heavenly Father give us the Holy Spirit when we ask Him! (Luke 11:9-13).

Jesus did not limit His promise to the early disciples or to certain members of the body of Christ, such as preachers, teachers, or evangelists. He placed the responsibility of seeking upon each born-again believer with the assurance that He would answer our prayers and fulfill His promise to baptize us with the Holy Spirit. As we are created individually unique, the baptismal experience often times is also unique for each believer. For some of us the baptism may be a dramatic event in our lives with one or more of the gifts of the spirit being immediately manifested in us or to us or through us. For others it may be a more subtle blessing. But each one who receives the baptism with the Holy Spirit will know that the LORD fulfilled His promise of empowerment and each can speak in the supernatural language of the Spirit.

Unfortunately, many today do not seek the Lord with their whole hearts, but are swayed by religious traditions or by every wind of doctrine that man or the devil propagates in the world. False teachings and false doctrines prevail in many religious settings, including many Christian denominations. Far too many individuals are unwilling to devote the time and effort to personally seek the truth in God's word under the guidance of the Holy Spirit.

Too often believers are willing to depend upon man rather than the Holy Spirit to teach them all things and to reveal to them an interpretation of Scripture. They tend to ignore the fact that Jesus said the Holy Spirit would be the One to teach and to guide us into the whole full truth, because He will not speak His own message—on His own authority. He will reveal the message to us that has been given to Him by the Father and the Son (John 16:13, 14). He will even declare to us the things that are to come or that will happen in the future, but He will never speak or act contrary to the Word of the Lord. Unless we become intimately acquainted with the Holy Spirit, how is it possible for us to be led by Him, particularly if we do not recognize His voice and are unaware of Who He is? We must remember that the Holy Spirit is He who imparts the abundant life that Jesus promised to us as His children (John 10:10).

Chapter Twenty Seven

The Spiritual Battle Continues to Intensify

Satan and his demon forces are spirit beings. They operate outside of the natural realm of human sensory perception and beyond natural law. Before the Son of Man was crucified, He prayed that we would be protected or delivered from the evil one (John 17:15).We are not to remain ignorant of Satan's devices, allowing him to take advantage of us (II Cor 2:11). We should not turn a blind eye to the reality that some deceived people are actively involved in the Church of Satan either openly or in an underground setting throughout the world. Not only do they knowingly worship Satan, but they look to him and respond to him in their worship and service as Christians do to the only true and living God. They have a counterfeit type of priesthood, subscribe to covenant oaths, and some even offer blood sacrifices to their god, Satan. They also have a form of liturgy and well as music that glorify Satan. They submit unto him to do his bidding through the spiritual power of evil and strongly oppose Christianity.

According to Scripture, the works of Satan will intensify as the return of the Son of Man approaches and the devil will enjoy a three and one-half year reign upon the earth through the antichrist when he appears upon the earth near the end of the age (Rev 13). More than ever, we as Christians must be strong in the Lord and in the power of His might. We are to put on the entire armor of God so that we may be able to stand against the deceptions and schemes of the devil. Our battle is not against each other as physical opponents, but against Satan and his spiritual host of wickedness, who rule over the kingdom of darkness in the supernatural realm in this age.

So we are commanded to put on the whole armor of God to enable us to withstand the devil and his wicked hosts when they come against us. After being fully clothed in the armor of God, we are to stand in resistance against the devil. We are to gird our waist with the belt of truth and to put on the breastplate of righteousness. We are to have our feet fitted with the preparation of the gospel of peace. Above all we are to take up the shield of faith, with which we can quench or extinguish all the fiery darts of the devil and we are to put on the helmet of salvation, and to be equipped with the sword of the Spirit, which is the word of God. We are to pray always, with all prayer and supplication in the Spirit and to remain alert as we continue praying with all perseverance and supplication for all the sanctified believers in Christ Jesus (Eph 6:10-18).

The whole armor of God speaks of the necessity for each believer to put on or be clothed in the fullness of the Lord Jesus Christ. For He is the Truth, and the Way and the Life; He is our Righteousness; He is the good news of Peace; He is the Shield of our faith to enable us to defend ourselves against the enemy of our souls; He is our Salvation; He is the living Word which is the sword of the Spirit, and He is the One who empowers us to pray in the Spirit. We as believers in Christ should seek the empowerment that only He can bestow upon us through the baptism with the Holy Spirit to become fully equipped to stand against the devious schemes of the devil and his demonic forces.

Because our bodies are members of Christ (1 Cor 6:15) and He is the head of every believer and the head of Christ is God (1 Cor 11:3), we will face the wicked opposition of the enemy of God. So we must be spiritually prepared through the revelation knowledge of the Word of God and the empowerment of the Holy Spirit to wage spiritual warfare against the devil, who violently opposes the Kingdom of God. Since we have become partakers of Christ's divine nature, we are to hold our original confidence in Him steadfast to the end. Even though we function in the natural realm of the flesh, we do not conduct warfare according to the world by using material weapons, as Satan induces men to do. For the weapons of our warfare *are not* of this natural world, but mighty in God for tearing down and destroying the enemy's spiritual strongholds, casting down arguments and every lofty thing that is contrary to the word of God, bringing every thought into captivity to the obedience of Christ (2 Cor 10:3-5).

The devil wages warfare in our minds, whereas the Lord moves upon us through our spirits, Spirit to spirit. Satan seeks to enslave and to exercise control over us through the sinful desires of the flesh and persistently tempts us to degrade our bodies and ourselves in disobedience to God's law and commandments. He attempts to seduce us to follow him in his occult pathway, to morally corrupt us and to ultimately destroy us. His methods of enticing us to enjoy forbidden earthly pleasure or to engage in religious worship of idols or to enter into bondage through the practice of false or satanic worship remains effective in the world today. Scripture emphasizes that we have the free will to make moral choices that have a good or evil affect upon our lives in this world. Our choices will determine our eternal future and our moral choices will come under attack by evil supernatural powers of Satan.

Are we to think that because a person is religious, he cannot be deceived? Jesus revealed that one of the most pervasive forms of deception is found in religious practice. During His ministry He was speaking about Himself to the religious Jews and to their leaders who claimed to know God the Father, but they could not discern who Jesus was. He told them that they were of their father, the devil and their desire was to do his bidding, which was to kill Him. Jesus described their father the devil as a liar and the originator of lies because he does not abide in the truth (John 8:44).

After Jesus ascended into heaven, the Apostle Paul warned believers that false apostles and deceitful workers will appear who are able to transform themselves into apostles of Christ. He further commented that it was no wonder that they were able to do so, for Satan transforms himself into an angel of light. His ministers are also able to transform themselves into coun-terfeit ministers of righteousness (2 Cor 11:13-15).

Paul warned us that some religious followers of Christ would seek those who would teach that which pleased them as opposed to the revealed biblical truth of God. He told the evangelist, Timothy, that the time would come when believers would not abide in sound doctrine. He said they would seek teachers to teach and to preach that which satisfied their own desires, because they would have itching ears to hear other than revealed biblical truth. They would choose for themselves unscriptural teachers and would turn away from the truth (2 Tim 4:2-4).

The apostle Peter likewise issued a warning that there were false prophets among the people in his time. He said that false teachers would be among us also and would secretly introduce destructive heresies. He said they will even deny the Lord who purchased them with His own shed blood and they would bring swift destruction upon themselves (2 Peter 2:1-3). Jesus also warned that false christs and false prophets would rise and display great signs and wonders in order to deceive some of those who follow Him (Matt 24:24, 25).

Satan devises many subtle schemes and methods to deceive even the elect of God, if that be possible. As the prince of the power of the air, Satan is the father of the occult realm and rules over it. The occult involves hidden or concealed evil spiritual activity in the supernatural realm, which cannot be readily discerned by the human mind. Certain mystic arts are manifested by demonic spirits through mediums to deceive and to ensnare unsuspecting individuals. The mystic or magic arts employed by the devil include white magic, black magic, astrology, witchcraft, palm readers, fortune tellers, tarot card readers, and many, many others.

Examples of Satan's power and authority were manifested in the time of Pharaoh in Egypt. In response to the Lord's command, Aaron threw down his rod before Pharaoh and his servants and it became a serpent. The wise men and the sorcerers, the magicians of Egypt, at the command of Pharaoh did likewise with their enchantments and their rods became serpents. On the second occasion Aaron lifted up the rod and struck the waters in the river and all the waters of the river were turned to blood. Then Pharaoh's magicians did the same with their enchantments. On the third occasion Aaron held the rod over the streams, over the rivers and over the ponds and frogs came up and covered the land of Egypt. The magicians did the same thing with their enchantments (Ex 7:10-22, Ex 8:5-7).

Most people do not realize that Satan has power and authority over his kingdom of darkness. When individuals knowingly or unknowingly dabble in occult activity, they discover that the supernatural or spirit realm is real. As people discover that actual events occur in the spirit realm, as in the case of the magicians who controlled the Pharaoh of Egypt, they become even more anxious to exercise more power and authority in their occult roles. Satan takes advantage of their weakness due to their worldly nature of greed, envy, vanity, lust and pride and makes them a captive to do his will.

In the ages past, God sternly warned His people that when they arrived in the land He had promised to Abraham and his descendants, they were forbidden to learn to follow the abominations of those who resided there. God forbade any of them to follow their heathen practice of making their sons or daughters to pass through the fire. The Israelites were commanded not to practice witchcraft, or to seek the advice of a soothsayer, or of one who interprets omens, or a sorcerer, or one who summons a demon or spirit by a magic spell, or a medium, or a spiritist, or one who calls up the dead. The LORD emphasized that all who do these things are an abomination to Him and because of these abominations, He would drive out from before them the people who engaged in such occult practices. God commanded His people to be blameless before Him. God's people were warned to listen to Him and not to be drawn away by Satan's impersonators, the soothsayers and diviners (Deut 18:9-14, Gal 5:20). God has not changed and His warnings apply to all of us. He, who is the LORD our GOD, commands us not to turn to mediums or to seek out spiritists, for we will be defiled by them (Lev 19:31). A spiritist is one who engages in the magic of calling spirits or holding séances, during which they try to communicate with the dead.

Many people unknowingly become involved in occult practices because they think it involves the true God of the universe. Today occult activity appeals to a multitude of people because Satan and his demonic forces exist in the unseen spirit realm and endeavor to mimic the Holy Spirit by displaying their power and authority. Those who are unfamiliar with the reality of the occult fall prey to Satan's demonic spirits who attempt to counterfeit or mimic God's kingdom of light. Many people try to contact deceased relatives to receive advice or comfort through mediums, who are empowered by demons.

The lack of biblical knowledge and understanding of the supernatural, or spirit realm, exposes us to the deceptions of Satan. Those who consult diviners, fortune tellers and other mediums of the devil instead of looking to God for their answer become enslaved to the power of evil and become an enemy of the Lord. Consulting with psychics, fortune tellers or sorcerers provides demonic spirits the opportunity to enter a person spiritually.

Satan then succeeds in accomplishing his goal of separating believers from their relationship with the only true and living God. To be delivered from occult bondages, the individual must renounce his allegiance to and involvement in each type of magic art or occult practice in which he is involved. He must confess his repentance before God and request Him to forgive his sins. Then he must accept and receive Christ Jesus as his Lord and Savior. For the work of casting off the occult stronghold over one's life can only be performed by the Holy Spirit. Not only will the Lord set you free, but He will also baptize you with His Holy Spirit to empower you to resist the devil and remain free from further attacks.

One of the most dynamic events of my Christian experience occurred during a teaching session relating to the operation of the gifts of the Holy

Spirit in the body of Christ. The Holy Spirit told me He was giving us a message. As our heads were bowed and our eyes were closed; the Lord gave a message in tongues to a member of the class and the interpretation of the message in tongues was given to another member by Him. As the second person was voicing the interpretation of the message from the Lord, a noticeable thud sounded and the cement floor vibrated. Over 60 members of the class gasped as we looked up to see a young lady in her late twenties spread-eagled face down in the middle of the aisle. She was facing the opposite direction from her seat on the aisle, which was about six rows back in the room. Dana remained motionless on the floor, with her arms fully outstretched forward and her legs fully outstretched together.

Based upon previous experience, I knew that Dana was under the power of the Holy Spirit. The two members were asked to share their experience with the class as to how the Holy Spirit had moved upon them and had spoken through them. As the second person was finishing, Dana began to slowly arise from the floor with a noticeable glow on her face. She did not suffer any injury despite the forceful power of the Holy Spirit lifting her and slamming her to the thinly carpeted cement floor. She was requested to share with the class what she had experienced. She explained that she and all members of her family were involved in the practice of witchcraft, with her mother having been a witch during Dana's entire lifetime. As the Holy Spirit was moving upon the other two members of the class, the Lord told her three times to "let go" of her involvement in witchcraft. But each time she drew back, refusing to do so since she knew that the power that she and members of her family experienced was real and she did not want to give it up.

Dana said after she refused for the third time, the Holy Spirit demonstrated God's greater power by lifting her up and slamming her face first onto the floor without causing any bruise or injury. Upon experiencing God's awesome power, while on the floor she repented and surrendered her life to the Lord Jesus, who not only saved her, but immediately baptized her with the Holy Spirit. A few months later she shared with the class how through her testimony eight members of her family had been saved by the Lord and delivered from witchcraft. A few weeks afterward Dana accompanied her mother to the altar of the church. Her mother expressed her desire to accept the Lord Jesus as her Savior. After I led her in prayer to renounce and to repent of her commitment to and involvement in witchcraft, she prayed to accept and receive the Lord Jesus, whereupon He not only saved her, but also baptized her with the Holy Spirit.

The Lord was demonstrating that even though He hates sin, He loves each one of us with a great and intense love (Eph 2:4). His desire is for each of us to turn from our wicked ways and return to Him. He again bore witness to His word that if *we confess our sins, He is faithful and just to forgive us our sins and to cleanse us from all unrighteousness (1 John 1:9).*

If our faith in God and His promises are based upon emotional feelings, false doctrines or traditions rather than faith derived through the word of God, we are subject to becoming as the ancient Israelites, who turned from God to obey the devil. We must remain open to the Lord and the Holy Spirit and shun the works of the evil one. We are exhorted not to believe every spirit, but we are to test the spirits to discern whether they are of God, because many false prophets are present in the world (1 John 4:1).

We are clearly warned in God's word to not allow our hearts to become evil and to depart from the living God. Instead we are to exhort each other daily to prevent our hearts from becoming hardened through the deceitfulness of sin. We become partakers of Christ if we hold the beginning of our confidence steadfast to the end. Every day we are to listen to His voice, and not to allow our hearts to become hardened as the Israelites did in their rebellion against God in the wilderness. Even though they heard the commands of the Lord and entered into covenant relationship with Him, they rebelled, thus arousing the anger of God. As a result, they spent 40 years in the wilderness and those who sinned died there. Those who did not obey God did not enter His rest because of unbelief in His word (Heb 3:12-19).

Idol and demon worship is the worship of a manmade god. We are commanded not to make an idol for ourselves in any form that is in heaven or that is in the earth or that is in the water. We must not bow to them or serve them (Exo 20:4, 5). You may ask: how can I know if I am involved in idol worship or serve an idol? If we consider the command of the Lord Jesus that we are to love the Lord our God with all our heart, all our soul, all our mind and all our strength, then anything in our lives to which we devote excessive devotion would constitute an idol. This would include anyone or anything that takes priority over the Lord God and His kingdom of righteousness. For example it could be our career, the love of money, the love of fame, the love of sports, the love of mind altering substances, the love of Satan or one of his idols, or any person, place or thing that we exalt above the Lord in our daily lives. The devil also sends temptations through various forms of the media, as well as through electronic devices that can become idols in our lives or that will influence us to violate God's commands.

We are to trust in the Lord with all our heart and not to rely upon our own understanding. In all our ways we are to acknowledge Him and the Lord will direct our paths. We are warned not to be wise in our own eyes, but to fear the Lord and turn from evil (Prov 3:5-7).

Chapter Twenty Eight

The Return of the SON of MAN

In the time of the prophet David, God, foreseeing the future, said, "Why do the nations rage and the people devise an empty scheme against Me? The rulers of the world assume their stand and conspire together against Me and against my Anointed. The rulers will say, 'Let us remove His restraints and shatter His control over us.'" God, who is enthroned in heaven, shall laugh and in contempt mock them. Then He will respond to them in His wrath and He will vent His anger upon them. He will tell them that He has set His King on His holy hill of Zion. God will declare His Son, whom He will beget in the flesh, to be the King of kings and Lord of lords. The Son will ask of the Father and He will give to His Son the nations of the world for His inheritance and the entire earth for His possession. He will rule over them with an iron scepter and will smash them to pieces like a clay pot. God issued a warning to the rulers of the world to be wise and to be instructed in His ways and to serve Him with fear and to rejoice with trembling before Him. He instructed the nations to pay homage to His Son and to honor Him, lest He become angry and they perish in their way because of His wrath. He said that all those who put their trust in Him will be blessed (Ps 2:1-12).

Christ was sent into the world as the Son of Man by God the Father, not to destroy man, but to seek and save the lost (Luke19:10). He endured the wrath of man as the Son of Man (Mark 9:9-12, Matt17:12). He was condemned to death as the Son of Man (Matt 20:18). He was crucified as the Son of Man (Matt 17:21, 22). He died as the Son of Man (Mt 20:18). He was sentenced to the second death in hell as the Son of Man (Matt 12:40). He endured the punishing wrath of God as the Son of Man. He defeated Satan and destroyed his works as the Son of Man (Rev 1:17, 18); He was raised from the dead as the Son of Man (Mark 10:34, Matt 17:9); He ascended into heaven as the Son of Man (John 3:13); He deposited His blood on the mercy seat of the Ark of the Covenant as the Son of Man and He sat down at the right hand of the Father as the Son of Man (Luke 22:69, 70; Matt 19:28, 26:64). He will return to Earth to rule and to reign as the Son of Man (Matt 24:27-31) and He will execute judgment as the Son of Man (John 5: 26, 27).

During His first advent, the Son of Man was faithful in fulfilling the prophecies of the Bible as pertaining to Himself. He encouraged us to be at peace and to believe in God and also in Him. He affirmed that in His Father's house are many mansions. He said He was going to prepare us a place and would return again to receive us unto Himself so that we could be with Him (John 14:1-3). Christ was offered once to bear our sins, but upon His second appearance, He will impart the fullness of salvation to all of us who are eagerly looking forward to His return and are waiting for Him (Heb 9:28 NKJV, AMP). The Son of Man provided every man, woman and child an opportunity to become a member of His body and to enter into the kingdom of God. During His second advent, He must put down all rebellion in the natural and supernatural realms and cleanse the earth of all sin and evil together with the corruptive and destructive effects that sin had upon the earth. Almost 2,000 years ago He promised to return to finish His work as the Son of Man. He provided identifiable clues to help us recognize the approximate time of His final appearance.

Signs of the Son of Man's Return to Earth

The Second Coming of the Son of Man is foretold in the four Gospels, in the book of Acts and in the epistles of John, Paul, James and Peter. His return is the central point of the book of Revelation. For those of us who have seen the fulfillment of scripture and have partaken of His divine nature, we believe that Christ will return according to the promises of God. He will return to the Mount of Olives in the city of Jerusalem to fulfill that which God commanded the first Adam and his wife Eve to do—that being to subdue Satan and his evil forces and to establish the eternal kingdom of God upon planet Earth.

While Jesus was sitting on the Mount of Olives, His disciples privately asked Him what would be the sign of His coming at the end of the age. Jesus said that the first sign will be the arising of those who will impersonate Christ. He urged us to be careful to prevent anyone from deceiving us, for many will come representing Him and in His name, identifying themselves as the Christ and many people will be deceived by individuals who claim to represent Him. He said the second sign will be wars and rumors of wars, all of which prevail in the world today. He cautioned us to not be troubled by the events that occur in the world because all biblical prophesies must be fulfilled before the end of the age. He said unrest would arise, pitting nation against nation and kingdoms against each other (Matt 26:3-7). Presently in the world we witness ever increasing wickedness and evil being visited upon mankind with millions of people being slain in civil wars, religious wars, and under the leadership of godless dictators as well as the suppression of human rights and enslavement, contrary to the commandments of God.

In other nations, including the United States of America, we are witnessing an unparalleled rebellion against God and His moral laws. We also see an upsurge in criminal activity, lawlessness, civil disobedience, and anti-God and immoral activities that would cause Sodom and Gomorrah to blush. When we consider the sacrifice of multimillions of aborted babies created in the image of God as a convenience and relief from irresponsible as well as immoral behavior, how long do we think God will condone such unconscionable disregard for human life? Yet the majority of people seem indifferent to the sinful slaughter of humanity that is taking place, while every effort is being made to prevent even the name of Jesus or God or His commandants from being publically mentioned or displayed.

The Apostle Paul forewarned us that

in the last days perilous times will come: for men will be lovers of themselves, lovers of money, boasters, proud, blasphemers, disobedient to parents, unthankful, unholy, unloving, unforgiving, slanderers, without self-control, brutal, despisers of good, traitors, headstrong, haughty, lovers of pleasure rather than lovers of God, having a form of godliness but denying its power. (2 Timothy 3:1-5)

Jesus told us that in the latter days there will be devastating famines, pestilences or plagues, and earthquakes in various parts of the world. We are witnessing the beginning of sorrows as Jesus described, for drastic changes are occurring in weather patterns with droughts, raging forest fires, floods, tornadoes, severe storms, and hurricanes wreaking havoc more frequently than ever. In a similar manner, destructive earthquakes are increasing and famine is prevalent in most third world countries as well as in many other places. As God punishes sinful nations for their disobedience, we can expect most severe famines, pestilences and earthquakes to take place, especially in the United States of America, which teeters on the brink of moral and financial bankruptcy, as leaders try to replace the role of God with government regulations and institutions.

Jesus foretold that Godly Christian believers would be delivered up to tribulation and death and would be hated by all nations for His name's sake. We see clear evidence of increasing animosity towards Christianity around the world. Yet religions, organizations and individuals are being embraced and extolled that do not honor or glorify God. He said many believers will become offended because of persecution and tribulation and will turn away from God, betraying one another and hating one another. True believers will be persecuted near the end of the age much like the early Christians, many of whom were martyred. Jesus said if the world hated Him, it would hate us because we are not of the world (John 15:18, 19). Such an environment is developing that will enable false prophets to rise up and to deceive many. The love of many will become cold because of increased lawlessness and iniquity. But each one who endures to the end shall enter into an eternal righteous relationship with God (Matt 24:3-13).

Jesus said that the Gospel of the kingdom of God would be preached throughout the world as a testimony of God's love and grace and then the end will come. At no other time in history has the Gospel been broadcast by so many forms of media. The Gospel is declared to the whole world by way of radio, television, the internet, telephone, and by other personal and written means. This prerequisite for the return of the Lord is on the very threshold of being fulfilled.

As the end of the age is about to close, Jesus said we would see the abomination that causes desolation, who is the Antichrist spoken of by Daniel the prophet, standing in the holy place in the Jewish Temple in Jerusalem (Matt 24:14, 15). The Lord told the prophet Daniel that in the latter days when the transgressors have reached their fullness, a king of fierce countenance shall arise. He will employ sinister schemes of craftiness and will be mightily empowered, but not of himself. His destructive acts will be fearful and he shall be successful in corrupting and destroying mighty men and the holy people of God. Through his deception he shall prosper and exalt himself in his heart. He shall corrupt and destroy many who feel secure. He shall even oppose the Prince of princes. He shall not be defeated by man, but by the Son of Man, who will consume him with the breath of His mouth and will destroy him with the brightness of His coming (Dan 8:23-25, Rev 13:4-10, 2 Thes 2:8).

We are told in Revelation that the Antichrist will speak great things and blasphemies. He will exercise his authority upon the earth for 42 months. He will blaspheme God, His name, His tabernacle, and those who dwell in heaven. He will be given power to make war with the saints and to overpower them. He will rule over every tribe, tongue, and nation. Everyone upon the earth will be compelled to worship him, except for those whose names have been written in the Book of Life of the Lamb, slain from the foundation of the world (Rev 13:5-8).

Apostle Paul cautioned us to not allow anyone to deceive us by any means. For the day of great tribulation will not come before the falling away of believers and the man of sin or the Antichrist is revealed, who is the son of perdition. He will oppose and exalt himself above all that is of God or that men worship. He will sit as God in the temple of God, proclaiming himself to be God (2 Thes 2:3, 4).

The Islamist movements have recently gained momentum, with the ultimate goal of establishing the Caliphate by uniting Muslim nations. Could it be that the antichrist will be the Islamic Mahdi, the promised messiah? Will he be the one who unites the Muslim people when he appears to rule and reign under the authority of the god of this world in his efforts to impersonate Christ Jesus, the true Messiah? It is of interest to note that the Mahdi will come through the lineage of Ishmael, whereas Christ Jesus came through the lineage of Isaac, both of whom are from the lineage of Abraham.

The coming of the lawless one or the Antichrist will be the work of Satan. He will be empowered by Satan to perform signs and lying wonders with all unrighteous deception among the unbelievers, who will perish. They will perish because they will not receive the loving truth of God's word that would impart salvation to them. *And for this reason God will send them strong delusion, that they should believe the lies of the Antichrist, that they all may be condemned who did not believe the truth but had pleasure in unrighteousness (2 Thes 2:9-12).*

The Antichrist will display awesome supernatural power to deceive all people, if that be possible. He will have the ability to perform great miracles, impersonating the Son of man. Then great tribulation, worse than any known to man or ever shall be again, will follow. And unless the days of tribulation are limited, no human being will be saved from the destructive power of the Antichrist, but for the sake of the children of God those days will be shortened (Matt 24:16-22, Rev 14:9-11, 20:4-6).

Jesus told His disciples and us as well not to believe anyone who says, "Here *is* the Christ" or "There He is," for false christs and false prophets will appear near the end time and will counterfeit great signs and wonders to deceive, if possible, even the elect of God. He stressed that all would recognize and know of His coming for as the lightning comes from the east and flashes to the west, His coming as the Son of Man will be in like manner. He described additional signs which would appear immediately after the tribulation of those days. The sun will be darkened, which will cause the moon not to shine; *stars will fall from heaven, and the powers of the heavens will be shaken* (Matt 24:23-29, Luke 21:25, 26).

After the tribulation, during which the wrath of Satan is visited upon mankind and after the heavenly signs appear in the heavens, the Day of the Lord will follow. The wrath of God will be poured out upon the earth as never before experienced by mankind (Rev 8-16). Satan's counterfeit religious system and kingdom of darkness upon the earth will be destroyed by the Son of Man upon His return.

When the Son of Man appears in the heavens, then all the tribes of the earth will mourn. They will see Him coming on the clouds of heaven, displaying His power and His brilliant splendor. He will send out His angels with a loud trumpet call and they will gather together His children from throughout the world and the heavens. Christ gave a parable of the fig tree to describe the sign of His coming. When its branch becomes tender and it puts forth its leaves, then one knows that the season of summer is near. So we also, when we see all these signs He mentioned, should know that His return is near or imminent (Matt 24:30-33).

Jesus declared that heaven and earth will pass away, but His words will never pass away. But with regards to the day and hour of His return, no one knows but His Father. But just as in the days of Noah, so shall be the return of the Son of Man to the earth. People will be as they were in the days before the flood, they ate and drank, they married and were given in marriage, until the very day that Noah entered into the ark. They did not comprehend the foreboding disaster until the flood arose and destroyed them.

So it will be with the coming of the Son of Man. On that day two *men* will be working in the field: one will be taken up and the other will be left behind. Two *women will be* grinding at the mill; one will be taken up and the other will remain. We are therefore warned to watch because we will not know what hour our Lord is coming. But we are to remain alert and to be ready for the Son of Man will come at an hour we do not expect (Matt 24:35-44). We are commanded to remain watchful and to pray always that we may be counted worthy to escape all the horrendous things that will come to pass and to be able to stand before *the Son of Man* (Luke 21:36).

John described the coming of the Son of Man. He saw heaven opened and sitting on a white horse was He who is called Faithful and True, who will judge and make war in righteousness. His eyes were like a flame of fire and He wore many crowns on His head. His name was written, but no one knew the meaning except Himself. He wore a robe that had been dipped in blood and He is called by the name, *The Word of God*. The armies in heaven were clothed in fine linen, white and clean. They followed Him on white horses. Now out of His mouth goes a sharp sword, which is the word of God and with it He will strike the nations. With an iron scepter He will rule all nations and He will tread the winepress of the fierceness and wrath of Almighty God. The name written on His robe and on His thigh is: *KING OF KINGS AND LORD OF LORDS* (Rev 19:11-16).

The return of Jesus will be as the mighty warrior, the Lion of the tribe of Judah and not as the Lamb of God, as when He came to earth the first time (Rev 5:5). He will come to punish the rebellious and disobedient and to subdue Satan and his wicked spirits. He will capture the beast and the false prophet of the devil and will throw the two of them into the lake of fire. The others will be killed by the sword of the Spirit that comes out of the mouth of the Son of Man (Rev 19:20, 21).

His angel will seize the dragon who is the ancient serpent, the devil or Satan. Satan will be bound for a thousand years and locked and sealed in the Abyss (Rev 20:1-3). At the end of a thousand years he will be released for a short time. Upon his release, Satan will continue his efforts to deceive the nations on the earth and will gather them for battle against the Lord. They will be innumerable as the sand on the seashore. They will assemble together and surround the camp of God's people, in the city of Jerusalem. But fire will come down from heaven and devour them as it did Sodom and Gomorrah. Satan, who deceived them, will be thrown into the lake of burning sulfur to be with the beast and the false prophet and they will be forever tormented (Rev 20:7-10).

God's original plan and purpose for creating man will be fulfilled when the Son of Man has purged the Earth and the heavens of all sin and unrighteousness by His holy fire (2 Pet 3:10-13). For John, to whom the revelation was given, said he saw a new heaven and a new earth, because the original heaven and earth had passed away. The sea had also disappeared. Then He saw the holy city, the New Jerusalem descending from God out of heaven. It appeared as a bride adorned for her husband. He heard a voice loudly proclaiming from heaven, *Behold, the tabernacle of God is with men, and He will dwell with them, and they shall be His people. God Himself will be with them and be their God. And God will wipe away every tear from their eyes; there shall be no more death, nor sorrow, nor crying. There shall be no more pain, for the former things have passed away.*

Then He who sat on the throne in heaven said, *Behold, I make all things new.* And He told John to write His words because they were true and faithful. Then He pronounced that it was finished. He declared that He is the Alpha and the Omega, which means the Beginning and the End. He said He would give the fountain of the water of life freely to the person who thirsts. He promised that he who overcomes in this life shall inherit all things promised to him, and He will be his God and the over-comer shall be His son. But He warned that the cowardly, unbelieving, abominable, murderers, sexually immoral, sorcerers, idolaters, and all liars shall have their part in the lake that burns with fire and brimstone, which is the second death (Rev 21:1-8).

He described to John the astounding New Jerusalem, which will come down from heaven. It will not have a temple, because the Lord God Almighty and the Lamb, the Son of Man, will be its temple. The glory of God will give it light and the Lamb will be its lamp. Nothing that is sinful or of a sinful nature will ever enter it, but only the people whose names are written in the Lamb's book of life. The Father and the Son of Man will dwell eternally on earth in the New Jerusalem with His saints (Rev 21:22-27).

Three times in the last chapter of Revelation Jesus said He was coming quickly or suddenly. He promised that each one who keeps the words of this prophecy will be blessed. He said His reward *is* with Him to give to everyone according to his work. He repeated that He *is the Alpha and the Omega, the Beginning and the End, the First and the Last.* He will bless those who do His commandments and will give them the right to the Tree of Life that they may enter through the gates into the city, the New Jerusalem. But dogs and sorcerers and sexually immoral and murderers and idolaters, and whoever loves and practices a lie will not be permitted to enter. Jesus, the Bright and Morning Star, and the Spirit say *Come! And let him who hears say, Come! And let him who thirsts come. Whoever desires, let him take the water of life freely* (Rev 22:7-20).

Chapter Twenty Nine

The Son of Man
Will Judge the World and All Mankind

God judged each one of us in the Son of Man when He united us with Him on the cross. The Son of Man will be He who judges each one of us, for we will all stand before Him on Judgment day. Since all believers are members of His body, He will know who belongs to Him and who does not. If we have been spiritually united with Him, we have already been judged by God, sentenced by God to the second death, and punished by God and raised in newness of life in Him.

God has appointed a day on which He will judge the world in righteousness by the Son of Man whom He has ordained. He has given us assurance of this by raising Him from the dead (Acts 17:31). We shall all stand before the judgment seat of Christ. For it is written: *As I live, says the Lord, every knee shall bow to Me, and every tongue shall confess to God. So then each of us shall give account of himself to God (Rom 14:10-12).* All of us must appear before the judgment seat of Christ so that each one of us may receive that which is due us for the things that we have done while living in the flesh, according to whether it is good or bad (2 Cor 5:10).

Christ Jesus said that the Father does not judge any of us, but He has committed the judgment of us all to the Son, that we should honor the Son just as we honor the Father. We who do not honor the Son do not honor God the Father who sent Him. Jesus gave us His assurance that we who hear His word and believe in the Father who sent Him have eternal life. We shall not come into judgment because we were judged in Him and have passed from death into life upon being spiritually baptized into His body. With total assurance Jesus said that the hour was coming, and now is, when we who receive His message and believe in and cling to and rely on the Father who sent Him will hear the voice of the Son of God and those who hear Him will be raised from spiritual death and will possess eternal life.

Because Jesus is the Son of Man, the Father has given Him authority to execute judgment also. We are not to marvel at this, for the time will arrive when all who have died will hear His voice and will be brought to life. Those who have done good will experience the resurrection of life and those who have done evil will experience the resurrection of condemnation (John 5:22-30).

Jesus said a good man brings forth good things out of his heart, but an evil man brings forth evil things out of his heart. He warned us that we will give an account for every idle word that we may speak in the day of judgment and our words will either justify us or condemn us (Matt 12:35-37). *He* said if we hear His words and refuse to believe what He says, we will not be judged by Him because He did not come to judge the world, but to save it. We who reject Him do not receive His word, yet the very words of Jesus will judge us in the last day (John 12:47, 48).

Jesus issued this stern warning to all mankind. He said that not everyone who calls Him *Lord, Lord* will enter the kingdom of heaven or the kingdom of

God. But the person who complies with the will of His Father will enter His kingdom of heaven. Many will say to Him on judgment day, "Lord, Lord, did we not prophesy in Your name; did we not cast out demons in Your name, and perform wonders in Your name?" Yet He will declare unto them, *"I never knew you; depart from Me, you who practice lawlessness!"* Whoever hears His sayings or teachings and does them, He will liken him to a wise man who constructed his house on the rock: and the rain came down, the floods arose, the winds howled and buffeted that house, but it remained standing because it was founded on the rock. Everyone who hears His sayings or teachings and refuses to obey them will be like the foolish man who built his house upon the sand. When the rain descended, the floods arose and the winds blew against that house it fell. And devastating was its collapse (Matt 7:21-27).

When the Son of man comes in His glory accompanied by all of His holy angels, He will then sit upon the throne in His glory. All of the nations shall be gathered before Him. He will separate each nation, one from another just as a shepherd divides his sheep from the goats. He will place His sheep on His right hand, but the goats will be on His left. He will say to His sheep, the faithful believers who have been born again from above, these heartwarming words, *"Come, you blessed of My Father, inherit the kingdom prepared for you from the foundation of the world."* He will say to the goats, those who have denied Him and refused to obey Him these heartbreaking words, *"Depart from Me, you cursed, into the everlasting fire prepared for the devil and his angels"* (Matt. 25:31-46).

For the most part we are prone to seek the things of this world and to ignore the command of Christ Jesus to seek first the kingdom of God and His righteousness. Yet the mercy and grace of God together with His blessings are offered to all of us through Christ Jesus by the Holy Spirit. But they can become ours only when we accept and appropriate them. Our heart and our will must be yielded to God before we can receive the word of God and obey it. Otherwise we will be seeking Him in vain. If we are willing to humble ourselves and to turn from our sinful ways and fervently seek the Lord with all our heart through prayer and the study of His word, the Holy Spirit will reveal the things of God to us and will make Jesus known to us.

Since Christ Jesus, as the Son of Man, established His and His saints' title to the kingdom of God on earth at the cost of His own life and sufferings He will reign over the world as King of Kings and Lord of Lords and shall judge all of mankind, including the living and the dead (1 Cor. 15:22-28, 45-47; Rev. 5:9, 10; 17:14). Ironically, He who, as the Son of Man, was judged by the world to be a sinner shall become judge of the world.

The final judgment will be when *the Son of man shall send forth His angels, and they shall gather out of His kingdom all things that offend, and them which do iniquity: and shall cast them into the furnace of fire: there shall be wailing and gnashing of teeth (Matt. 13:41).* The kingdom will be His and all the angels of God will be His obedient servants.

Because death came by man, the resurrection of the dead also came by man. As in Adam all die, all shall be made alive in Christ Jesus that is each one in his own order: Christ, the first fruits, who is the firstborn from the dead; then when He comes, those who belong to Him. The end will then come when He will deliver the Kingdom to God the Father after He has put an end to all rule and all power and all authority of Satan, his wicked spirits and his followers. Christ will reign until He has placed all enemies of God under His feet. Death will be the last enemy that He will destroy. All things will be put under

Him except God the Father. Once all things have been made subject to Him, then Jesus will also be made subject to the Father, who put all things under Him, and God will then be all in all (I Cor 15:22-28). Jesus will become the ruler over the earthly world as the Son of Man and over the entire universe as the Second Person of the Trinity under the authority of God the Father.

Chapter Thirty

Is Your Name Written in the Book of Life?

What is the most critical and ultimate question that each of us faces today? The answer will determine where we will spend our eternal future. Is your name written in the Book of Life? Jesus said He came down from heaven not to do His own will, but the will of the Father who sent Him. He said the will of the Father is that everyone who sees the Son and believes in Him will have eternal life with Him and He will raise them up at the end of the age (John 6:38-40). Christ declared that whoever is ashamed of Him and His words, then the Son of Man will be ashamed of him when He returns to Earth in His own glory (Luke 9:26).

Jesus pronounced that He is the First and the Last. He is the one *who* came to earth and who lived and died, but is now eternally alive. He holds the keys of Hades and of Death (Rev 1:9-18). Jesus was raised from the dead in possession of the keys of hell and death inasmuch as He became the only Truth and the only Life and the only Way to God and no man can come unto the Father but by Him (John 14:6). He is the door and if anyone enters by Him, he will be saved... (John 10:9). Keys represent the power and authority vested in the possessor. No longer can Satan lord it over us as sinners by holding us prisoner through the power of sin, for the Son of Man died and suffered to redeem all of us. Those who choose to obey God by accepting His plan of salvation will become one with the Conqueror, who defeated Satan and robbed him of his power to condemn us.

Christ Jesus, the Son of Man, in order to qualify as Mediator and High Priest to represent us before God, was subjected to and experienced in our stead, every trial, tribulation, rejection, suffering, torment and punishment that any person will ever encounter or experience. If we as an offspring of the first Adam refuse to repent and to accept Jesus as our atoning sacrifice, we will be without excuse when we stand before the judgment seat of Christ following our physical death. Each one of us will determine our own eternal destiny by virtue of the decision we make as to whether we accept or reject God's provision for our redemption from Satan's kingdom of darkness. Our eternal spiritual future rests in our own hands and therefore God cannot be accused of sending anyone to hell to face His eternal wrath.

Scripture clearly states that

...the wrath of God is revealed from heaven against all ungodliness and unrighteousness of men, who suppress the truth in unrighteousness, because what may be known of God is manifest in them, for God has shown it to them. For since the creation of the world His invisible attributes are clearly seen, being understood by the things that are made, even His eternal power and Godhead, so that they are without excuse, because, although they knew God, they did not glorify Him as God, nor were thankful, but became futile in their thoughts, and their foolish hearts were darkened. Professing to be wise, they became fools... (Romans 1:18-22)

God our Savior desires all men to be saved and to come to the knowledge of the truth (I Tim 2:3, 4). Scripture makes our position with God crystal clear. *The Father loves the Son, and has given all things into His hand. He who believes in the Son has everlasting life; and he who does not believe the Son shall not see life, but the wrath of God abides on him* (John 3:35, 36). God did not appoint us to wrath. His desire and plan for us is to obtain salvation through our Lord Jesus Christ, who died for us, that we should be totally committed to live united in relationship with Him (I Thes 5:9, 10).

The Lord said that we who overcome shall be clothed in white garments and He will not blot out our name from the Book of Life, but He will confess our name before His Father and before His angels (Rev 3:5). We who overcome are those who remain faithful to God by accepting His only begotten Son as our Savior and Lord and by remaining obedient to His commands. We will be clothed in white garments, which represent a righteous relationship with God through Christ Jesus, the Son of Man.

In the Old Testament of the Bible, the Lord told Moses that whoever has sinned against Him, He will blot out of His book *(Exo 32:33)*. King David, who was also a prophet, had this to say about evil doers: *Let them be blotted out of the book of the living, and not be written with the righteous* (Ps 69:29, 109:13). Daniel prophesied that at end of the age: The Arch angel Michael, the great prince who stands watch over the sons of God's people, would stand up. At that time there will be trouble such as not seen before or afterwards since a nation existed upon the earth. Then God's people will be delivered—that is everyone whose name was found written in God's book (Dan 12:1).

Scripture reveals more than one book will be opened at the final judgment by the Son of Man who will judge the living and the dead, but the key book to be opened will be the Book of Life. The apostle John, who received revelation from the Lord, said:

> Then I saw a great white throne and Him who was seated on it. Earth and sky fled from His presence, and there was no place for them. And I saw the dead, great and small standing before the throne, and books were opened. Another book was opened, which is the Book of Life. The dead were judged according to what they had done as recorded in the books. The sea gave up the dead that were in it, and death and Hades gave up the dead that were in them, and each person was judged according to what he had done. Then death and Hades were thrown into the lake of fire. The lake of fire is the second death. If anyone's name was not found written in the book of life, he was thrown into the lake of fire. (Revelation 20:11-15, NIV)

The Lord God repeatedly confirmed that the names of unrepentant sinners who reject the Lord Jesus Christ and His substitutionary sacrifice will die in their sins. Their names will be blotted out of the Book of Life and their names will not be found written therein on judgment day. When a person stands before the Son of Man on Judgment Day, the question will not be are you a Jew, or a Catholic, or a Baptist, or a Presbyterian, or a Methodist, or a Mormon, or a Jehovah Witness, or a Muslim or a Buddhist of some other religious denomination or sect, but is your name found written in the Book of Life?

Since Christ Jesus, the Son of Man, suffered the wrath of God, once for all, the name of every person regardless of the sins committed was written in the Book of Life. The initial judgment for all of mankind will be based upon whether the individual accepted or rejected God's provision for his salvation. Those who reject Him will have their names blotted out of the Book of Life by God and will be condemned to the second death, where they will experience eternal punishment with Satan in the lake of fire.

To be blotted out, according to words used in the Scripture, conveys the meaning that in the Book of Life it will appear as if their names were never written in it. Many individuals, void of spiritual understanding, cringe in disbelief that a loving God would sentence anyone to hell. In truth and in fact God made provision for all mankind to escape being sentenced to hell by being spiritually born again from above by the Holy Spirit out of Satan's kingdom of darkness into the kingdom of His dear Son. We become eternal heirs and joint heirs with Jesus providing we continue to abide in Him. Each individual determines his final destiny by the ultimate decision that he alone makes as to whom he will obey and serve—either God the Creator of all things, or Satan, the great deceiver and liar, who is the god of this world. When man dies a physical death, he either dies spiritually united with Christ Jesus or in his sins. The latter will subject him to the eternal wrath of God, together with Satan and his evil spirits.

We alone condemn ourselves to hell and remove our name from the Book of Life by rejecting Christ Jesus as Savior and Lord of our life. When Jesus was spiritually united with every man to be born upon planet Earth as man's sin bearer on the cross, He became legally obligated to pay the sin debt once for all of us. The name of every person to ever be born of man was written in the Book of Life in heaven. As a result, only we can exercise the authority to remove our name from the Book of Life by rejecting God's provision for our redemption and our salvation.

Lightning Source UK Ltd.
Milton Keynes UK
UKOW02f0953190314

228407UK00003B/18/P

9 781628 716573